CHOOSIN

Non-State Actors in International Law, Politics and Governance Series

Series Editors:
Math Noortmann, Erasmus University, Rotterdam, The Netherlands
Bob Reinalda, Radboud University Nijmegen, The Netherlands
Bas Arts, Radboud University Nijmegen, The Netherlands
Peter Willetts, City University, London, UK

The proliferation of non-state actors in the international system over the last three decades has increased the need for a broader theoretical analysis and empirical validation. The series explores the capabilities and impact of non-state actors, such as privately-based transnational corporations, non-governmental organizations (NGOs), international criminal organizations, and liberation movements, as well as intergovernmental organizations (in which NGOs often participate). The series seeks to address this need and to deepen the knowledge and understanding of non-state actors by scholars, practitioners and students in the fields of international law, politics and governance. By emphasizing legal, political and governance aspects of non-state actors' activities at the international (global and regional) level, the series intends to transcend traditional disciplinary and organizational boundaries.

Also in the series:

**Surviving Global Change?: Agricultural Interest Groups
in Comparative Perspective**
Darren Halpin
978 0 7546 4204 6

**The Romani Voice in World Politics: The United Nations
and Non-State Actors**
Ilona Klímová-Alexander
978 0 7546 4173 5

Non-State Actors in International Relations
Bas Arts, Math Noortmann and Bob Reinalda
978 0 7546 1848 5

**Agents of Altruism: The Expansion of Humanitarian NGOs
in Rwanda and Afghanistan**
Katarina West
978 0 7546 1839 3

Choosing the Lesser Evil
Understanding Decision Making in Humanitarian Aid NGOs

LIESBET HEYSE
Twente University, The Netherlands and Groningen University,
The Netherlands

ASHGATE

Published by
Ashgate Publishing Limited
Gower House
Croft Road
Aldershot
Hampshire GU11 3HR
England

Ashgate Publishing Company
Suite 420
101 Cherry Street
Burlington, VT 05401-4405
USA

Ashgate website: http://www.ashgate.com

British Library Cataloguing in Publication Data
Heyse, Liesbet, 1973-
  Choosing the lesser evil : understanding decision making in
  humanitarian aid NGOs. - (Non-state actors in international
  law, politics and governance series)
  1. Medecins sans frontieres (Association). Holland
  2. Action by Churches Together (Organization). Netherlands
  3. Humanitarian assistance - Decision making
  4. Humanitarian assistance - Decision making - Case studies
  5. Non-governmental organizations - Decision making
  6. Non-governmental organizations - Decision making - Case
  studies
  I. Title
  361.7'7'0684

Library of Congress Cataloging-in-Publication Data
Heyse, Liesbet, 1973-
  Choosing the lesser evil : understanding decision making in humanitarian aid NGOs /
by Liesbet Heyse.
        p. cm. -- (Non-state actors in international law, politics, and governance
series)
  Includes bibliographical references and index.
  ISBN-13: 978-0-7546-4612-9 1. Humanitarian assistance--Decision
making. 2. Humanitarian assistance--Decision making--Case studies. 3. Non-
governmental organizations--Decision making. 4. Non-governmental organizations--
Decision making--Case studies. 5. Medecins sans frontieres (Association). Holland. 6.
Action by Churches Together (Organization). Netherlands. I. Title.

HV553.H49 2006
361.2'60684--dc22

                                                                2006031449

ISBN-13: 9780754646129

Printed and bound in Great Britain by Antony Rowe Ltd, Chippenham, Wiltshire.

Contents

List of Figures

List of Tables

List of Boxes

Preface

This book is anything but a product of hours of isolated work in 'the ivory towers of academia', although the arguments made and the line of reasoning presented are my sole responsibility. This book is the result of the input and support of many people.

I first and foremost thank the employees of the two NGOs that I studied. This book would not exist without their cooperation, which was extraordinary considering their hectic jobs. I thank Jacques Willemse for welcoming me at ACT Netherlands and Austen Davis for opening MSF's doors to me in Amsterdam and the field. I am grateful to all the ACT and MSF employees who granted me interviews or helped me otherwise. I owe special thanks to Arjan and Farida, Ayam, and Kostas for their hospitality and open attitude in the field.

This book was started at Leiden University, The Netherlands. I especially thank Paul 't Hart and Uri Rosenthal, as well as Mark Bovens, Arjen Boin, Mathilde Meijers, Marc Otten, all members of the Leiden University Crisis Research Center, and all members of the Public Administration seminar for their feedback and support. Petra Schreurs's enthusiasm and humor has especially been motivating during and after my time in Leiden. It is therefore so sad that we no longer can experience her energy and personality anymore. Outside Leiden, the NIG PhD students were a great support group throughout the whole process, especially because of the *Provo's* Ellen van Bueren, Monique Esselbrugge, and Mathilde Meijers. This book was finished at Twente University, The Netherlands. I thank my colleagues from Sociology who not only waited patiently for this book to finally finish, but also provided input for the conclusion and the epilogue. In my personal life, I especially thank my parents, my two brothers, and my good friend Lilian.

I dedicate this book to Arjan Bons, an extraordinarily dedicated, critical, and motivated humanitarian aid worker. I was lucky to meet him during my fieldwork in 2001. He and his wife Farida made me feel so welcome when they invited me into their lives. He not only made me experience the real world of humanitarian aid, but he also shared his personal thoughts and doubts about his work during the field trips, his office work, and the (email) conversations we have had. I was shocked to hear that he unexpectedly passed away last year. To me, he was the living example of how humanitarian aid workers can do their work: experiencing a permanent, personal, and sincere struggle between idealism and realism, while finding ways to choose, and live with, the lesser evil. To him I dedicate this book, in memory of his life and work.

July 2006

In Memory of Arjan Bons

Chapter 1

Choosing the Lesser Evil:
Selecting Humanitarian Aid Projects

Deciding on humanitarian aid projects involves difficult choices about life and death. Humanitarian aid providers permanently face violent conflicts, famines, and natural disasters, all of which concern people in need of food, medical treatment, and shelter. Yearly reports of the United Nations, International Red Cross (ICRC), and other international organizations show proof of large numbers of people in need. For example, in the year 2005 alone, more than twenty million people had either fled their country or were internally displaced (UNHCR, 2005:14).

As a result, humanitarian aid organizations need to select where to go and what to do, if only because the demand for humanitarian aid often exceeds the supply of humanitarian aid activities (in terms of money and manpower). Humanitarian aid organizations therefore constantly face difficult decisions about whom to help and what to do in a situation of serious time constraints. This forces humanitarian aid organizations to select locations and groups for aid provision on a daily basis, making humanitarian aid provision a continuous selection process. In this sense, it could be argued that humanitarian aid organizations always face 'tragic choices' (Calabresi & Bobbitt, 1978). The aim of this study is to gain more insight in the way these difficult decisions are taken.

Humanitarian aid provision as constrained decision-making processes

Selecting humanitarian aid projects requires decisions about where to go (location), what to do (activities), when to start (initiation) or not (rejection), and when to extend or end activities (prolongation and termination). These decisions need to be made in contexts which can be characterized as 'complex humanitarian crises', referring to the fact that these crises are both complex in cause and consequence (Duffield & Prendergast, 1994; Harriss (ed.) 1995; Albala-Bertrand, 2000). Most humanitarian crises develop from a series of interrelated causes, such as inter- or intrasocietal tensions, a colonial heritage, environmental degradation, economic decline, and an unequal distribution of power and economic resources (see for example, Field (ed.), 1993; Duffield & Prendergast, 1994). These often result in conflict, hunger, destruction of political, social and economic infrastructures, and population movements within or crossing the national borders.

In such a complex context, the decision-making process about humanitarian aid interventions is constrained by many obstacles (see for example, Cuny, 1983; Smillie, 1995). Access is the first obstacle to conquer, obstructing humanitarian aid organizations to independently decide about their project locations. Humanitarian aid organizations often have to deal with the absence of political structures and regularly have to negotiate and renegotiate their access. Besides, the local ruling elite sometimes tries to use the aid organization for its own benefit by allowing the organization to provide aid to some groups while not to others.

If access is granted, infrastructural and security problems regularly hamper access to the populations in need, thereby further restricting the range of alternatives for humanitarian aid provision. Roads may be destroyed or covered with landmines, and the air not safe enough to organize an airlift (aside from the fact that an airlift is extremely expensive). Even if it is possible to travel by road, violence is another impediment. Becoming hostages, being killed, being bribed or looted are all risks which humanitarian aid workers regularly have to face. In addition, rivaling factions regularly steal aid to feed their soldiers, which indirectly can contribute to the continuation or the exacerbation of the conflict (Anderson 1999; Aall *et al.*, 2000).

A massive influx of humanitarian aid agencies can complicate the decision-making process regarding humanitarian aid provision even more. Agencies of the United Nations (UN) – such as the UNHCR, Unicef and WFP – sometimes enter the country together with governmental humanitarian aid agencies of the European Union (ECHO) and national governments (for example, USAID, Danida, SIDA).[1] National and international non-governmental organizations also make their entry on the scene. Finally, the UN may be present in the form of UN peacekeeping or peace enforcing troops. This often creates coordination problems due to differences in mandate and work methods. It sometimes even results in rivalry among the many actors in humanitarian aid provision (Smillie, 1995).

Humanitarian aid organizations also have to take into account a set of organizational factors such as the wishes and conditions of their national or international donors (governments, EU, or the UN); the expectations of the public at home; the sensitive relationship with the press; their budget, human resources, expertise, and mandate; and the need to create a distinctive image compared to other aid agencies for the sake of funding (Burnell, 1991; Benthall, 1993; and De Waal, 1997). Donors sometimes provide funds for aid conditionally, demanding aid organizations to give aid to those groups or areas that donors favor for political reasons (Weiss & Gordenker, 1996:32). Another constraint is related to the 'funding game'. Crises that are neglected by the press, and therefore do not reach the public, raise less funds than those extensively covered by the media (Seaman, 1996).

The above organizational and situational constraints are part and parcel of the reality of humanitarian aid provision. This results in a complex context – both in the country of the headquarters and in the receiving country – in which decisions have to be made about the aid activities to employ and the target groups to reach. As a result, decision-making concerning humanitarian aid provision is not only difficult because it involves hard choices about life and death in a context of scarcity, but the difficulties are not over once a country or a target group has been selected. The next dilemma is how to distribute the aid. Should one stay out of specific areas because effective aid provision is difficult to achieve and this would be problematic for the organizational image and future fundraising? Or should one decide to provide aid, knowing that part of the relief effort may create adverse effects, which the donors, the public, and the press may feel is unacceptable?

In past decades, we have learnt a lot about the constraints of humanitarian aid provision as well as about their causes and consequences. A start has been made to find ways to better cope with these constraints (see for example Anderson, 1999; Wood *et al.*, 2001; ALNAP, 2002). What we do not know much about is how humanitarian aid agencies deal with these complex organizational and situational constraints when deciding about their humanitarian aid projects. Although there is a vast literature about humanitarian aid provision,[2] selection and decision-making processes of humanitarian aid actors are not often touched upon in detail. The central question of this book therefore is:

> How do humanitarian aid organizations decide on the selection of aid locations, target groups, and aid activities and why do they do so in a particular way?

This question is studied for one particular category of humanitarian aid agencies: international non-governmental organizations (INGOS).

NGOs: dominant players in the humanitarian aid community

The NGO sector is an important part of the international humanitarian aid community (West, 2001). NGOs are not-for-profit, private, self-governing organizations aiming at 'improving the life of disadvantaged people' (Vakil, 1997; see also Barrow & Jennings, 2001). Important characteristics shared by NGOs are the fact that they are 'organized, private, non profit distributing, self-governing' and of some voluntary character (Salamon & Anheier, 1997a; 1997b).[3]

As of 1996, over a thousand NGOs provide humanitarian aid (Haghebaert 1996). The participation of NGOs in humanitarian aid operations has substantially increased in the past decade. For example, during the emergency situation in Somalia (1991–1993) over fifty NGOs were involved in humanitarian aid activities (IOV 1994:100), whereas during the 1999 Kosovo crisis, already more than 400 NGOs participated in the humanitarian relief effort (Fitz-Gerald & Walthall, 1999). Currently, UNHCR efforts are implemented by more than 600 NGOs, receiving almost 270 million dollars, more than one fifth of UNHCR's annual budget (UNHCR, 2005:65).

Apart from the sheer number of NGOs involved in humanitarian aid activities, a further development makes these organizations of interest for this research: NGOs are often funded by government agencies. From 1975 to 1992, global government contributions to NGOs rose from 1 percent to 28 percent of total government expenditures for humanitarian aid (Borton 1993:192). The European Union is another important money source for NGOs: in the year 2005, for example, the EU spent more than €653 million on humanitarian aid, of which 51 percent was distributed through NGOs from within the EU (European Commision, 2005; http://ec.europa. eu/echo/statistics/echo_en.htm, date of entry 17 July 2006).

Humanitarian aid projects can hence be characterized as partially public projects, paid for by taxpayers' money. It is remarkable in this respect that NGOs do not have to account for their activities to the general public the way governmental organizations (Ministries of Foreign Affairs, agencies of the United Nations, and the European Union) are supposed to. For example, the agencies of the United Nations have been scrutinized extensively concerning their humanitarian aid performances in countries such as Somalia and Rwanda (Sommer, 1994; Whitman & Pocock, 1996).

In addition, more information seems to be available about selection processes and outcomes within governmental organizations, such as with regard to the UN and the United States in the Cambodian case (Shawcross, 1983), the WFP (Charlton, 1997) and bilateral humanitarian aid (ODI, 2000).[4] Little is known about the way non-governmental actors select their humanitarian aid activities, since the literature that touches upon NGOs in humanitarian crises does not focus on the internal work processes of these organizations in detail.[5]

Filling a void in NGO research: A study of diversity in NGO behavior

The lack of knowledge on internal work processes of NGOs does not only exist with concern to *humanitarian* NGOs, it is characteristic for the NGO literature in general (Lewis, 2001; Dijkzeul & Beigbeder, 2001). The NGO literature focuses on explaining the existence, growth, role, and behavior of the NGO community as a whole in comparison to state and market organizations. In these explanations, NGOs are often presented as a coherent group of actors that are similar in nature and behavior. For example, NGOs are presented to be better in providing some services than state and market organizations because they are better suited to accommodate information asymmetry or they are better able to reach persons in need (Hansmann, 1987; Douglas, 1987; James, 1990; Anheier, 1990). The other way around, it is regularly argued that problems in NGO performance are the result of their common nature: NGOs are characterized by multiple stakeholders and goals that result in internal conflicts and an internal structure that is loosely coupled (DiMaggio & Anheier, 1990; Edwards & Hulme, 1996).

One could wonder to what extent this unified picture of NGOs is suitable for the purposes of our study, because the two NGOs of this study differ in decision-making outcomes, such as will be shown in the following sections. Hence, we looked for clues in the NGO literature that could guide our attempt to understand differences between these two NGOs. This part of the literature is much less developed; it predominantly focuses on differences in national contexts and fields of expertise. Such differences are argued to be of influence of an NGO's structures, goals, and work methods (see, for example, DiMaggio & Anheier, 1990). However, this relationship is not explored explicitly and the impact of these differences on the decisions and performance of

NGOs is hardly studied. It is also suggested that the organizational set up of NGOs in terms of field of expertise, level of operation, work method, and ideology is related to the decisions and operations of NGOs as well (Fisher, 1997; Vakil, 1997). Unfortunately, explicit hypotheses about this relationship are lacking as well.

This study aims to fill this void in knowledge by studying differences in NGO decisions regarding one specific field of expertise: humanitarian aid provision. This study departs from the assumption that NGO structures are related to the outcomes of such organizations, such as suggested in the NGO literature. By studying NGOs in this way, this study hopes to contribute to the knowledge about the internal work processes of NGOs in general, and to the understanding of the assumed relationship between NGO structures and NGO decision outcomes in humanitarian aid in particular (see also Chapter 2).

Exploring NGO diversity: Research design

In order to accomplish the abovementioned aims, we have conducted an exploratory study of the Dutch branches of two non-governmental international humanitarian aid organizations – Médécins sans Frontières (MSF) and Acting with Churches Together (ACT). MSF Holland and ACT Netherlands represent two extremes in the diverse community of humanitarian aid NGOs (see Figure 1.1), except for the fact that they both participate in larger international networks of humanitarian aid organizations.[6]

MSF Holland

MSF Holland belongs to the category of the *operational* NGO that focuses on *a specialized form of aid* provision and on *one phase* in particular, i.e. the immediate emergency phase. MSF Holland is a medical organization that mainly provides medical aid directly to populations in need. The organization therefore has its own teams on the ground manned by expatriate and local team members. The organization was founded on the idea that proximity to people in need is a way to express solidarity. The aim of aid provision is to help people to safeguard or re-establish their human dignity and to make their situation known to the world. At the time of the study, more than 160 people worked in the Amsterdam headquarters and another 4 to 500 expats work in the field. In 2000, the total expenditures exceeded €50 million. In 2004, the expenditures had risen to more than €75 million.

Act Netherlands

ACT Netherlands fits the category of the *non-operational* NGO that subsidizes local organizations and the humanitarian aid projects they implement. The organization believes that solidarity to people in need should be expressed by providing local organizations the means to develop their own capacities and skills to prevent and battle humanitarian emergencies. By funding the humanitarian aid projects of these local organizations, these NGOs hope to contribute to more resilient Third World societies. The local partner organizations therefore often receive *a more permanent form of aid*, even though there is no immediate humanitarian emergency. ACT Netherlands supports *various kinds of aid* efforts, such as shelter, food, education, prevention, and preparedness. During the case study period, ACT Netherlands consisted of seven project officers in charge of geographically divided project portfolios. Another three persons provided administrative assistance. ACT Netherlands spent a little less than €12 million on its projects in the year 2000. In 2004, this was approximately €7,5 million.

	MSF Holland	ACT Netherlands
Founding members	Medical professionals	Protestant churches and the old catholic churches
Founding year	1984	1952
Solidarity through	Proximity and ensuring human dignity of people in need	Support of local organizations
Work method	Operational teams of expats in the field	Transfer of money to local partner organizations
Principal focus in phase	Acute emergency + some prevention and rehabilitation activities	Prevention & preparedness, emergency, rehabilitation and development
Principal focus in aid	Medical/medically related such as vaccination, supplementary feeding, water and sanitation, education & training	All kinds of aid, such as food, shelter, organizational development, training and education, human rights
Aid budget	± €50 million in 2000	± €12 million in 2000
Number of employees	160 in headquarters 500 expats in the field thousands of local workers in the field	7 project officers 3 administrative assistants 1 head of department 3 liaison officers

Figure 1.1   The two NGOs selected for this study

These two organizations were selected from a population of a group of ten humanitarian aid NGOs in The Netherlands.[7] The selection of these two NGOs represents a form of maximum variation sampling. Maximum variation sampling has the advantage that it allows the researcher to 'describe the variation in the group and to understand variations in experiences while also investigating core elements and shared outcomes' (Patton, 1990:172). This case selection method is particularly useful in exploratory studies like this, since the study of these two 'extreme' NGOs will offer us a broad and diverse picture of decision-making processes regarding humanitarian aid provision, while at the same time providing us the opportunity to check for common patterns, there where they are to be expected least (see further the Appendix).

The two cases selected also offer the possibility to systematically study the relationship between NGO organizational set up and selection outcomes in order to fill the gap in knowledge about internal work processes in NGOs. The two NGOs selected for this study represent two common NGO categories in the humanitarian aid community (Natsios, 1994): MSF Holland represents the operational, specialist humanitarian aid NGO whereas ACT Holland represents the non-operational (more developmental) generalist humanitarian aid NGO. These two international NGOs operate in the same field of expertise (humanitarian aid) and in the same national headquarters context (The Netherlands). We can therefore explore to what extent differences in the organizational set up influences the organization's selection outcomes, since the variables 'field of expertise' and 'national context' – also believed to be of influence on the decisions and performance of NGOs – are kept constant (see also Chapter 2).

Hence, this research design allows theoretical generalization, meaning that the results of the study of these two cases may have wider theoretical implications for the study of (humanitarian aid) NGOs in general (Yin, 1994). The theoretical replication logic of this study is to explore whether differences in the organizational setting of humanitarian NGOs is related to differences in decision-making outcomes.

The data used in this study have been collected by means of qualitative interviewing (Weiss, 1994), document analysis of policy papers and project files, and observation of decision-making in practice, especially at the headquarters level. The data collection took place from the beginning of 1998 to the end of 2001 and was concluded by a two month observation period in each organization (two months per organization). In addition, the decision-making practices of both organizations were followed somewhere in Africa in the fall of 2001.

Different as night and day: MSF and ACT selection outcomes

Studying the expenditures of the two NGOs selected for this study, we see how these organizations not only differ in their outlook and work methods, but also in their focus on countries and continents that receive aid.[8]

First, the organizations prioritize the four continents differently throughout the years. During the Kosovo crisis in 1999, for example, ACT Netherlands spent 44,1 percent of its budget on Europe and the Middle East and 24,2 percent on Africa, whereas MSF Holland spent 19,4 percent of its budget on the former continent and 43,2 percent on the latter (see Table 1a and 1b). Apparently, both organizations focus on different continents.

Secondly, there are differences in expenditure trends throughout the years. If we look at the expenditures for Africa per organization for the years 1996–2000 (see Figure 1.2), we can conclude that MSF Holland has a pretty stable budget for Africa ranging between 43,1 percent and 54,6 percent of the total aid budget. ACT Netherlands is less stable (though declining) with budgets ranging between 24,2 percent to 74,2 percent of their total aid budget.

Table 1.1a   ACT's expenditures per continent in percent of total expenditure per year (1996–2000)

Continent	1996	1997	1998	1999	2000
Africa	74,2%	40,0%	41,5%	24,2%	23,8%
Asia	13,8%	23,1%	31,1%	21,0%	26,1%
Latin America	10,1%	27,4%	16,5%	10,7%	6,5%
Europe and Middle East	1,9%	9,5%	10,9%	44,1%	43,6%
Totals	**100,0%**	**100,0%**	**100,0%**	**100,0%**	**100,0%**

Table 1.1b   MSF's expenditures per continent in percent of total expenditure per year (1996–2000)

Continent	1996	1997	1998	1999	2000
Africa	54,6%	53,6%	52,1%	43,1%	50,5%
Asia	20,4%	23,3%	30,8%	24,9%	28,6%
Latin America	6,6%	11,2%	11,6%	12,6%	11,9%
Europe and Middle East	8,4%	11,9%	5,5%	19,4%	9,0%
Totals	**100,0%**	**100,0%**	**100,0%**	**100,0%**	**100,0%**

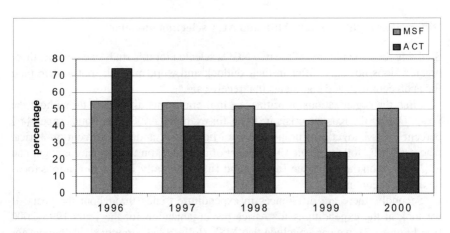

Figure 1.2   MSF and ACT expenditures on Africa in percent of total budget (1996–2000)

Third, the organizations vary in the number of countries receiving continuous aid per continent. For the Latin American continent, for example, a fairly large part of the Latin American aid budget of ACT Netherlands (between 51,1 percent to 91,2 percent) is spent on countries receiving continuous aid, whereas the MSF budget spent on Latin American countries receiving continuous aid has decreased from 81,3 percent in 1996 to 20,9 percent in 2000 (see Figure 1.3).

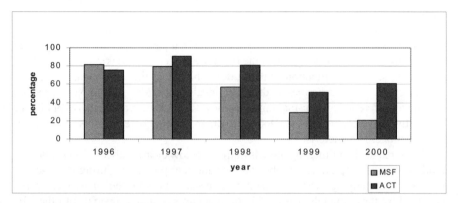

Figure 1.3   MSF and ACT expenditures on countries receiving continuous aid in Latin America (in percent of the total Latin American aid budget)

The countries that receive continuous aid also differ per organization. For example, there are four Latin American countries that received ACT money continuously from 1996 to 2000 – Colombia, Mexico, Nicaragua and Peru – whereas MSF sponsored two countries continuously in that period, i.e. Peru and Brazil. Peru is the only country both organizations had aid projects in from 1996 to 2000.

Finally, when we look at the top three countries in expenditure per organization throughout the years, it becomes clear that the organizations prioritize different countries. During the time span of five years studied for this research, only Sudan, Chechnya and Afghanistan were in the top three of both organizations. In 2000, for example, MSF's top three consisted of Sudan, the Democratic Republic of Congo and Chechnya, whereas ACT's top three countries were Kosovo, Afghanistan, and Liberia.

The above information illustrates how different MSF Holland and ACT Netherlands are, not only in background, but also in selection outcomes. In this study, we will look into the question how the selection processes that produced these outcomes unfolded and what factors influenced their course and outcomes. Based on the NGO literature, we try to explore what the relationship is between the organizational set ups of both NGOs and their decision-making outcomes. In order to do this, we need a 'tool' to open up the black box of NGO decision-making processes. This 'tool' has been developed on the basis of organizational decision-making theories.

Opening the black box of NGO decision-making dynamics

The literature on organizational decision-making provides useful clues for understanding how these two humanitarian aid NGOs select the locations and activities of their aid projects, and how they decide on the initiation, termination, rejection, and prolongation of their activities. The theoretical framework of this study (see Chapter 3) consists of insights gained from this literature in general and from the work of decision-making scholars such as March, Simon, and Olsen in particular.

The two theoretical questions deriving from the empirical research question are how decisions are made and why they are made in a particular way. Roughly three answers to this question are given in the literature on decision-making (March, 1994; 1997). These answers function as the building blocks of the theoretical framework of this study. Each describes a different ideal-typical decision-making process, leading to different decision-making outcomes. These three models also explicitly or implicitly formulate hypotheses about the organizational determinants of decision-making process characteristics.

The three decision-making models outlined below clearly reflect ideal types. The models were used to guide my observations and interpretations during the research process. By studying decision-making processes through the analytical lenses provided by these models, I was able to generate systematic insight into the *way* decisions were taken, *why* they were taken in a specific way, and how that related to the *outcomes* of the decision-making process.

The logic of consequence

Some authors, such as Downs (1967) and Quade (1975) assume that people act on the basis of instrumental rationality. March (1988; 1994) labels this idea of instrumental rationality in decision-making as reasoning according to a *logic of consequence*. Put briefly, people make decisions on the basis of their preferences, the available alternatives, and the possible consequences of these alternatives. Decision-making is therefore prospective, because one connects alternatives to desired future consequences.

In this study, it is hypothesized that the logic of consequence is a characteristic of Herbert Simon's concept of the *administrative organization* (1945/1997), since according to Simon the criterion of efficiency is the driving force behind decision-making in this organizational context. In order to achieve the organizational goals with the lowest cost, a consequential decision-making mode is applied. The organizational structure of the administrative organization is designed to ensure that organizational members will act rationally, efficiently, and goal-oriented.

The logic of appropriateness

Other authors argue that decision-making is based on rules and identities (see for example Burns & Flam, 1987). These authors argue that individuals, when they try to decide, do not take into account their preferences, the alternative choices available or the possible consequences of their choices. Instead, they take into account what they think they are expected to do in a given situation. People accordingly act upon their identity and role in a specific situation by following rules that apply to that situation. Action is determined by former experience, and not by taking into account future consequences. March (1994) describes this model of decision-making as reasoning according to *a logic of appropriateness*.

In this study, the hypothesis is formulated that the logic of appropriateness is characteristic for Selznick's interpretation of 'the institution'. An institution is not a rational instrument, but rather a 'natural product of social needs and pressures' (Selznick 1957:5), in which 'choices are structured by socially mediated values and normative frameworks', not by self-interest or prospective reasoning (Scott 1995:39).

Garbage can decision-making

A third group of researchers claims that there is actually hardly any logic in decision-making processes (see for example Cohen, March and Olsen, 1972). Decision-making is more or less coincidental, as several aspects of the process develop quite independently from each other. The formulation of problems and solutions is not chronologically ordered (first problems, then solutions), as is assumed in both the logic of consequence and the logic of appropriateness. Instead, solutions co-exist independent from problems, problems independent from choice opportunities, and choice opportunities independent from solutions. Sometimes all of these aspects coincide accidentally at a certain moment, and action follows. Sometimes they never coincide, and no decisions are taken. This type of coincidental decision-making is called *garbage can decision-making*.

In this study, it is assumed that garbage can decision-making is a characteristic of March and Olsen's ambiguous organization. The ambiguous organization is characterized by unstructured work processes, decentralized decision-making, an unclear technology and problematic preferences. In such organizations work processes, organizational goals, and decision-making procedures have not fully taken shape yet. In such circumstances, garbage can decision-making may occur.

Coping with complexities

This book sheds light on how two international non governmental organizations deal differently with the complexities of aid provision through their decision-making processes. The two NGOs of this study clearly have different dominant modes of decision-making. These dominant decision-making modes influence their selection outcomes. Hence, we refute the assumption often found in NGO research that NGOs are similar in nature and behavior. The differences are not only related to their differences in outlook and work method, but also by the way these two NGOs are structured organizationally. By studying the characteristics of the decision-making processes within these two NGOs, we gain more understanding of why certain countries are prioritized and others not, why certain projects are preferred above others, and why the expenditures are more stable in one NGO than the other.

This study also reveals that the dominant decision-making modes were sometimes set aside due to organizational and contextual constraints in aid provision. Then secondary decision-making patterns evolved. This book offers insight into how and why decision modes within MSF Holland and ACT Netherlands shifted.

Theoretically, this book shows that the three 'decision-making logics' are helpful analytical tools for a study of decision-making processes. In addition, this book illustrates how all three decision-making logics can coincide in one organization. This helps us to formulate some theoretical generalizations about diversity in NGO behavior. It also brings to the fore that decision-making modes might have various functions in the decision-making process. This study indicates that some 'logics' – in this case the logic of consequence and appropriateness – can serve as complexity reducing mechanisms, whereas others – i.e. the logic of the garbage can – seem to provide a last resort decision-making strategy in a context of very limited alternatives for action.

A reader's guide

This book consists of thirteen chapters, an epilogue, and an appendix. Those who are interested in the theoretical considerations of this study, are recommended to read Chapter 2 to 4 of this book. Those who are not, can directly proceed to Chapter 5.

In Chapter 2, we will review the NGO literature in order to search for potential answers on the question how to explain diversity in NGO decisions on humanitarian aid. The review serves as input for the legitimization of the focus of this research on the explanation of diversity in NGOs that operate in the same field of expertise. It is argued that we need to open up the black box of NGO decision-making in order to explain diversity. In Chapter 3, we use organizational decision-making theories to construct a theoretical framework that can guide our observations. We will first argue why the literature on organizational decision-making is useful for this study and why we chose to work with the three 'logics', before we turn to a fuller description of the three decision-making logics and their organizational settings. In Chapter 4, an attempt is made to translate the fairly abstract notions of organizational decision-making theory to the reality of humanitarian aid provision.

For those interested in the daily practice of decision-making within the two NGOs studied, Chapter 5 to 11 are most relevant to read. In these chapters, we describe the decision-making processes in the two Dutch humanitarian aid NGOs. Chapters 5 to 8 focus on MSF Holland and Chapters 9 to 11 on ACT Netherlands. First, we present a sketch of the organizational features of both organizations (Chapter 5 and 9), before we proceed to a description of their dominant and secondary decision-making modes. These chapters include some extensive case descriptions in order to show how these decision-making modes work in practice (Chapter 6, 7 and 8 for MSF, and Chapters 10 and 11 for ACT).

In the final part of the book, we compare ACT and MSF's decision-making dynamics and evaluate the theoretical framework of this study (Chapter 12). In Chapter 13, we take a look beyond the horizon of this study and formulate some theoretical generalizations. In the epilogue, we discuss some final thoughts about the implications of this study for the larger context of NGO humanitarian aid provision. In the appendix, one can read about the methodological considerations of this study, as well as about the operationalization of the theoretical framework and the data collection process.

Notes

1 UNHCR stands for the United Nations High Commisioner for Refugees, Unicef means the United Nations Children's Fund and WFP stands for World Food Program. ECHO is the Humanitarian Aid Office of the European Union. USAID stands for the United States Agency for International Development, DANIDA is the Danish Agency for Development Assistance and SIDA is the Swedish International Development Cooperation Agency.

2 See for example: Macrae, J. and A. Zwi (eds). 1994. *War and Hunger: Rethinking International Responses to Complex Emergencies*. London: Zed Books; Prendergast, J. 1996. *Frontline Diplomacy, Humanitarian Aid and Conflict in Africa*. Boulder/London: Lynne Rienner Publishers; DeWaal, A. 1997. *Famine Crimes: Politics and the Disaster Humanitarian Industry in Africa*. London/Bloomington/Indianapolis: African Rights, The International African Institute and Indiana University Press.

3 NGOs are also referred to as part of the 'third sector', 'civil society', or the 'non profit sector', referring to the sector existing next to the state and the market (Lewis, 2001).

4 For the Cambodian case, Shawcross (1983) already showed the existence and relevance of different selection outcomes in humanitarian aid. He studied the patterns in aid distribution of the various UN and American government agencies in terms of locations and target groups in and around Cambodia. Donors and agencies showed a remarkable preference for providing aid to refugees on the Thai side of the border (Shawcross 1983:392). Shawcross makes his point by comparing the amount of dollars spent on each refugee in different locations in the conflict area. A more recent publication by Mark Charlton (1997) deals with selection outcomes of the United Nations' World Food Program. The author shows remarkable shifts in the regional focus of WFP aid distributions over time: from the 1950s to the 1970s most food aid was directed primarily at Asia (about 75 percent), whereas Africa only received 5 percent of the budget. In 1994 this focus had changed completely: Africa received 36 percent of the WFP food aid budget and Asia 28 percent. The author also notices differences in individual donor preferences. The Australian government for example does not direct any food aid to the European continent via WFP programs, whereas the United States earmarks one third of its budget for WFP food aid in this region. With concern to bilateral humanitarian assistance, it is interesting to note that in the year 2000, people living in South-Eastern Europe received an average of $ 185,9 per affected person, whereas $37 per affected person was spent in Sierra Leone, and $9,6 per affected person in Somalia (ODI Briefing Paper, April 2002).

5   There are publications that deal with particular NGOs. See for example: De Milliano, J. 1991. *Tussen Korenvelden en Puinhopen: Onderweg met Artsen zonder Grenzen*. Amsterdam: Balans/Lannoo; Duffield, M. and J. Prendergast. 1994. *Without Troops and Tanks: the Emergency Humanitarian Desk and the Cross Border Operation into Eritrea and Tigray*. Lawrenceville NJ: The Red Sea Press; Berendsen, L. 1996. *Kroniek van Artsen zonder Grenzen*; Willemsen, J. 1996. *Van Tentoonstelling tot Wereldorganisatie, De Geschiedenis van de Stichtingen Memisa and Medicus Mundi Nederland 1925-1995*. Nijmegen: Valkhof Pers. However, these publications do not provide detailed insight in the organizations' internal workprocesses concerning the selection of aid activities, locations, and target groups.

6   This community consists of many different types of NGOs that approach humanitarian emergencies in substantially different ways. Therefore, many different typologies of NGOs have been developed. See for example Seaman's typology (1996) of humanitarian aid organizations in which he makes the distinction between the developmental and relief approach. Natsios (1997) further divides the humanitarian aid NGOs into religious versus secular NGOs and adds distinctions by focus of sector and region. Others provide more general typologies for the NGO community as a whole, such as Smillie (1996); Weiss & Gordenker (1996); and Salamon & Anheier (1997).

7   These included Caritas Holland, World Vision, War Child, ZOA Refugee Care, Tear Fund, the Dutch Disaster and Relief Agency, Memisa, and Stichting Vluchteling. Exploratory interviews were conducted with representatives of nine of these aid NGOs. On the basis of these interviews, three NGOs were approached for a first short preliminary study of a week in order to establish to what extent the data required for the research was available in these organizations. The main reason for selecting these three organizations was that they were the three biggest humanitarian aid NGOs in the country in terms of budget. Access was another important reason to select these three NGOs. The preliminary study resulted in the conclusion that the data required for the research were availabe in all three organizations. Eventually, the number of cases was limited to two organizations, because two of the three NGOs studied belonged to the same extreme NGO type (the religious, non-operational one). In addition, these two organizations provided access to their headquarters and were open for more intensive research methods, including observation of decision-making processes.

8   These numbers are based on the annual reports of both organizations.

PART I
NGO Decision Making in Theory

Chapter 2

Filling a Void in NGO Research: Understanding Diversity in NGO Behavior[1]

Non-governmental organizations (NGOs) have become relevant and interesting subjects of study in the social sciences, not only because of their substantial growth in numbers, but also because NGOs are claimed to represent a distinctive category of organizations that differs from market or state organizations. Many attempts have been made to categorize and study non-governmental organizations in comparison to state and market actors (Vakil, 1997; Salamon & Anheier, 1997a, 1997b; Lewis, 2001).

The literature is just as diverse as the NGO community itself. The NGO literature roughly focuses on four topics. First, the literature tries to explain why NGOs exist in the first place. Various explanations exist, but they all are functional in character; NGOs exist because they are believed to perform better than state and market organizations or to complement state and market activities. Second, the literature focuses on explaining the expansion of the NGO community in the past decades. This expansion is predominantly explained by the promise for successful performance of NGOs. However, this promise did not uphold, the performance of NGOs appeared problematic. This initiated a third strand of NGO research into the exploration of NGO problems in relation to NGO characteristics and NGO behavior. However, there is legitimate reason to question the assumption that NGOs can be treated as a coherent group of actors. A fourth strand of research therefore focuses on the study of diversity within the NGO community, as a way to explore causes of variety in NGO behavior and performance.

These topics are approached from various perspectives and disciplines: we find sociological and economic publications on the role and position of NGOs in society, as well as organizational studies about a specific NGO or the NGO community as a whole (see, for example, Hansmann, 1987, Douglas 1987, DiMaggio & Anheier, 1990, Seibel & Anheier, 1990). The nature of the studies differs as well: there are classification studies and comparative studies presenting overviews of the NGO community as a whole or per country, as well as single case studies (see, for example, Salamon et al., 2003, for the former, and Ebrahim, 2003, for the latter).

This chapter provides a basic overview of the latest NGO research relevant to the research questions posed in this study which are predominantly of an organizational nature. We explore the four topics of NGO research. The literature review leads to the conclusion that considerable academic progress has been made with concern to the question why NGOs exist and how they behave as a distinctive category of organizations. However, there is less attention to diversity in the NGO community. Although progress has been made in comparing NGOs that operate in different fields of expertise (such as the environment, development, or health care) and in different national contexts, the question remains unanswered how differences between NGOs that operate in the same field of expertise can be explained. This question is relevant since NGOs differ in behavior, even if they operate in the same sector, such as the two NGOs of this study. This book aims to contribute to fill this void in knowledge.

The promise of successful NGO action

NGOs are often presented to be the solution to many problems: they are believed to be able to complement, substitute, or countervail state or market organizations, thereby compensating for market or state failure. Various theoretical explanations are given for this. For example, NGOs would meet 'residual demand' not covered by state organizations (public goods theory); or NGOs are the logical providers of services that are characterized by information asymmetry, because for profit organizations can take advantage of this asymmetry (contract failure theory) (Hansmann, 1987, 1990; see also James, 1990; Badelt, 1990). Others argue that NGOs are capable to 'work easily with or complement the resources of family and informal networks' (Douglas, 1987:43). It is also argued that NGOs are solutions to the free-rider problem that the state often experiences and it gives the state a way out to deal with diversity, to minimize bureaucratization, and to enhance experimentation. In addition, it gives the state a way out with concern to insoluble, political, and sensitive social problems (Anheier, 1990).

     These various advantages of NGOs can be categorized in two perspectives on the function of NGOs: a political view and an instrumental view (Seibel & Anheier, 1990; Fisher, 1998). In the latter view, the NGO community is perceived as purely instrumental: it comprises of clusters of organizations that provide support and services which the state or the market does not provide at all or not as well (James, 1989). From this perspective, NGOs are studied as effective and efficient service providers doing the job better than state or market organizations.

    In contrast, the political perspective focuses on the political role of NGOs. Within this perspective we find nuanced differences in views. One idea is that NGOs function as a countervailing power to the market or/and the state, adding to the creation of a system of checks and balances in society (Gordenker & Weiss, 1997). The political function of NGOs is then to 'strengthen civil society and hence democracy by improving interest articulation and representation' (Clarke, 1998:50). A slightly different perspective on NGOs as political actors is that they represent 'the institutionalization of existing patterns of political contestation between civil society and the state and within civil society itself' (Clarke, 1998:50). In addition, NGOs are also described as 'a collection of individuals engaged in a struggle for respect and recognition as human beings with dignity' (Fisher, 1997:446).

Related to the academic discussion summarized above, one can also identify various political views on the functions of NGOs. Liberals perceive NGOs as preferred channels of *substitution* of state or market action aiming at socio-economic development. Neoliberals see NGOs as channels of service provision *complementary* to the state (Edwards & Hulme, 1996; & Salamon & Anheier, 1997b; Clarke 1998). From a more leftist stand, NGOs are perceived as vehicles for democratisation contributing to the transformation of society (Edwards & Hulme, 1995; Vakil, 1997; Clarke 1998). In other words, NGOs either fill in a vacuum between market and the state or become arenas of 'political contestation' as a 'response to the hegemony of formal institutions' (Clarke, 1998:45, 41).

Table 2.1   Various perspectives on the role and function of NGOs

Academic perspectives	Political perspectives
NGOs are political in nature	Leftist view: NGOs as vehicles of democratization

– they strengthen civil society and add to the creation of checks and balances in society
  – they represent the institutionalization of existing patterns of political contestation between the state and civil society and within civil society
  – they represent a collection of individuals engaged in the struggle for human dignity	

NGOs are instrumental in nature	Liberals: NGOs as substitution of the state or market
	Neoliberals: NGOs as complementary to the state or the market

The debate about the role and function of NGOs has not been resolved. Moreover, the question is whether this debate is a matter of 'either … or'. Some argue that NGOs are both instrumental and political in character by characterizing the role of non profit organizations as 'protectors of both pluralism and privilege, sites of democracy and control, sources of innovation and paralysis, instruments of and competitors to states' (Di Maggio and Anheier,1990:153).

Nevertheless, the outlook is predominantly optimistic: NGOs are perceived as promising actors on the global scene. They would either be better service providers than state or market organization or they would contribute to a better and fairer world. It was this optimism that induced the growth of the NGO community in the past decades.

The expansion of the NGO community

The promise for successful NGO performance manifested itself in the expansion of the
NGO community (Skjelsbaek, 1971; Iriye, 1999). For example, the number of NGOs
has increased from 832 in 1951 to 16,208 NGOs in 1990 (Yearbook of International
Organization 1989-1990 in Beigbeder (1991)). This expansion is related to various
societal, political, and economic developments (Salamon & Anheier, 1997b; Fisher,
1997; Vakil, 1997). Societal changes, such as an increase in alphabetism and the
globalization of communication, enhanced the possibility for speedy and worldwide
(non-governmental) organization and action. Economic growth facilitated the rise
of a commercial, professional, 'bourgeois' class. This created material improvement
and a group of people capable to organize non-governmental action in the Western
and non-Western world.

In addition, various economic and political 'crises' have contributed to a growing
demand of third sector organizations (Salamon, 1994; Lewis, 2001). Especially the
crisis in the welfare state and in development, as well as political crises in Eastern
Europe are important in this respect. In the 1980s and 1990s, the Western world
experienced a crisis in the western welfare state originating in disappointment about
the effectiveness and efficiency of the public sector (DiMaggio & Anheier, 1990;
Salamon & Anheier, 1997; Vakil, 1997). This resulted in 'a neoliberal climate of
disenchantment with the state' (Clarke, 1998:37) focusing on the privatization
and marketization of government tasks. This neoliberal climate also spread to the
development sector, which was confronted with a lagging economic growth in
Third World countries. This was blamed, among other things, on the ineffectiveness
of bilateral and multilateral development aid programs implemented by national
governments. NGOs were believed to be better capable in reaching the poor and
to be more cost-effective because of their flexibility, their specific expertise, and
their small scale approach to development (Smith, 1996; Gordenker & Weiss, 1997).
Ideas such as participatory development, empowerment, and 'assisted self-reliance'
emerged and governments started to fund NGOs with the aim to materialize these
ideas in the Third World (Salamon, 1994; Weiss & Gordenker, 1997). In addition,
the crisis of communism, highlighted by the fall of the Berlin Wall in 1989, led to a
decrease of state support for social security arrangements in former Eastern Europe.
The void was filled with market initiatives and the emergence of civil society actors
in these former communist states, which in turn were funded by Western NGOs.

Hence, the rise of the NGO community is related to changing attitudes and
behavior of various actors, such as nation states, international organizations, and
Western NGOs (Salamon, 1994). Nation states and international organizations were
responsible for increased NGO funding. The disappointment in the effectiveness of
state interventions led to political decisions to subsidize NGOs as a substitution of
or complementary to state action (Edwards & Hulme, 1996). The increased funding
of western NGOs by western governments allowed these NGOs in turn to fund local
NGOs in the developing world and in Eastern Europe.

In conclusion, the growth of the NGO community is explained predominantly from the instrumental perspective. NGOs were increasingly perceived to be efficient and effective service providers by their donors and hence they received more funding. However, the promise for successful NGO service provision appeared to be problematic, as will be discussed in the next section.

Broken promises: Explaining problematic NGO performance

For a long time, the optimism for successful NGO performance was shared by academics. This resulted in fairly rosy accounts of NGO actions and behavior (Clarke, 1998). Since the 1980s, however, the political and instrumental role and behavior of NGO has been studied more critically. This led to studies pinpointing not only the strengths but also the weaknesses and problems of NGOs: NGOs failed to reach the poor, worked in some places but not in other places, or lacked internal democracy or downward accountability (Edwards and Hulme,1996). Various organizational problems were identified, such as problems of establishing legitimacy and ensuring accountability, of buttressing the philanthropic base, and of balancing professionalization with voluntarism (Salamon and Anheier,1997b:116-128). In other words, NGOs were accused of not fulfilling both their political and instrumental roles satisfactory.

The identification of not only the strengths but also the weaknesses of NGOs resulted in a heated and continuing debate about NGO performance and accountability (see for example, Edwards & Hulme, 1996; Brown & Moore, 2001; Choudhury & Ahmed, 2002). This led to a new question in NGO research: how to explain these problems in NGO performance? The explanation for these problems is often sought in the common nature of NGOs which is argued to induce problematic performance. One explanation is that NGOs do not solely focus on representing the interests of disadvantaged groups, but also on defending their own organizational interests (Uphoff, 1996). In other words, the disappointing performance of NGOs is explained by the quality or budget maximizing behavior of NGOs (Hansmann, 1987; Beigbeder, 1991). Another explanation is that NGOs are responsible and accountable to multiple stakeholders whose expectations range between an instrumental and a political view of NGOs. This creates multiple and conflicting accountabilities to various principals, such as donors, governments, beneficiaries, the board, and the employees (Brett, 1993; Edwards & Hulme, 1996; Fowler, 1996; Tandon, 1996; Wills, 1996; Vakil, 1997; Hilhorst, 2002). Stakeholders, such as the government, may even be internally divided about their expectations towards an NGO (Fisher, 1997). This forces NGOs to address all their stakeholders' accountabilities and expectations, demanding a multiplicity of activities and 'creative packaging' (Smith, 1996:326). The consequences of these contradicting expectations can be described as follows (Edwards and Hulme, 1996:13):

> Large-scale service provision [in instrumental terms, LH] requires standardised delivery mechanisms (to reduce unit costs), structures which can handle large amounts of external funding, and systems for speedy, and often hierarchical, decision-making; effective performance as an agent of democratisation [i.e. political action, LH] rests on organisational independence, closeness to the poor, representative structures, and a willingness to spend large amounts of time in awareness- raising and dialogue.

The above indicates that NGO structures and behavior are related to the expectations of the dominant coalition of stakeholders. Hence, stakeholders have an impact on the organization's structures and operations. Since these stakeholders have different interests and opinions, we may expect NGOs to be necessarily ambiguous, creating organization problems and hindering effective action (Edwards and Hulme, 1996; DiMaggio & Anheier, 1990).

Recently, it is argued that NGOs are increasingly confronted with stakeholders that emphasize the instrumental nature of NGOs – where NGOs are seen as cost-effective instruments for service delivery – whereas NGOs themselves are inclined to emphasize their political role. Biggs and Neame (1996), for example, argue that important stakeholders have developed 'a formal, linear, mainstream approach to development planning,' in which development is perceived as 'a set of predictable outcomes to be achieved through the ordering of project inputs and outputs …'. This approach inhibits a strong belief in the possibility to accurately measure development outcomes.

In summary, NGO researchers, in their search for explanations for NGO problems, often consider NGOs as a coherent group of actors that show similarities in their characteristics and behavior. This is illustrated in the availablity of many publications that discuss the common nature of NGOs. For example, economists try to explain why NGOs are inherently inefficient or slow to respond to growing demand due to the absence of ownership, constraints in access to capital, and lack of means to control the client and the worker (Hansmann, 1987). Publications studying NGOs from an organizational or management perspective discuss NGOs in relation to issues such as management and leadership (Lewis 2001, 2003; McClusky, 2002), learning capabilities (Edwards, 1997), organization change (Powell & Friedkin, 1987; Christensen & Molin, 1996) and innovative capabalities (Corder, 2001). However, the question is to what extent this assumption of NGOs as a coherent group is legitimate.

Understanding diversity in NGOs

Whereas the explanation of the existence and growth of the NGO community as well as their problematic performance was sought in the common character of NGOs, there is growing attention to the diversity in the NGO community. This attention is relevant since NGOs appear to differ in work methods, goals, and performance. How to explain these differences?

In current NGO research, differences between NGOs are explained by the national context in which they originate or by the field of expertise they operate in. Dimensions that matter in this respect are, for example, the variation in the nature of legal systems, the level of development, the degree of centralization, and the contents of governmental policies, in addition to varying degrees of religious, ethnic, and ideological heterogeneity, historical contingencies, intersectoral relations, and polity structures (James, 1989; DiMaggio and Anheier, 1990; Salamon and Anheier, 1997a).

The John Hopkins Comparative Nonprofit Project is an outstanding example of empirical research into national differences in NGO communities. This project defined NGOs as 'organized, private, non profit distributing, self-governing' and of some voluntary character (Salamon & Anheier, 1997a; 1997b). Based on this definition the project regularly analyzes non profit sectors in various countries, starting with six countries in 1997 (Salamon & Anheier, 1997b). A recent overview of global civil society of the project included a comparison of 35 countries in total (Salamon *et al.*, 2003). The countries are compared on issues such as the scale of the sector per country, the fields in which these NGOs were active, and their income base. This research confirms the argument that the NGO sector varies considerably per country.

However, NGOs also vary in functions, organizational structures, goals, and membership, even if they operate in the same national context (Fisher, 1997:447). Hence, diversity in the NGO community is not explained by national differences only. Korten (1986, 1990) was one of the first to explore differences between NGOs that originated in the same national context. He followed a historical line of reasoning by claiming that NGOs reflect the dominant values of the time in which they were established. So, whereas the first NGOs were predominantly organized to provide relief and welfare assistance, the second generation NGOs reflected ideas of democratization and empowerment that originated in the 1960s and 1970s, and the third generation focused more on issues of sustainability (Korten, 1986). Other authors have also tried to classify NGOs in order to grasp NGO diversity. We hear from government-organized NGOs (GONGOs), quasi-NGOs (Quangos), and donor-driven NGOs (DONGOs), next to community-based organizations, voluntary organizations, cooperatives, etc. (see, for example, Weiss & Gordenker, 1996; Fisher, 1997; Gordenker & Weiss, 1997; Clarke, 1998).

Vakil's (1997) review of various attempts of classification is of value in this respect. She bases her own new taxonomy on these previous attempts and argues that there are two 'essential descriptors' of NGOs, i.e. their orientation and their level of operation (see table 2.2). *Orientation* refers to the activities the organization is engaged in. Vakil (1997:2063) distinguishes six categories: welfare, development (divided into membership and service organizations), advocacy, development education, networking, and research. The *level of operations* is described in terms of international, national, and community-based NGOs. Beside these essential descriptors she also describes so-called contingent descriptors: the sectoral focus and evaluative descriptors (such as accountability, effectiveness, etc.).

Table 2.2   Vakil's categorization of NGOs (1997)

Orientation ↓	Level of operation →	International	National	Community-based
Welfare		Sectoral focus + Evaluative descriptors	Sectoral focus + Evaluative descriptors	Sectoral focus + Evaluative descriptors
Development		Sectoral focus + Evaluative descriptors	Sectoral focus + Evaluative descriptors	Sectoral focus + Evaluative descriptors
Advocacy		Sectoral focus + Evaluative descriptors	Sectoral focus + Evaluative descriptors	Sectoral focus + Evaluative descriptors
Development Education		Sectoral focus + Evaluative descriptors	Sectoral focus + Evaluative descriptors	Sectoral focus + Evaluative descriptors
Networking		Sectoral focus + Evaluative descriptors	Sectoral focus + Evaluative descriptors	Sectoral focus + Evaluative descriptors
Research		Sectoral focus + Evaluative descriptors	Sectoral focus + Evaluative descriptors	Sectoral focus + Evaluative descriptors

Distinguishing NGOs by these descriptors is of value because Vakil argues that differences in orientation, level of operation, sectoral focus, and evaluative descriptors might explain differences in the structure, operating procedures, and management of NGOs. In other words, differences in NGO behavior might be explained by the descriptors previously mentioned. However, *how* these differences might matter remains unexplored.

It can be concluded that the study of diversity in the NGO community has not progressed as much as the study of the existence and growth of the NGO community. We know more about the relationship between national differences and sectoral differences in the NGO community, but we know little about the consequences of these differences for NGO behavior. This has also to do with the fact that the collection of empirical data on NGOs has recently started (1990s) and is very laborious. Unfortunately, there is less attention to diversity in NGOs that operate in the same sector. Searching for explanations for diversity of that sort is relevant because there is evidence of variations in NGO decisions and performance, even if they operate in the same national context or field of expertise. The two NGOs of this study, for example, select different locations for their humanitarian aid projects, and yet operate in the same sector.

Those studies that go deeper into the internal dynamics of NGOs, which are often case studies, clearly show how diverse the NGO community is (see for example Hilhorst, 2004, and Ebrahim, 2003). However, these are hardly connected to larger N-studies, resulting in a lack of knowledge of (differences in) NGO behavior on an aggregate level. Important progress has been made by studying various subgroups in the NGO community, such as done by the John Hopkins project, but these studies do not focus on NGO behavior. Hence, there is yet little theoretical and systematic empirical understanding of differences between NGOs that operate in the same fields or sectors.

Filling a void in NGO research

If we follow the current state of the art literature on NGOs we should assume that NGOs have common organizational features and show similarities in their behavior. Based on existing classification efforts we could refine this assumption by adding that differences in organizational set ups might also explain differences in NGO behavior. How these differences in organizational set ups matter is not clear yet.

This book aims to make a start with the study of diversity in the NGO community and is a first attempt to come to an explanation of behavioral differences in NGOs by studying the internal decision-making processes of a specific group of NGOs: humanitarian aid NGOs. We do not take a stand on the question whether NGOs are of a predominantly instrumental or political nature. The argument in this book is that we first need to open the black box of NGOs in order to study what is driving the actions of NGOs before we can come to such a conclusion. This study also questions whether NGOs share similar organizational features as a category or not.

This exploratory study of two NGOs offers the opportunity to explore if and how organizational set ups influence NGO decision outcomes. The focus is on humanitarian aid NGOs only, thereby assuring that differences in field of operation/ expertise cannot explain differences in their behavior. The NGOs selected for this study also operate at the same level (i.e. the international level), meaning that they have their headquarters in the Western world and they predominantly operate in non-Western countries (see also Vakil, 1997). In addition, both organizations are member of a larger international network of humanitarian organizations. The national headquarters context of both NGOs is kept equal as well, because the literature suggests that differences in national context also create behavioral variation in NGO behavior. Variation in national context would hence undermine our purposes of studying the internal dynamics of NGOs in relation to variation in the organizational set up.

The national context in which these two NGOs selected for this study operate is The Netherlands. The Netherlands is a substantial player in the humanitarian aid system. Not only is The Netherlands a major donor of humanitarian funding (Randel & German, 2002), The Netherlands is also a relevant diplomatic actor regarding humanitarian issues. For example, The Netherlands support the Mine Ban Treaty (also known as the Ottawa Treaty) and successfully negotiated a Protocol in the Convention of Conventional Weapons about the issue of Explosive Remnants of War (ERW). Hence, this study focuses on NGOs in a country that is a substantial player in the humanitarian system. This particular national context may be of influence on the decision-making processes of both NGOs. In the conclusion of this book, we will therefore review to what extent the specifics of the Dutch context influences the research results as well as the possibilities for theoretical generalization.

Even though the sectoral focus of the two selected NGOs is clear – humanitarian aid provision is their common denominator – humanitarian aid consists of various sectoral specializations, such as medical aid, sanitary aid, food aid, and shelter. It can also consist of training and organizational support. It is therefore necessary to define the exact orientation of humanitarian NGOs, since humanitarian aid provision can have elements of welfare, development, advocacy, and networking activities.

A useful distinction in this respect is between the operational and the 'non-operational' NGO (Natsios, 1997). Those humanitarian aid NGOs that send (Western) expatriates to provide humanitarian aid are welfare organizations that deliver services to specific groups. However, there are also humanitarian aid NGOs that provide local or national NGOs with money to provide humanitarian aid. This group of NGOs can be said to be more developmental in character, since they aim at improving the capacities of local communities to deal with humanitarian emergencies. These NGOs are often more generalist in their aid activities, whereas the operational NGOs are more specialized. The two NGOs selected for this study, resemble the above distinction. One NGO represents the *operational, specialist* humanitarian aid NGO (MSF) whereas the other represents the *non operational, generalist* NGO (ACT) and hence differ in their (formal) orientation (welfare vs development, see Table 2.3).

By studying two NGOs with a different orientation we can explore to what extent NGOs that operate in the same sector , in the same national context, and on the same level show similarities in their behavior. If we find more differences than similarities then we have the opportunity to explore how these differences could be explained, thereby filling in a void in the state of the art of (humanitarian) NGO research. A study of these differences might help us gain some first understanding of differences in NGO decisions.

Table 2.3   The two humanitarian NGOs of this study

	Welfare (Operational)	Development (Non-operational)
International	MSF Holland	ACT Holland
	Specialist NGO focused on medical aid and sanitation, advocacy and training	Generalist NGO focused on organizational development, food, medicine, education and advocacy
	= welfare orientation	= developmental orientation

The research strategy followed in this book is neither a single case study nor a multiple N study, it is a study of two cases. On the one hand, this study is an attempt to make generalizations to the theory. On the other hand, this study is sympathetic to the claim that treating NGOs as stable sets of entities leads to only partial explanations of NGO behavior or structures, since the acts and behavior of agents within the organization do not receive much attention. Fisher (1997) pleads to 'avoid reductionist views of NGOs as fixed and generalizable entities with essential characteristics' (1997:442). He argues that it is more useful to approach NGOs as 'fluid webs of relationships' which may help to gain insight in the various relationships within and outside the organization. We therefore attempted to open the black box of internal NGO dynamics to see how structural factors influence internal processes by focusing on the agents within the organization, because it is these agents that constitute the behavior of NGOs. In order to do this, we need a 'tool' to open the black box of internal NGO dynamics. This 'tool' is developed in the next chapter in which a framework for studying NGO decision-making processes is formulated.

Notes

1   I thank Duco Bannink, Berber Lettinga, and Sandra Resodihardjo for their constructive comments on earlier versions of this chapter.

Chapter 3

Opening the Black Box of Internal NGO Dynamics: An Organizational Decision-Making Perspective

In the previous chapter, the state of the art on NGO research was discussed as far as relevant for this study. This literature review led to the conclusion that there is little understanding of the behavior of NGOs that operate in the same sector. We attempt to gain such understanding by means of a study of two Dutch humanitarian aid NGOs that represent two important organizational categories in humanitarian aid.

In order to study NGOs behavior in more detail, this chapter sets out an analytical framework of organizational decision-making processes. The focus on decision-making was chosen since this can be considered an important aspect of NGO behavior in humanitarian aid provision. NGOs need to decide first where to go, whom to help and what to do, before they can implement their projects.

The organizational decision-making perspective set out in this chapter is based on the work of James March. He distinguished between a logic of consequence, a logic of appropriateness, and a garbage can decision-making perspective. These three images of decision-making are helpful in studying decision-making processes in the two NGOs of this study. They serve as organizing concepts that facilitate the construction of an overarching framework of decision-making processes, capturing a substantial part of the organization decision-making literature. In this way, the blackbox of internal NGO dynamics can be opened.

Three images of organizational decision-making

The two theoretical questions deriving from the empirical research question of this study are how decisions are made within organizations and what the determinants for a specific decision-making outcome are. Students of decision-making are exposed to a variety of answers to these questions. This variety can be explained by the presence of many theories of and approaches to the issue, as well as by the many disciplines in social science that study decision-making processes.

Decision-making studies are conducted by scholars in economics, political science, sociology, organization studies, psychology, law, and public administration. The research question of this study directs our attention to the organizational dimension of decision-making processes since we distinguish between an operational, specialist NGO with a welfare orientation and a non-operational, generalist NGO with a development orientation. We need a theoretical framework to further study the differences in organizational set up between these two NGOs. Hence, the focus in this study is on those decision-making theories that have been developed in the field of public administration, sociology, and organization studies.

However, even within the fields of organization studies, public administration, and sociology, many different views on organizational decision-making exist. For this study, we chose three images of organizational decision-making to guide my observations (see Figure 3.1). These three images have been labeled by James March (1988, 1994) as the logic of consequence, the logic of appropriateness, and decision-making as a 'garbage can'. The use of March's three images places this study in the tradition of organizational decision-making research as developed by scholars such as March, Simon, and Olsen. This tradition is characterized by a predominantly theoretical debate about organizational decision-making (Kriger & Barnes, 1992).

This study differs from the existing literature in this tradition because it is an attempt to use parts of these theories to explore an empirical phenomenon. The three decision-making modes provide a means to systematically study decision-making processes in organizations we do not yet know much about. As we argued previously, not much is known about the internal dynamics in non governmental humanitarian aid organizations in general, and their decision-making processes in particular. It is therefore hardly possible to formulate hypotheses about the characteristics of the decision-making processes beforehand. Because of this lack of information, the most suitable research option was to conduct an exploratory study. For this we needed a heuristic framework to guide our observations, which March's categorization provides.

	Time dimension	Process characteristics	Determinants of outcomes
LoC	Prospective	Formulation of alternatives and cost-benefit analysis	Organizational goals and structures
LoA	Retrospective	Matching rules to situations and identities	Rules of appropriate behavior
GC	Simultaneous	Coupling problems, solutions and decision makers	Timing, coupling and coincidence

Figure 3.1   Decision-making in three

Another research tradition of organizational decision-making which could have been useful for my study evolved through the work of scholars such as Mintzberg *et al.* (1976), Nutt (1984), Shrivastava & Grant (1985), Hickson *et al.* (1986), and Heller *et al.* (1988). Their studies are predominantly quantitative in character and search for general patterns in organizational decision-making processes by studying a large(r) number of cases. These studies are less suitable for the purpose of this research for two reasons.

First, these large(r) N studies focus on decision-making processes with hardly any attention to the organizational setting they take place in (see, for example, Heller *et al.*, 1988). When scholars do study the impact of organizational factors on decision-making, they pay attention to broad categories of organizational factors, such as the private-public distinction and the distinction between manufacturing and service delivery (Hickson *et al.*, 1986; Nutt, 2000). Since this study focuses on two organizations that are both non-governmental and focus on service-delivery, these distinctions are not helpful in understanding the impact of the organizational setting on decision-making processes about humanitarian aid projects.

Second, these general patterns in decision-making tell us something about what decision-making processes look like, but they do not seem to provide tools to open up the black box of decision-making in such a detailed way as March's categorization does. Although these studies provide insight into some determinants of decision-making outcomes, such as the nature of the decisions to be taken and the problem to be encountered, they do not show *how* these determinants influence the character of the decision-making process and *why* they do so in a particular way.

March's categorization seems to be more promising in this respect, since the three decision-making modes offer three different descriptions of decision-making processes which enable me to open up the black box of decision-making in more detail. In addition, they define organizational determinants of decision-making outcomes. The three decision-making modes provide a way to combine organization theory with organizational decision-making literature. These two literatures have evolved quite independently from each other, which is surprising because of their shared interest in organizational behavior.[1] This study is an attempt to combine the two in order to gain more insight into how organizational determinants influence decision-making processes.

The choice for March's categorization limits the range of decision-making models applied in this study to a certain extent, but still represents a substantial part of the existing theoretical and empirical literature on organizational decision-making. For example, many studies of organizational decision-making focus on the consequential aspect of decision-making in the sense that they view decision-making as a sequential and prospective process (March & Shapira, 1982:92). These studies pay attention to how problems and alternatives for action are formulated and how they are weighed in the decision-making process. Although these studies make adjustments and refinements to the original idea of consequential decision-making, they still adhere to the idea that decision-making processes are sequential and prospective in character. Other scholars focus more on rule application and appropriate behavior in organizations, such as Kaufman (1960), Miller (1994), and Messick (1999). These authors describe decision-making as a process of recognizing situations and applying rules to these situations retrospectively. The application of rules happens instantly and almost unconsciously. Yet others pay attention to the garbage can character of organizational decision-making such as Padgett (1980), Kingdon (1984), Pinfield (1986), Sproull *et al.* (1987), Mc Grath & More (2001), and Lai (2003). These authors show how solutions and problems chase each other simultaneously and how decision-making is dependent upon timing, coincidence, and coupling. In addition, we see (part of) these three decision-making models back in other categorizations of organizational decision-making theories. Koopman and Pool (1992), for example, categorize decision-making processes into an arena model, an open-ending model, a bureaucratic model, and a neo-rational model; Lipshitz (1994) distinguishes consequential choice, matching and reassessment models; and Browne (1993) discusses rational, organizational, and political decision-making models (see also Grandori, 1984; Brunsson, 1985; Choo 1998; Nutt, 2005).

In summary, March's categorization seems to be a helpful analytical tool to study organizational decision-making in relatively understudied organizations that operate in the same context and work in the same sector, such as humanitarian aid NGOs. In addition, his categorization promises a fruitful combination of organizational decision-making and organization theory literature. The three images of March are used as an heuristic tool and provide an overarching framework to describe three modes of decision-making that represent dominant views on organizational decision-making in the literature.

At the end of the chapter, we will look into the question if and how the three decision-making modes are interconnected. But first we will describe March's three images of decision-making. Per decision-making mode, we will first describe the process characteristics of each decision-making mode, followed by a description of the organizational setting of the decision-making mode.

The logic of consequence

The idea of the 'logic of consequence' became widespread after James March introduced this notion in the 1980s. The concept is closely related to ideas on instrumental rationality in decision-making (White in Schreurs 2000:163).

Instrumental rationality is one of the defining characteristics of the model of consequential decision-making. Instrumental rationality assumes that human beings maximize their individual preferences. Human beings are considered to be self-interested actors that weigh costs against benefits when making decisions. They are capable of making such a cost-benefit analysis by acquiring complete information on alternatives of action and the consequences of those alternatives. In addition, human beings are capable of weighing alternatives against their preferences in a systematic manner, so that only one alternative will prevail.

In the past decades, these ideas on pure instrumental rationality have been adjusted. March and Simon, for example, argued that human beings are cognitively incapable of overseeing all alternatives for action or their future consequences (March 1994:10; Simon 1945/1997:93,94; Kahneman, Slovic & Tversky, 1982). Human beings can at most intend to act rationally. In addition, Simon, March, and others argued that instrumental rationality cannot be achieved because preferences contradict each other, are vaguely defined, or cannot be hierarchically ordered (Simon 1945/1997:74; Lindblom 1959). Scholars of decision-making processes therefore attempted to create a more precise description of decision-making practices. Simon (1945), for example, introduced the concepts of bounded rationality and satisficing, while Etzioni described a model of mixed scanning (1967).[2]

Today, there is a substantial group of social scientists that adhere to the principles of instrumental rationality and use these to study decision-making processes. For example, the rational choice school of thought, in spite of its many different methods and views, derives a substantial part of its theoretical assumptions from the notion of instrumental rationality and consequential decision-making (Zey 1998:41).[3] A study of decision-making, such as this, would therefore not be complete without the inclusion of the model of consequential, rational behavior.

Process characteristics: Anticipatory action in a self-interest world

In a model of consequential decision-making, the aim of the decision-making enterprise is to maximize organizational goals in an efficient way (Edwards, 1954; March 1994; Allison & Zelikow 1999). The organizational goals are formulated with an eye on desired future accomplishments. When individuals in an organization need to decide on a matter, an analytical process will unfold. This process contains the definition of a problem and a search for as many solutions for this problem as possible. This is followed by an analysis of the future consequences of the formulated solutions. The solutions and their consequences will be analyzed in relation to the organizational goals and preferences. Organizational members will study which solutions meet the organizational goals at what costs. Ideally, decision-making should then result in optimal decisions. Hence, the following questions are at the center of decision-making processes (March 1994:2, 3):

- What actions are possible?
- What future consequences might follow from each alternative?
- How likely is each consequence to happen?
- How valuable are the consequences associated with each of the alternatives to the decision maker (in relation to the goals, LH)?
- How is a choice to be made among the alternatives?

According to the consequential decision-making model the most efficient solution, i.e. the solution ensuring maximum goal attainment against the lowest costs, will be chosen. The decision-making process can hence be characterized by instrumentality, sequentiality, and prospective and anticipatory reasoning (Perrow 1986:121; March and Olson 1989:23; Scott 1995:50).

Nowadays, it is acknowledged that human beings are not capable of maximizing their preferences completely, because of cognitive and organizational constraints (see for example, Holmstrom & Tirole (1989) and Kreps (1990) in March, 1997). Simon redefined rational behavior therefore as human beings *attempting* to maximize their preferences. One can only speak of people *intending* to behave rationally as a result of organizationally and cognitively bounded rationality (Simon 1945/1997:88). However, these two adjustments still allow decision-makers to try to answer the questions mentioned above within the boundaries of their own capabilities and those of the organization. This indicates that the result of the decision-making process might be less optimal than was aimed for, but the process of decision-making will still follow the logic that has been described.

In this study, we define consequential decision-making as a prospective and sequential process. In this model, efficiency and goal achievement are the driving forces of decision-making. The task of the individual is to systematically calculate what alternative is the best solution to the problem in relation to desired future accomplishments. Decision-making is an analytical task, predominantly performed by experts on the job. We will therefore label a decision-making process as consequential when we observe:

- *Sequential reasoning*: Decision-makers first define a problem and then define multiple alternative courses of action before deciding what to do.
- *Prospective reasoning*: Decision-makers decide by taking into account the possible future consequences of these alternatives.
- *Maximizing and anticipatory behavior*: Decision-makers weigh these consequences, together with the proposed alternatives, with an eye to the organizational goals.
- *Information-driven decision-making*: Decision-making is closely related to collecting and analyzing information on the problem, the possible alternatives, and consequences.
- *Optimal decisions*: Because the organization seeks to maximize its organizational goals, one expects to find decisions that are optimal. These decisions can vary in content, but will reflect a striving for the most efficient way of achieving the organizational goals.

Organizational characteristics: Simon's administrative organization

Since the main research question of this study has to do with organizational decision-making, we should ask ourselves in what organizational setting consequential decision-making can be found. The model of consequential decision-making is closely related to Herbert Simon's theory of the administrative organization (Simon 1945/1997; Scott, 1992:45), because it shares assumptions about instrumental rationality, attempts to maximize behavior, and consequentiality in action.

Selznick (1957) already made an analytical distinction between the 'organization' and the 'institution'. The organization is a structure of people working together to accomplish a specific goal. The organization serves as a technical tool designed to accomplish these goals in the most efficient and effective way (Selznick 1957:5). Herbert Simon adheres to this notion of the organization in his theory of the administrative organization. This theory reflects an instrumental interpretation of organizational processes (Denhardt 1993:89).[4]

In the administrative organization, the criterion of efficiency is the driving force behind the organization of work. The organization is designed in such a way that the organizational goals will be accomplished with the lowest costs. An administrative organization has a consequential logic of decision-making, in which one choice is made from among many alternatives (Simon 1945/1997:72,77). The focus of the higher-level administrators in the organization is therefore to make sure that its members choose the desired alternatives.

The organizational structure of the administrative organization is designed in such a way that the organizational members will act rationally, efficiently, and goal-oriented. Such a structure requires a clear statement of the organizational goals as well as specialization of its operations. The organization takes away some of the individual's decision-making authority in order to achieve organizational rationality. The individual can no longer decide on his own, but is constrained by the 'vocabulary' of the organization (Simon 1945/1997:47). This vocabulary consists of three aspects: authority, communication, and organizational identification.

Authority is important to secure *high quality* decisions in terms of rationality and effectiveness (Simon 1945/1997:188). This is achieved by specialization. Specialization is a means to optimally use specialized skills in the organization. The work of the organization is subdivided in such a manner that processes requiring a specific skill are handled by the person most specialized in that skill (Simon 1945/1997: 189). The function of the individual is specified in terms of the scope and nature of his job, and the duties connected to it (Simon 1945/1997:7). Authority is also important to guarantee that the organizational members make the *same* decisions. This is done with the help of procedural coordination, such as standard operation procedures, and with aid of substantive coordination, such as manuals (Simon 1945/1997:190,191). Authority also means that some persons have the power to impose sanctions or to create incentives. In addition, there are additional methods, such as training, that lead to the internalization of the organizational objectives (Simon 1945/1997:112). In this way, the premises of decision-making for the individual are created and organizational rationality can be accomplished.

The organizational structure states clearly which expert has to decide on what kind of problems by means of specialization. It also ensures that the decision-making rules are clear by standardization of procedures and by assigning decision-making authority. This prevents discussion and conflict about solutions and consequences.[5] In such a setting, decision-making processes and fora are characterized by a focus on technical issues and information exchange.

If a decision-making process is consequential in character, we expect to find the following characteristics of the organizational setting in which decision-making takes place:

- *The formal structure prescribes behavior, norms and rules, and dictates the decision-making process:* Daily decision-making processes correspond closely to the formal procedures for decision-making in the organization, and the decision-making outcomes correspond closely to the formal (i.e. paper) objectives of the organization.

- *Compliance is secured through sanctions and incentives*: People are sanctioned if they do not make decisions according to the formal policies and procedures.
- *Specialization and hierarchy coordinate the decision-making process with help of procedural and substantive mechanisms*: The decision-making process is facilitated by specialization on the basis of expertise and skills required to decide, i.e. decision-making is partly decentralized to the person who has the expertise to decide. Nevertheless, there is also some element of hierarchical decision-making. Decisions are made with help of standard operating procedures and/or manuals.
- *Decision-making fora have a technical character and focus on information exchange*: Since decision-making is information-driven and based on expertise, decision-making fora are meetings of experts exchanging information.
- *Decision-making is characterized by a low degree of conflict*: There is a clear understanding of decision-making authority: there is little conflict about who should decide, even in the case of disagreement
- *Decision-making is an intra-organizational process:* Because the organization defines its own goals, decision-making is only related to those goals. There is no interest for outside pressures and demands that are not related to those goals.

This image of the consequential organization is related to well-known classifications of organizations, such as the mechanistic organization (Burns & Stalker, 1961; see also Morgan, 1986) and the machine bureaucracy (Mintzberg, 1983).

The logic of appropriateness

Decision-making theories are closely related to the classic debate on the nature of man. The basic issue in this debate is whether the individual is a *homo economicus* or a *homo sociologicus* (Searing 1991:1240). The core assumption of the consequential model of decision-making is that the individual is the former. This explains the notions of self-interested and anticipatory behavior in the model. The idea of the *homo sociologicus* brings us to another strand of decision-making theory, which I will call a model of appropriate decision-making. The *homo sociologicus* is not occupied with self-interested and maximizing behavior, but is a product of its environment that imposes rules, norms, and roles upon the individual (Scott 1995:51).

Various research traditions have developed from notions of the *homo sociologicus*. In these traditions, 'the logic of appropriateness' (March, 1988, 1994, 1997) is the dominant pattern of human behavior, meaning that 'action is often based more on identifying the normatively appropriate behavior than on calculating the return expected from alternative choices' (March and Olsen 1989:22).[6] The above-mentioned ideas form the basis of an alternative, sociological mode of deciding that will be used in this study.

Process characteristics: Obligatory action in a rule-based world

A model of appropriate decision-making contradicts many (but not all) assumptions of the model of consequential decision-making. The aim of decision-making in this model is to make appropriate decisions, i.e. to behave as is expected from the individual in a given situation (Scott, 1995:39, March, 1994:57). In order to do this, the individual matches situations to socially constructed rules that in turn provide guidelines for decision-making. Hence, the following questions are at the center of the decision-making process (March, 1981:228; March 1994:58; see also Burns and Flam 1987:36):

- What kind of situation is this?
- What kind of person am I?
- What kind of organization is this?
- What does a person such as I, or an organization such as this, do in a situation such as this?

The individual will collect situational data to recognize and define a situation. A set of socially and organizationally shared rules is used to select and analyze these data, so that the situation can be defined. Once that has been done, an appropriate rule regime will be chosen and applied, and a decision is taken (Burns and Flam 1987:41,42).[7] A rule regime is 'a social rule system enforced and sustained by legal as well as non-legal sanctions' (Burns and Flam 1987:100). A rule regime consists of rules that specify which actors should act; how they should act; when and where they should act; what roles and obligations they have; which stakeholders should be involved; and what their activities should be. In short, rule regimes define the actors, the decision-making processes and procedures, the stakeholders, the communication channels, and the resources (see Figure 3.2).

It is these types of rules that create patterned behavior among individuals. They have a specific character because they reflect duties and obligations that are part of the contextual setting of the decision to be taken. These duties and obligations define the set of norms and roles that constrain the individual in the decision-making process (March and Olsen 1989; Searing 1991:1241; March 1994). They are the products of a historical process of organizational learning and adjustment (March and Olsen 1989:38; Biddle 1986:67, 69).

The choice of a rule regime defines the type and amount of information needed to decide, and the actions to be taken. In order to define the situation correctly and to choose the proper rule system individuals use reasoning mechanisms, such as thinking by means of analogy and metaphors (March and Olsen 1989:25, Neustadt & May, 1986; Houghton, 1998). Hence, decision-making is retrospective in character.

Who? (actors)
Rules defining who may participate and not in a given social relationship, defined in
categories of participants and roles (connected to purposes of action, types of activities,
and resources)

Why? (purposes)
Rules specifying appropriate or legitimate values, purposes or problems which are to
motivate actors to act in a relationship. These might be specified to specific categories
of actors. These rules specify what outcomes and results are appropriate or valid in
connection with actions and interactions.

What action? (activities/outcomes)
Rules specifying acceptable activities, related to communication, exchange, conflict and
power processes. They also define the rights and obligations of different categories of
actors, or may exclude certain behavior

How?(process/procedures)
Rules specifying how social decision-making and transactions are to be carried and what
procedures are to be followed in a specific situation.

With what means? (instruments)
A further specification of appropriate and legitimate activities and procedures, defining
acceptable resources, technologies and instruments that may be employed.

When and where?(context)
Rules specifying appropriate or legitimate contexts for the activities, actors and resources,
in particular the time and the place of the activities.

**Figure 3.2   Universal rule categories of institution grammars
               (Burns and Flam 1987:102)**

The matching of situations to rules should ideally result in one option for action,
contrary to the logic of consequence that leads to the search for as many alternatives
as possible. Ideally, the rules are clear and known by all organizational members,
resulting in instant decision-making.

   In summary, the model of appropriate decision-making can be defined as a process
of instant, retrospective reasoning in combination with obligatory, rule-based, and
value-driven action (March and Olson 1989:23). In this study, we define appropriate
decision-making as a retrospective process in which the institutional members almost
instantly know what to do and how to decide as a result of shared rules, beliefs, and
values, which create patterned behavior (Brunsson 1985; Zhou, 1997). The driving
force behind decision-making is the urge to act according to perceived organizational
and environmental expectations. The task of the individual is to match situations
to existing rules that reflect the norms and expectations associated to these norms
(Lipshitz, 1994:49). Decision-making is a task that requires thinking with help of
analogies and past experiences. Since individuals have a shared system of rules and

norms, this leads to great conformity in the decisions taken. This indicates that there is little variation in individual decision-making processes and outcomes.

In this study, we will define a decision-making process as 'appropriate' when we observe:

- *Instant reasoning*: Decision-makers define a situation, immediately know the appropriate rule system to use, and almost unconsciously apply that rule system to the situation at hand.
- *Retrospective reasoning*: As rules develop through time, decision-making is a process of looking back into history in order to decide what to do in a current situation.
- *Obligatory, rule-based behavior*: Decision-makers decide on the basis of rules that reflect their roles, duties and obligations in a specific situation.
- *Decision-making by analogy*: Decision-making is a process of comparing current situations to comparable situations; decision-makers consider whether the decision taken in a former and comparable situation is applicable to the current situation. In addition, decision-makers have to make up their mind which rule system applies to a specific situation.
- *Congruent decisions*: Because the individual will act on the basis of values, expectations, and rules that have been internalized through time, basically every individual can decide. In addition, people will make the same decisions, whatever their position in the organization, as a result of their shared values and beliefs.

Organizational characteristics: Selznick's idealtype of the institution

In what organizational setting can we expect to find appropriate decision-making? The logic of appropriateness is a typical feature of the ideal type of the institution, as defined by Selznick (1957). The institution is, contrary to the administrative organization, 'a natural product of social needs and pressures – a responsive, adaptive organism' (Selznick 1957:5). It is a valued product of interaction and adaptation that provides a source of personal satisfaction to its members (Selznick 1957:17; Scott 1987).

The organization is an expendable tool: whenever the job is done, or somebody else can do the job better, then the organization is no longer needed. An institution has a value and a character of its own, for its members and for its environment. Even if the technical task in an institution would be accomplished or no longer needed, an institution has become so valuable to its members and its environment, that change or abolishment will be resisted.

In the institution, there is a clear idea of the purpose of the organization. Contrary to the administrative organization, this purpose is not so much related to formal goals, but to the 'critical problem' at hand, meaning the problem that is 'most frequently and persistently encountered by administrators in their daily environment' (Boin 1998:45). Hence, this purpose can differ from, or even contradict, the formal goals.

In addition, there is a consistent set of beliefs and assumptions within the institution that reflect internal and external pressures and expectations (Scott, 1992:66). This leads to a clear understanding of the standard rules for behavior within the institution. Individuals apply these rules because they perceive an intrinsic value in them (Burns and Flam 1987:66, see also Brunsson 1985). The result is a consistent, patterned way of working that has evolved through the years and that guides individual behavior and actions. This pattern differs from the rational, formal way of working in the administrative organization because the individual is provided with 'an ordered approach to his day-to-day problems, responding to the world consistently yet involuntarily, in accordance with approved perspectives yet without continuous reference to explicit and formalized rules' (Selznick 1957:18). This implies that decision-making is a fairly unconscious, invisible process.

In addition to this internal dimension of the institution, there is an important external dimension: an institution is not only valued by its members but also by its environment. In the institution one recognizes the importance of outside support from politicians, the public, and other stakeholders (Brunsson, 1989; see also Boin, 2001). The interests of these outside groups are taken into account, but only to a certain degree, as an institution is not only characterized by a high level of legitimacy, but also by a fair degree of autonomy to act.

In the institution we can distinguish a clear and common value system (Peters 1999: 40; see also Brunsson, 1989). Individuals act according to these shared beliefs, values, and rules that are perceived as proper and valuable. Therefore, we argue, decision-making processes in institutions follow a logic of appropriateness (Peters 1999:29). The question is, however, how members of an institution know what is expected from them. How is appropriateness achieved in the institution? Selznick (1957) mentions several mechanisms for achieving appropriate behavior. One mechanism important for acquiring appropriate behavior is the recruitment procedure (Selznick 1957:57; March 1994:60). In institutions, people are not so much recruited for their expertise and technical competence, as is the case in the administrative organization, but for their shared outlook on the job at hand and the world in general. Second, when people are recruited and enter the organization they are taken care of by means of training and other socialization processes. This ensures that the new employees internalize the values of the organization and learn how to act accordingly (Selznick 1957:58; Peters 1999:35). Training is therefore not a process of communicating formal rules and technical procedures, as in the administrative organization, but a mechanism that ensures that the individual will act according to the proper role. This is done, for example, by providing newcomers with role models and mentors, and by teaching them the proper categories to think in (March 1994:94). Third, there are informal mechanisms of social control, such as self criticism or peer review (Miller in Boin 2001:32). Fourth, internal group interests are fairly represented (Selznick 1957:59), because internal differences of opinion are perceived as reflections of outside pressures which the institution has to deal with in order to ensure its legitimacy (DiMaggio & Powell, 1983).

If a decision-making process can be defined as an appropriate decision-making process, we expect to find the following ideal typical characteristics of the organizational setting in which decision-making takes place:

- *The formal structure reflects the organizational values and norms, and facilitates decision-making*: Decision-making will occur without the help of formal rules and procedures. It is a coherent value system, in combination with strong socialization mechanisms, that determines the decision-making process. In other words, decision-making is a quite invisible, unconscious process.
- *Compliance is achieved through socialization, training, and informal social control:* Compliance is guaranteed by providing newcomers with role models and mentors, and by teaching them the organizational history, language, and rules. New organizational members learn to appreciate and internalize the rules, norms, and values of the organization, and consequently act almost unconsciously. In addition, social control mechanisms ensure compliance.
- *Coordination is achieved through a clear and common value system:* Formal rules and procedures are not needed to achieve coordinated action in the organization. A shared understanding of the organization's mission and way of working results in coordinated action.
- *Decision-making fora either confirm the shared value system or pass these on to others:* Since the shared value system guides behavior in the organization, decision-making fora are in fact not needed to discuss decisions - these are obvious to all. Decision-making fora are places where the shared values, norms, and rules are confirmed or passed on to newcomers.
- *Decision-making is characterized by a low degree of conflict:* People know what is expected of them, share the values of the organization, and therefore hardly any conflict in the organization will arise. However, if there are value conflicts, they will have a fierce, and potentially destructive, character.
- *Decision-making is a contingent process:* An institution takes into account outside pressures from the public, interest groups, the media, and politics as well as inside pressures while making decisions.

This image of Selznick's institution is related to other organizational categorizations such as the organic organization (Burns & Stalker, 1961) as well as the idea of the professional organization.

Garbage can decision-making

The idea of 'garbage can' decision-making originates from an article by Cohen, March, and Olsen (1972). In this article, some generally accepted assumptions on decision-making were challenged by the authors, the most important one being the idea of decision-making according to a specific logic. Instead, the authors introduced the hypothesis that decision-making is largely coincidental and that problems, solutions, and choices are not connected to each other in an orderly way.

Process characteristics: Coincidental action in an unstructured world

The idea was launched that there are various 'streams' in the decision-making process, namely problems, solutions, participants, and choice opportunities, that exist quite independently from each other (Cohen, March, and Olsen, 1988:297). Cohen, March, and Olsen oppose the notion of sequential decision-making. They argue that the formulation of problems is not automatically followed by the formulation of solutions. These two streams in decision-making float around simultaneously in the organizational space (i.e. the garbage can), parallel to choice opportunities and participants.

Problems can be defined as the concerns of people inside and outside the organization. Not all problems will gain the attention of decision-makers; only those problems will be noticed that have an attractive solution and a choice opportunity attached to it.

Solutions are products made by people within the organization. 'It is an answer actively looking for a question', according to Cohen, March, and Olsen (1988:297). They argue that solutions create a need for problems. The stream of solutions is characterized by the entry time of the solutions and the access structure of the solutions to problems, choices, and participants. Those solutions will be chosen that are connected to a problem, to an attractive choice opportunity, and to participants who support this combination of problem and solution.

The group of participants in decision-making processes is never stable; participants come and go because of other demands on the participants' time. The streams of problems, solutions, participants, and choice opportunities are coupled whenever suitable and possible for participants who have the authority to decide:

> One can view a choice opportunity as a garbage can into which various kinds of problems and solutions are dumped by participants as they are generated. The mix of garbage in a single can depends on the mix of cans available, on the labels attached to the alternative cans, on what garbage is currently being produced, and on the speed with which garbage is collected and removed from the scene (Cohen, March, and Olsen, 1988:297).

Decision-making can therefore be characterized by a process of coupling problems, solutions, choice opportunities, and participants to each other. Participants will only pay attention to those issues that are interrelated in the streams, i.e. those issues that connect problems to solutions and participants. A decision will be taken if these streams can be coupled. Hence, the following questions are at heart of garbage can decision-making processes:

- Is there a solution looking for a problem?
- Are there solutions matching a specific problem?
- If a solution matches a problem, which participants are in favor of this coupling?

- If so, are these participants in a position to influence the decision-making process?
- If so, is there a choice opportunity available in which the problem can be coupled to the solution?

Timing is an important element in a garbage can decision-making process. It depends on the entrance time of problems, solutions, and participants as to what couplings can be made between these streams (Cohen, March, and Olsen, 1976:27).

In the original version of the garbage can model, participants did not have a significant role in the decision-making process. Moreover, the individual was practically left out of the analysis (Bendor *et al.*, 2001: 172,174). However, it is individual participants who eventually make the decisions. Hence, it is important who participates in the decision-making process, which problems these participants think need most attention, and which solution they prefer. Kingdon recognized this important omission in the model of garbage can decision-making and added the notion of entrepreneurial behavior to the garbage can model. Entrepreneurs can push their concerns about certain problems higher on the agenda; they can also push their proposals during a process of softening up the system; they can make couplings; and they can bring in crucial resources (Kingdon, 1995:203). Hence, the agenda setting phase and the formulation of alternatives is crucial in the garbage can model of decision-making. The agenda setting phase is important because it determines what situations will be defined as problems that need to be solved.

In summary, the garbage can model reflects a process of simultaneous and contextual decision-making, in which timing, persuasion, and entrepreneurial action are important factors in the process of coupling problems, choice opportunities, solutions, and participants. In this study, we define garbage can decision-making as a simultaneous and contextual process of decision-making, in which an absence of agreed upon goals and values leads to the generation of many problems and solutions. The decision-making process is a matter of persuading those with decision-making authority. Entrepreneurs can have a substantial impact on the outcome of the decision-making process. Timing, for example with regard to the entrance of problems and solutions, is another important defining factor in the process. In this study, we will define a decision-making process as a garbage can in case we observe:

- *Simultaneous reasoning*: There is a simultaneous existence of the four 'streams' of decision-making: the formulation of alternatives, the definition of problems, making decisions, and the actions of participants.
- *Individual and departmental prospective reasoning*: Since there is a lack of shared and agreed upon goals in the organization, individuals do not strive for collective instrumental rationality. Hence, there is more room for individual or departmental interests to influence the decision-making process.
- *Entrepreneurial, persuasive behavior*: The coupling of problems, solutions, and participants can be influenced by the actors involved in the decision-making process. Persuasion is an important mechanism during the coupling

process. People have to be convinced that certain solutions are more suitable for certain problems than others. Entrepreneurial action is therefore a crucial factor in the decision-making process.

- *Decision-making by coupling*: Decision-making can take place if there are problems, solutions, and participants that can be coupled.
- *Coincidental decisions*: Because the decision-making process is dependent upon the dynamics in the various streams, the decisions taken are to a large extent coincidental. The outcome of the process depends on who is available and present during the decision-making process, and on what problems can be matched to certain solutions.

Organizational characteristics: March and Olsen's ambiguous organization

Although garbage can decision-making is characterized by coincidence and timing in decision-making, this does not mean that March, Cohen, and Olsen believe decision-making processes to be completely unstructured. Decision-making always takes place in an organizational structure. Cohen, March, and Olsen argue that the organizational structure affects the outcomes of decision-making processes by means of the access structure of the problem and the decision structure of the choice. The access structure represents all choices available at the moment a problem is defined (Cohen, March, and Olsen, 1988:296). The decision structure is determined by the participants present in a particular decision-making occasion (Cohen, March, and Olsen, 1988:299). So, the question is: who decides and what choices (solutions) are available, and, most importantly, in what way are these two structured organizationally?

The authors describe three ideal types of organizational decision structures: unsegmented participation, hierarchical participation, and specialized participation (Cohen, March, and Olsen, 1988:304; Cohen, March, and Olsen, 1976:28,29). In an unsegmented setting, any decision-maker can participate in decision-making. In a hierarchical setting, important choices are made by the important decision-makers, and important decision-makers can participate in all decision-making processes. A specialized decision structure means that 'each decision-maker is associated with a single choice and each choice has a single decision-maker. Decision makers specialize in the choices to which they attend' (Cohen, March, and Olsen, 1976:29). The access structure can also be described ideal-typically in terms of unsegmented, hierarchical, or specialized access (Cohen, March, and Olsen, 1976:30).

The type of decision structure and access structure is influenced by the degree to which the organization has been able to regulate the connections between the streams by means of hierarchy, specialization, information distribution, classifications, and agenda-building (Cohen, March, and Olsen 1976:31,32). The authors hypothesize that:

the less the organizational regulation of the four streams, the less the experience with the situation, and the higher the load on participants, the more important the timing of the four streams for a decision process and its outcome (Cohen, March, and Olsen, 1976:32).

This implies that we have more chance to observe garbage can decision-making in organizations that deal with relatively new issues, have a high workload, and a fairly unstructured work process than in organizations that deal with routine issues, have an average workload, and a fairly structured work process.

In addition, Cohen, March, and Olsen argue that garbage decision-making is characteristic for organizations that have problematic preferences, an unclear technology, and fluid participation (Cohen, March, and Olsen, 1988:294). These preferences are considered to be 'problematic' because they are inconsistent and ill-defined. The organization is a 'loose collection of ideas', which results in goal ambiguity, conflict, and poorly-understood problems (Cohen, March, and Olsen, 1988:295, 323). Unclear preferences also lead to an unclear technology. The members of the organization do not completely comprehend the organization's processes, and only have a fragmented understanding of the organization. The organization can therefore only operate on 'the basis of trial and error, learning from accidents of the past, and pragmatic invention' (Cohen, March, and Olsen, 1988:295). The third characteristic mentioned by the authors is fluid participation. This means that 'participants vary in the amount of time and effort they devote to different domains; involvement varies from one time to another' (Cohen, March, and Olsen, 1988:295). This results in an ever changing group of people involved in decision-making. The fact that these groups vary has also to do with how much time is needed to respond to outside demands by the decision-makers (Cohen, March, and Olsen, 1988:316).

This sketch of the organizational setting of garbage can decision-making fits the idea of the 'institutionalizing organization.' Earlier, we argued that both consequential and appropriate decision-making take place in a structured setting, either by means of hierarchy and specialization or by means of values. In these organizations the goals or mission, and the procedures or rules of the organization, are clear to its members. In the institutionalizing organization there is lack of structure and agreed upon goals. Hence, the organization is characterized by a low degree of institutionalization, which means that the organization

> harbors a significant level of uncertainty and ambiguity about the nature of desirable policies and mixes of policy instruments. What the organization does and why it happens is subject of continued discussion, ad-hoc decision-making, and fragmented sense-making processes (Boin, 2001:22).

These ideas of goal ambiguity and an unclear technology correspond with Cohen, March, and Olsen's description of the organizational setting of garbage can decision-making. We therefore argue that the garbage can decision-making model is present in an institutionalizing organization.

In the institutionalizing organization neither the formal setting nor a shared value system structures the daily work processes. Instead, the daily work process is fragmented and varies within the organization. Decisions can only be taken by groups, since decision-making is a matter of consensus-building. Since goals and work processes are unclear, there is no shared understanding or formal procedure to structure organizational action. This indicates a high degree of conflict and discussion in the organization. Since there is disagreement on the organizational purposes and work methods, we will find a tendency to 'emphasize the methods rather than goals' (Selznick, 1957:12). In addition, the organization will be characterized by a high turnover of staff.

If a decision-making process can be defined as garbage can decision-making, we expect to find the following characteristics of the organizational setting in which decision-making takes place:

- *There may be a formal structure, but this structure is debated and hardly influences decision-making:* Although formal policies, goals, and procedures might exist, we expect that these are debated constantly and do not have a significant impact on the decision-making process. Decision-making outcomes will hardly reflect the formal goals of the organization due to a lack of clear goals and work methods, as well as fluid participation.
- *Compliance mechanisms are absent or debated*: There might be formal compliance mechanisms, but when present these are debated and therefore do not influence decision-making.
- *Coordination mechanisms are absent or debated:* There might be formal coordination mechanisms, but when present these are debated and therefore do not influence decision-making.
- *Decision-making fora are places of discussion, persuasion, and compromising* Since there is a lack of agreement on goals and work methods, decision-making fora will be places where matters are discussed, people need to be persuaded, and compromises will be made.
- *Decision-making is characterized by a high degree of conflict*: An institutionalizing organization does not have a coherent framework that guide the actions of its members. Instead, there is continuous discussion and conflict with concern to problems and solutions.
- *Coincidental decision-making*: Timing is an important factor in the decision-making process: it depends on the entrance time of participants, problems, and solutions, as well as on the dynamics within each stream, as to what choice eventually will be made. Decision-making is therefore highly contextual. This is reinforced by fluid participation of organizational members.

This image of the ambiguous organization resembles other organizational categorizations, especially the idea of the loosely coupled system (Weick, 1976; Hasenfeld, 1983).

The three ideal types as a heuristic instrument

In the past decades, the three decision-making modes presented in this theoretical framework have been subject of criticism (see, for example, Goldmann, 2005). For example, scholars started doubting the possibility of consequential decision-making because of issues such as bounded rationality, ambiguity, and uncertainty about probabilities and preferences in decision-making (Kahneman, Slovic, and Tversky, 1982; March, 1994; Kunreuther & Meszaros, 1997). The logic of appropriateness presents us with a deterministic picture of the world in which deviations from rules and past methods are scarce. Hence, it cannot explain change very well. Moreover, both the logic of consequence and appropriateness assume that organizational members will obey the organizational goals and values, whether voluntarily or not. In both logics conflict is the absent factor and is judged to be dysfunctional to the organization's effectiveness. Garbage can theory has also received its share of criticism, not only for the lack of conceptual clarity in the model, but also for its neglect of formal structure and structural constraints, and the fact that it does not allow much room for human beings to influence decision-making outcomes (see Mucciaroni, 1992; Browne, 1993; Bendor et al, 2001).

From these criticisms, many adjustments of the decision-making modes have evolved, predominantly with the aim to adjust these three modes to the reality of decision-making. Examples of these are an attempt to combine garbage can decision-making with institutional theory (Levitt & Nass, 1989), Kingdon's refinement of garbage can decision-making (1984/1995); and recent applications of Selznick's idea of the institution (Boin, 2001). Since this is an exploratory study - which prevents us from determining in advance which adjustment might explain decision-making processes in the two NGOs of this study best -, we have chosen to use the three decision-making models as *ideal types* that serve as a heuristic instrument to guide our observations (see Figures 3.3 and 3.4 for an overview). This requires use to construct the three ideal types in their pure, original form, leaving out those criticisms referring to the applicability of the decision-making modes to social reality.

The relationship between the three decision-making modes

Although the three decision-making modes are used side by side in this study, one should be aware that they do not consist of completely comparable elements. First, the three decision-making modes focus on different decision-making units. The logic of consequence and the logic of appropriateness have evolved as decision-making models focusing on the micro level: the individual is the central decision-making unit (see also Bendor 2001). Garbage can theory pertains to the meso/macro level of decision-making: the organization as a whole is the central decision-making unit in the model.

Second, the degree of detail in the description of the decision-making modes varies. The logic of consequence gives us a very detailed description of how decisions are made. The logic does not only describe the order in which decisions are taken, but also the kind of goals that are important in the process, i.e. efficiency and instrumental rationality. The logic of appropriateness is less specific about what values are central in the decision-making process and what the contents of the rules is that people take into account when deciding. This implies that – on a more abstract level – consequential decision-making may be the appropriate decision-making rule in an organization. The logic of consequence can hence be said to be a specification of a particular type of appropriateness (see also Noordegraaf 2000:268). The garbage can mode is even more abstract because it describes the decision-making process on the organizational level.

Third, the three decision-making modes are not necessarily mutually exclusive. This study explores the relationship between the features of decision-making processes and their organizational setting. This does not automatically imply that the organizational setting is the only variable influencing the nature of decision-making processes. It may be possible that garbage can decision-making occurs in an organization that resembles Simon's administrative organization or Selznick's institution. However, it is less expected that appropriate or consequential decision-making will take place in an institutionalizing organization, since the organizational preconditions for such decision-making processes are lacking. It remains to be seen to what extent the organizational setting influences the characteristics of the decision-making making process or whether contextual factors are more dominant in this respect.

Fourth, the evaluation of the three decision-making modes in the public domain differs substantially from the way we apply the three modes in this study. The logic of consequence has a strong prescriptive element; it is widely believed to be the most desirable way of deciding in organizations. If decision-making processes deviate from this ideal, decision-making is evaluated to be of bad or lesser quality. The logic of appropriateness and the garbage can decision-making mode are descriptive models. Appropriate decision-making may be less desirable in some organizational settings and highly regarded in others, while garbage can decision-making – by its name only – is condemned to be undesirable to begin with. In this study, this evaluation of the three decision-making modes is not shared. The three modes are used to study the practice of decision-making in an attempt to establish what decision-making processes look like in reality and why they do so in a particular way, not to evaluate whether this is good or bad.

The issues raised above are important to keep in mind when reading the empirical chapters of this book. At the end of this book, we will return to the four issues raised above to see if and how these issues are related to the data analysis as well as to the conclusions of this study. In the next chapter we will try to translate these fairly abstract notions on decision-making to the reality of humanitarian aid provision.

	Consequential decision-making	Appropriate decision-making	Garbage can decision-making
Mode of reasoning	Sequential	Instant	Simultaneous individually or
	Organizationally prospective	Retrospective	Departmentally prospective
Type of behavior	Maximizing	Obligatory	Entrepreneurial
	Anticipatory	Rule-based	Persuasive
The inference pattern	Information-driven decision-making:	Decision-making by analogy:	Decision-making by coupling:
	What actions are possible?	What kind of situation is this?	Is there a solution looking for a problem?
	What future consequences might follow from these actions?	What kind of person am I? What kind of organization is this?	Are there solutions matching a specific problem?
	How likely is each consequence to happen?	What does a person such as I, in an organization such as this, do in a situation such as this?	If a solution matches a problem: which participants are in favor of this match?
	How valuable are the consequences in relation to the organizational goals?		If so, are these participants in a position to influence the decision-making process?
	How is a choice to be made among the alternatives?		
Important actors in decision-making	Experts	The more experienced organizational members	Entrepreneurs
Outcome of decision-making	Optimal decisions	Congruent decisions	Coincidental decisions

Figure 3.3   **Process characteristics of the three decision-making models of this study**

	Simon's administrative organization	**Selznick's institution**	**March & Olsen's ambiguous organization**
Role of formal structure in decision-making	The formal structure prescribes behavior, norms and rules, and dictates decision-making	The formal structure reflects the organizational values and norms, and facilitates decision-making	There may be a more or less organized formal structure, however, this is debated and hardly influences decision-making
Compliance mechanisms	Sanctions and incentives	Socialization, training, and informal social control	Compliance mechanisms are absent or not agreed upon
Coordination mechanisms	Formal authority, specialization, with help of substantive and procedural mechanisms	A clear and common value system	There are few formal mechanisms, and these hardly facilitate consistent coordinated action
Character of decision-making fora	….have a technical character in which information exchange is the main activity	….are places where the shared value system is either confirmed or passed on to others	….are places of discussion, persuasion and compromising
Degree of conflict	A low number of conflicts with low intensity	A low number of conflicts with the potential of high intensity	A high number of conflict with varying degrees of intensity
Impact of environment	Decision-making is an intra-organizational enterprise in which environmental pressures are not taken into account	Decision-making is a contingent process in which pressures from politics, the public and the press are taken into account	Decision-making is a coincidental process in which the dynamics in the generation of problems, solutions, participants, and choice opportunities affect the outcome of decision-making to a large extent

Figure 3.4   Organizational characteristics of the three decision-making modes

Notes

1   There are, of course, exceptions to this. See for example, Frederickson (1986) and Pool (1992) who both studied the relationship between organizational structures and the nature of decision-making processes. Fredericksson studied the impact of the degree of centralization, formalization and complexity on the character of decision-making processes.

2   On the other hand, some authors felt the criticism of this rationality concept to be fundamental, that they developed new models of decision-making, such as incrementalism (Lindblom 1959) and garbage can theory (Cohen, March, and Olsen 1979).

3   Other examples of decision-making theories related to the ideal of instrumental rationality and consequential decision-making are game theory and principle-agent theory (for example, see Schick (1997); Halperin & Stern (1998); and Zey (1998)). See also, Carley (1980).

4   It must be noted that Herbert Simon cannot be regarded as a rational thinker who dismissed the existence and usefulness of values and beliefs in organizations. He acknowledged the importance of institutionalization processes and roles in organizations (Simon 1945/1997: 11). However, Simon emphasized the efficiency criterion and rational behavior in the organization, and made all other aspects of organizational life subordinate to these two dimensions. In addition, Simon did not pay attention to possible external constraints to organization rationality, such as the political environment can create. In that sense, Simon is still an instrumental thinker, opposite to Selznick who was more interested in the institution in which internal and external social needs and pressures define organizational action (Selznick 1957:5)

5   This elaboration of the model of consequential decision-making in the administrative organization resembles Thompson and Tuden's category of 'computation in the bureaucracy' (1959), in which the organizational members agree on the preferences about outcomes and beliefs about causation. Thompson and Tuden define three other categories of consequential decision-making that take into account that organizational members may not agree on these two dimensions. These three categories are not used for this study, because the model of consequential decision-making is brought back to its basic assumptions here. Thompson and Tuden's three categories contain an adjustment to the original model.

6   Founding fathers of this tradition have been Weber, Parsons, and Selznick (Scott 1995:16). Institutionalists, such as March and Olsen, have been important scholars in this regard, as they studied the way that norms and values regulate behavior in organizational settings (Boin 1998:41). More social-psychological approaches in this tradition are social identity theory and role theory (Biddle 1986; Ashforth and Mael 1989), in which human beings are studied in relation to the social context they operate in. For example, social identity theory argues that people classify themselves and others into various social categories. People tend to 'choose activities congruent with salient aspects of their identities' (Ashforth and Mael 1989:25). Role theory assumes that persons hold social positions and have expectations for their own actions and those of other persons based on these social positions.

7   Burns and Flam (1987) did not develop a specific decision-making model based on rule following, as their social rule system theory applies to all forms of human interaction, whether on a global or an individual level. For this study, their ideas on rule-based behavior are used to construct a model of organizational decision-making.

Chapter 4

Towards the Reality of Humanitarian Aid Provision: Three Sketches of NGO Behavior

In the previous chapter we have constructed an analytical framework of organizational decision-making processes which serves as a means to open the black box of internal NGO dynamics. Now the question arises what kind of decision-making mode could be expected to be present in the two humanitarian aid NGOs of our study.

The current state of the art on NGO research would lead us to assume that NGO internal decision-making processes probably resemble garbage can decision-making most. Since the NGO literature formulates the expectation that NGOs are confronted with the multiple stakeholders problem, they are 'necessarily ambiguous' as Edwards and Hulme (1996) argued. They therefore will have loosely coupled structures, characterized by internal conflicts about the goals and work methods of the organization (see Chapter 2). If the above holds true, we expect to find that the decision-making processes in both NGOs frequently resembles garbage can decision-making and that their organizations resemble the 'ambiguous' or 'institutionalizing' organization.

However, there are also some clues in the NGO literature that we can find differences between the two NGOs of this study, due to their different organizational set ups in terms of level of operationality and degree of specialization (see Chapter 2). Unfortunately, the literature does not provide hypotheses about how these differences are related to differences in NGO decision-making behavior or outcomes. We are therefore unable to formulate such hypotheses. Instead, we will sketch the characteristics of the humanitarian aid NGO in the ideal worlds of consequential, appropriate, and garbage can decision-making as well as their expected consequences for the patterns in aid provision as a way to study decision-making processes in humanitarian aid NGOs (see Figure 4.1).

The consequential humanitarian aid NGO

If decision-making follows a logic of consequence, we should find sequential reasoning, prospective reasoning, maximizing behavior, information-driven decision-making, and expert decision-making. Decision-makers in an NGO with a consequential mode of decision-making perceive their work as providing aid where they feel they can be most effective with a particular budget. Effectiveness can be defined in many ways, but an NGO will at any time try to meet their organizational goals in an efficient way. For example, an NGO might start projects that are believed to help the largest number of people; or an NGO might go there where others do not come. A project is ended if the goals of the project are accomplished, or if the project is problematic in terms of effectiveness and efficiency.

The decision to start humanitarian aid projects is made on the basis of information. Experts formulate various alternatives for action and a decision is made by assessing information on issues such as the scope of a humanitarian crisis, the number of people in need, the needs in terms of hunger, illness or displacement, and the number of other aid agencies present in the area. These issues will be evaluated with an eye to the goals and the future plans of the organization. The organizational goals form the basis for the budget and the formal policy plans of the organization. These describe in which global areas the NGO plans to be active, and with what type of activities.

We expect the NGO to attach a lot of value to detailed written project proposals that entail a budget, a project plan, and a deadline. The locations and humanitarian activities will probably be selected based on information about the humanitarian crisis situation and related to the goals and policies of the organization. This implies that both the location and the activities might vary through time, depending on the policies, the situation, and the needs at hand.

The termination of projects will be based on an extensive formal evaluation of a project in order to determine whether a project has achieved its goals or whether there are legitimate reasons to terminate the project because of ineffeciency and ineffectivity. This indicates that an NGO in which consequential decision-making is dominant will end projects quite regularly. Important indicators of success of projects are for example: the number of people who received aid; the fact that the implementation of the project activities corresponded with the formal project plan; that the project spendings did not cross the planned budget; and timely implementation of the project.

We expect the organizational policies and procedures to closely match the actual decision-making outcomes and processes. The organizational members will regularly use policy papers, procedures, and guidelines in the decision-making process. The NGO has several specialized departments, such as regional or thematic departments, in which people with the same kind of expertise (per region or type of aid) are brought together. This expertise is a defining factor in decision-making.

The hierarchical line of decision-making is clear to all organizational members. In addition, the organization has an administrative system that facilitates the collection and exchange of information. Filing and documenting decisions, next to evaluation and assessment mechanisms, are important means to control the decision-making process. We expect that projects will be closely monitored through regular financial and activities reports.

The appropriate humanitarian aid NGO

If decision-making follows a logic of appropriateness, we should find rule-based decision-making based on instant, analogous, and retrospective reasoning, and obligatory behavior. Decision makers in humanitarian aid NGOs that resemble the model of appropriate decision-making will make decisions based on organizational experiences. Hence, those organizational members who have been working in the organization for a substantial period of time, and therefore know the organizational experiences, have a defining impact on the outcome of decision-making.

Actions in the past determine the decisions for the future. There is a clear understanding of what the organization should do or should not do. People decide in an appropriate way, because they are convinced that there is only one right way to act in relation to the organization's purpose. There is an almost unconscious way of acting. This way of working has developed through time and reflects the organization's history.

We expect humanitarian aid NGOs with an appropriate decision-making mode to help those countries where they feel they are obliged to go. The urge to go somewhere is a result of a consideration process in which the expectations of the public, the press, the receiving countries, and the organizational values and beliefs are taken into account. Former experiences are also important factors in the decision-making process. If the organization had a presence in the area before, we expect that the decision to initiate humanitarian projects will be taken quite automatically. In addition, project activities will be regularly extended. If a project has been successful in the past, in the sense that the organization's trust has not been damaged, we expect an almost automatic approval of the project.

The decision-making process is an individual activity. Internalized rules provide the organizational members with clues for how to act. Most of the time, the decision-maker will immediately know what to do. Since the organizational values of trust and obligatory action are so much engrained in the individual, we hypothesize that there will be few conflicts within the organization. Project proposals and other decisions regarding the initiation and termination of project activities will not be debated. The organizational members make decisions based on the internalized value system. We will not see the use of manuals, decision-making procedures, and policy plans describing the organization's future plans. There is little specialization of work, and the organization has a low degree of hierarchy.

We hypothesize that the aid flow to countries and organizations is relatively stable. As the NGO provides aid, expectations for the future are created in the recipient countries and the NGO will feel a commitment to continue its activities. We also expect that the organization's activities are relatively stable; as the organizational members have a clear sense of what kind of aid projects fit the organizational purposes. Hence, NGOs develop long-lasting relationships with the recipient countries. Ending projects will not happen easily and regularly, because the feelings of commitment in the organization are strong. Whenever projects end this is only after a long process of deliberation and consultation. In case a project is ended, the organization will ensure that the project is taken over by others or that the people on the spot can take care of themselves.

The garbage can humanitarian aid NGO

The defining characteristics of garbage can decision-making are simultaneous and individually prospective reasoning, entrepreneurial behavior, and decision-making by coupling. If an NGO has a garbage can model of decision-making we expect to find the organization to be very dynamic and turbulent. There will be lots of discussions about decisions to be taken. Decisions are highly debated because there is no agreement on goals and organizational preferences. We expect that every now and then this internal turbulence is part of newspaper headlines, as some participants might have an interest in making the turbulent dynamics within the organization public. In addition, we expect to find fluid participation in decision-making fora, for instance, in the form of high turnover of staff.

Decision-making is largely informal. In such a context, we expect to find decisions that do not reflect the formal goals and policies, if they exist. Therefore, the decisions taken will not reflect a coherent pattern regarding the selection of locations, target groups, and activities of humanitarian aid projects. This is a result of the coincidental character of the decision-making process. The activities will not be focused but spread broadly, depending on individual ideas about humanitarian aid.

Every project proposal will lead to a discussion on the values and mission of the organization. There will be lack of agreement on questions such as: What is good humanitarian aid? What kind of activities should we employ and which not? When do we leave somewhere? Where should we go and where not? When should we start a project? The initiation and termination, as well as the location and activities, of humanitarian aid projects will to a large extent be arbitrary, and can better be explained by group dynamics than by the organization's structure and policies or a shared value system.

Towards the reality of humanitarian aid provision

Now we have sketched the process and organizational characteristics of humanitarian aid NGOs that resemble one of the three decision-making modes, we can turn to the reality of humanitarian aid provision by MSF Holland and ACT Netherlands. We will present our empirical data in the following chapters in order to establish if the NGOs indeed match the 'ambiguous organization' and to what extent the two NGOs differ with concern to their decision-making processes and their organizational characteristics.

We will first sketch the formal organizational characteristics before turning to an analysis of the process characteristics of each NGO. We then analyze the relationship between process and organization in order to establish whether the theoretical relationships assumed in Chapter 2 and 3 hold. We will reflect upon the hypothesis

	Consequential decision-making	Appropriate decision-making	Garbage Can decision-making
Pattern in aid activities in relation to the organizational setting	The locations, target groups, and activities will closely correspond to formal goals and policies	The locations, target groups, and activities will reflect the organizational value system	The locations, target groups, and activities will reflect various group interests
Degree of consistency in locations, target groups and activities over time	The aid provision is consistent with the policy plans, manuals, and procedures	There is a consistent pattern in aid activities, based on the shared value system	There is no consistency in aid activities
Degree of congruency in the decisions within the organization	Experts in the same area of expertise will make the same kinds of decisions	Decision-makers make the same choices as a result of a shared value system	Many different decisions – if they are the same, it is a coincidence
Length of projects	The length of projects will vary, depending on the project objectives	Projects will last long as a result of long-lasting commitments	The length of projects will vary

Figure 4.1   Predicted patterns in aid provision per decision-making mode

about the presence of garbage can decision-making in humanitarian aid NGOs. In the final chapters, we will conclude with a comparison between the two NGOs and an attempt to contribute to the existing knowledge and understanding of potential differences in behavior between NGOs that operate in the same sector and at the same level.

PART 2
MSF Holland Decision Making in Practice

Chapter 5

Traces of the Administrative Organization: MSF's Organizational Features

MSF Holland was established in 1984 in Amsterdam by a group of six Dutch doctors. This group was inspired by the French branch of Medécins sans Frontières founded by French doctors in 1971. These doctors believed it was necessary to establish a non-military, non-governmental organization specialized in emergency medical assistance in order

> to rectify what they perceive as the shortcomings of international aid: that it offers too little medical assistance and that aid agencies are overly reticent in the face of the many legal and administrative obstacles to the provision of effective humanitarian relief. The founders of MSF also distinguish themselves from other aid workers by their awareness of the role of the media in bringing the plight of populations to the attention of the general public (www.msf.org/msf/history).

In 1985, MSF Holland implemented its first aid project in Sudan, independently from other national MSF branches (De Milliano, 1991; De Haan *et al.* 1995).[1] Shortly thereafter, the organization initiated many interventions, for example, after an earthquake in Mexico (1986), a volcanic eruption in Colombia (1986), the famine in Ethiopia (1987), and an earthquake in Armenia (1987).

The budget increased equally fast from five million Dutch guilders (€2,3 million) in 1985, to eighteen million (€8,2 million) in 1988, to almost 116 million guilders (€52,7 million) in 2000. As a result, MSF Holland grew rapidly from nine office employees and seventy expatriates in the field in 1986 to 179 office employees (occupying 129 full time jobs) and 613 expats (occupying 353 full time jobs) in 2000. The project portfolio of the organization expanded as well from twelve project countries in 1989 to 41 project countries in 2000.[2]

How is an operational and specialist organization, with such a large budget and so many employees in the headquarters and the field, structured and organized? Do we find features of the 'ambiguous' organization as assumed by current NGO research? This is the question at the heart of this chapter. In order to find an answer to this question, we studied MSF Holland's formal organizational features. We studied MSF's internal formal structure, formal coordination and compliance mechanisms, and the decision-making fora and actors (see Figures 3.3 and 3.4 in Chapter 3). This information is needed to understand MSF Holland's decision-making processes in practice as discussed in the following chapters.

A brief history of MSF Holland's organizational development[3]

Since its foundation, the high growth rate within MSF Holland affected the organization's structure and functioning in such a way that it required the organization to adapt its policies and management structures several times.

In 1986, two years after MSF Holland was founded, a second director was appointed to be responsible for internal affairs. This position was eliminated three years later. By the end of the 1980s, the organization started a process of professionalization. Various handbooks and procedures were introduced and the first training course for expats was organized. At the same time, a separate emergency desk was set up in order to respond more effectively and speedily to humanitarian emergencies.

In 1990, MSF Holland organized a meeting to discuss new MSF policies. Three categories of aid projects were defined: unstable area projects; refugee and displaced persons projects; and epidemic and other disease-related projects. In 1991, this categorization of projects was replaced by two new project categories: medical humanitarian aid projects in acute emergencies with a time span of three months at most (A projects); and B projects, meaning medical humanitarian aid projects in chronically unstable areas with a maximum time span of one and a half years.

Development projects were no longer considered to be a core activity of the organization. This created a problem, because the organization had been implementing this type of projects for quite some time. MSF Holland therefore looked for a way to transfer her development projects to other organizations. However, existing developmental organizations did not have enough expertise to engage in development activities in relatively unstable areas, which was characteristic for MSF's development projects. Hence, MSF Holland decided in October 1992 to found a new organization specialized in developmental activities in post-conflict situations: *Health Net International*. Up until 2000, an average of 5 percent of all MSF projects was transferred to this organization every year (MSF policy document 1996).[4]

In 1993, the general director needed more help to manage the growing organization. Therefore, a five person management team was established which consisted of the heads of the Operations, HRM, Control, and Marketing and Communication departments. At that time, the office in Amsterdam consisted of various 'country desks' that initiated and monitored all MSF Holland projects. These desks were regionally divided and responsible for the management of all MSF's projects in the field. The field teams had only limited decision-making authority.

In 1996, the organization changed its organizational structure from top to bottom. A decentralized structure was introduced which was called the 'demand driven system'. The country desks disappeared and the MSF country teams were expanded and given more responsibilities instead. The idea behind this organizational change was that the field teams were better able to identify the needs on the ground. The heads of mission in the field were therefore given the decision-making responsibility concerning the operational aspects of projects. Their operational directors at headquarters remained their supervisors but more distantly. The other departments in the head office changed into advisory departments to the field (see Figure 5.1). In 1997, the dual directorship was reinstated.

The demand driven system: a focus on information and specialization

After the introduction of the demand driven structure, the top of the organization consisted of a management team (see Figure 5.1). At the time of the study, members of this team were the director of external affairs, the director of internal (HRM) affairs, and four operational directors (ODs).

Each operational director had a portfolio of project countries and supervised projects in specific areas in the world.[5] This division of labor, however, was never stable, because the regional focus per director depended on workload and on current trends. Whenever one operational director was overloaded with work, another OD took over an area of focus. It could also occur that new humanitarian crisis areas emerged. The portfolio of countries therefore changed approximately every nine months. It was decided not to divide tasks according to a consistent regional logic, because it was believed that each operational director could learn more by supervising different regions. Coherency in project portfolios was acquired by a thematic approach, for example, through allocating all sleeping sickness projects in one portfolio.

At the time of the study, the Amsterdam office contained several supporting departments. There was a Control & Financing Department; a HRM department; a Context and Evaluation department; a Communication & Fundraising Department; a Logistics department; and a Public Health department (see Figure 5.1). The Context & Evaluation Department analyzed sources of conflict and emergencies in the world in order to give MSF the opportunity to intervene timely and effectively. In addition, the department promoted, planned, and implemented project evaluations for the organization.[6] The Public Health department had subdivisions specialized in water and sanitation issues, humanitarian affairs, and medical issues. All these departments had an advisory role in that they evaluated and advised country teams.[7] Then there was the Emergency Desk, which consisted of experienced expat personnel who could be brought into action to assist the local MSF teams whenever needed. The Emergency Desk had a special position within MSF Holland, because it could initiate new projects in areas where no MSF teams were present.

As a demand driven organization, MSF Holland worked bottom up: it was the field that defined the need for interventions, and the top of the organization that facilitated these interventions. The management team (MT), however, had the final responsibility for major project decisions. The MT had the task to guard the organization's budget and human resources and therefore had the authority to approve or reject project proposals.

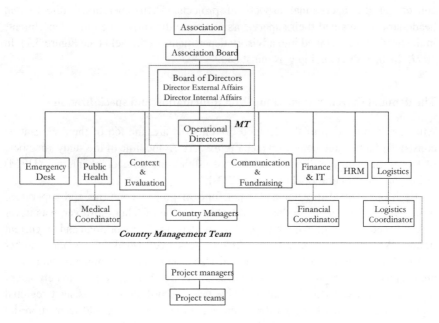

Figure 5.1   MSF Holland's organizational structure in 2001

In each country where MSF had a substantial presence, one could find a country management team (CMT), headed by a Country Manager (CM) who was responsible for the management of the country team and the project managers. The country management team often consisted of various experts: a medical coordinator (medco), a financial coordinator (finco), and a logistics coordinator (logco). These experts had an advisory role towards the country manager and the project managers. They often contacted the medical, financial, and logistics advisors at headquarters. The formal line of authority led from project manager to country manager to the operational director at headquarters (see also Figure 5.1). The country manager supervised various projects in the country, which in turn were managed by project managers. The project staff often consisted of local and expatriate staff, such as doctors, nurses, nutritionists, as well as financial, administrative, and logistics team members. Sometimes communication advisors or humanitarian affairs experts were added to these teams.

From the above, it could be concluded that MSF Holland structured its organization according to principles of specialization through the various advisory departments at headquarters and the expert members of the country management teams. In addition, information collection was important, since there was a special unit to fulfill this task in the organization. Finally, there was a formal line of authority from project managers, to country managers, to the operational director, and the management team.

An abundance of coordination mechanisms

During the case study period, MSF Holland had a large number of procedural and substantive coordination mechanisms. The procedural coordination mechanisms consisted of a general policy plan, an annual planning process, and country policies. The substantive coordination mechanisms entailed policy papers, guidelines, and manuals.

The Mid Term Policy

Strategic policymaking within MSF Holland takes place in cycles of three years. Every three years the management team produces a new policy document that envisions the goals and activities of the organization in the coming years. This is the so-called Mid Term Policy (MTP). As of 2001, the organization had produced three of these policy documents (in 1993, 1996, and 1999). The Midterm Policy is designed to provide the foundation for all other – subordinate – decision-making processes.

At the time of the study, the 1999 Mid Term Policy was in use (written for the period 2000–2002). The mission of MSF for these years was summarized as the will to 'be present, relevant and effective in the major humanitarian crises of the day' (MTP 1999:6). MSF Holland aimed to

> show compassion to Populations in Danger; to work alongside Populations in Danger; to provide them with excellent medical assistance they clearly value; to provide a much valued voice to the voiceless; and to play a meaningful role in the social life of our supporting publics (MTP 1999:6).

The guiding principles for the organization's actions were: humanity (all human beings require a minimum level of basic and fundamental needs); medical ethics; international humanitarian law; and human rights norms and laws. MSF core values were defined as: independence, impartiality, and neutrality in action; volunteerism and an associative nature (MSF Holland is a volunteer organization). Its operational principles were proximity (medical assistance is not only a technical activity, it is also an act of compassion, solidarity and protest); accountability; and transparancy (MTP 1999:8–11, 31).

MSF recognized in its Midterm Policy that it cannot respond to every need identified and tried to deal with this in a manner which can be labeled as an attempt to maximize available resources efficiently:

> We are unable to react and serve all needs, therefore we need to identify the type of crisis where we have the strongest humanitarian impulse and the greatest chance for a medical impression – and act to ensure that the capacity is present, relevant, and effective (MTP 1999:13).

The MTP contained a framework with general intervention criteria that should guide the discussion whether to intervene or not in specific situations (MTP 1999:15,16).

Broadly spoken, these criteria were: the scope of the disaster and the needs (scale, severity, duration, and abnormality); the causes of the needs (i.e. the nature of the crisis in relation to vulnerable groups in the society); and the role of MSF. MSF's role to play was defined by (MTP 1999:16):

- the requirement for a humanitarian as well as a medical emergency response
- the willingness and capacities of others to respond
- the failure of formal authorities to meet their formal responsibilities
- denial of humanitarian access or degrading of humanitarian principles
- a high level need for the protection of victims
- forgotten crisis, not in the public eye

So, MSF Holland aimed to intervene in crises where there was social injustice or a violation of human rights, in combination with a significant medical and humanitarian crisis where MSF had an important role to play (MTP 1999:17). MSF's core activities can hence be defined as emergency medical aid, témoignage (to bear witness), and upholding humanitarian principles and action. The MTP formulated the aim to spend 65 percent of the budget on conflicts and emergencies, 25 percent on other medical humanitarian crises, and another 20 percent on unplanned emergencies. Another target was to allocate 60 percent of the yearly budget to Africa.

Project activities would be terminated if the crisis of needs had diminished; when others were adequately fulfilling the needs; when there was an opportunity to hand over the project to more appropriate partners; or when the target population was able to cope with the situation (MTP 1999:17). Local capacity building was a means to an end and not an end in itself.

The Annual Planning Process and Country Policies

Based on the Mid Term Policy, the operational directors each year formulated an annual plan (AP) for which they asked their country managers to make estimates of expenditures for the coming year. This annual plan was the point of departure for the budgetary process that followed accordingly (see Figure 5.2). Most newly planned activities were launched by means of the annual plan. In the annual plan, an overview was presented of the results planned for each country in the coming year. This consisted of continuing projects and newly planned projects. The intended results were stated in terms of indicators for success. In case of new projects, a motivation for starting the project had to be added. The country team also needed to plan evaluations and exploratory missions.

In order to decide on the allocation of resources in the annual plan, the operational directors and country managers used country policies. The country policy was the guideline for decision-making concerning the allocation of the yearly budget and the activities per country. This policy should exist for every country in which MSF Holland was involved. In these policies it was clarified what activities had priority for MSF in a specific country. The prioritization of activities was based on a context analysis of the country's political and humanitarian situation. One could find summaries of these policies in the annual plan.

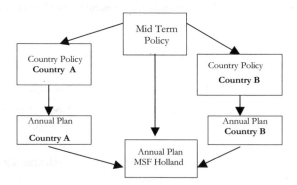

Figure 5.2   A flowchart of the annual planning process within MSF Holland

The draft annual plan per country was made in the field. The country managers sent their draft annual plans to their operational director for approval. The management team then sat down to discuss the annual plans per country in order to decide whether the budgets fit within the total planned budget of the organization. Projects were approved if they matched the MTP and country policy, and if enough funds were available.

In the yearly budget, approximately 80 percent was reserved for the implementation of projects and 20 percent for 'unplanned emergencies'. If more money was needed than originally planned for, and the money was available, MSF could extend its original budget. The Emergency Desk had the freedom to spend 20 percent for unplanned emergencies. Of course not all interventions could be anticipated in the annual plan. In case a country team saw a need to initiate a project that was not planned for, separate approval had to be asked from the operational director and the management team. These proposals were then discussed in weekly MT meetings at headquarters.

Thematic policy papers, guidelines, and manuals

Beside the MTP and country policy, the organization also produced thematic policy papers. These policy papers, approximately 20 at the moment of the study, dealt with more general topics, such as how to act in different kinds of crisis situations, how to prepare for specific emergencies, and how to deal with various diseases (see Table 5.1).

In addition, there were procedures that encompassed the practicalities at the operational level, the so-called guidelines and manuals. Guidelines were concerned with the project level of interventions and mostly involved medical and logistics issues. In 2001, 88 of these guidelines could be counted, of which 43 dealt with medical issues, 19 with logistics, 8 with HRM, 4 with Context & Evaluation topics, and 3 with security and Emergency Desk issues. Other themes touched upon in guidelines were psychosocial care, training, IT, finances, and humanitarian affairs.

Table 5.1   Overview of MSF policy papers topics

Public health issues	Management issues	Emergency issues
HIV/AIDS	Code of conduct	Flood interventions
Mental health policy	General security policy	Emergency preparedness policy
Local purchase of pharmaceuticals	Donor strategy	Earthquake interventions
Tuberculosis	ICT field policy	Handling abduction cases
Female genital cutting	Code of conduct	
Operational policies for water and sanitation projects		
Public Health department policies		

From proposal to project and beyond

For each project that MSF employees wanted to start, a project proposal was required. In this proposal, the authors had to provide a problem analysis, for example by presenting morbidity and mortality rates for a specific disease, or for a specific population. The target population had to be described, as well as a general project objective and specific project objectives (SOs). A 'logical framework' followed the objectives (see Figure 5.3). This required a translation of the project objectives into (measurable) indicators, sources of verification, and assumptions (i.e. requirements for success).

The project proposal could be formulated by a project manager, but the country manager was responsible for the final draft before it was sent to the Amsterdam headquarters. Most of the time, the advice of the medical, financial, and logistic coordinator in the country management team was asked before the proposal was sent off to Amsterdam. These coordinators, for their part, often had been in touch with their advisors in the headquarters about the specifics of the project proposal.

Formal approval of a project proposal could not be given before the Amsterdam management team had discussed the proposal in one of their weekly meetings. Although the operational directors and the management team had the formal authority to decide, these actors often discussed their plans with the advisory departments in meetings that were called Operational Support Teams. These teams consisted of financial, health, logistics, humanitarian, and other experts from various departments at headquarters. In these meetings, the operational director exchanged information about the status of the projects in his or her project portfolio. The experts were free to express their opinion and advice to the operational director. However, the director was not obliged to follow up on the advice given.

Objectives	indicators of success	Sources of Verification	Assumption
SO 1: control of mortality and morbidity of the refugee pop	CMR < 1/10.000/day < 5 CMR < 2-4/10.000/day	- MoH monthly stats - MSF monthly stats - graveyard monitor	community based health care program operational adequate general food ration 2100 Kcal per day
SO 2: mother and child health improved	still birth rate < 10/1000 births maternal mortality rate <200 per 100.000 births	- MSFH monthly antenatal stats - graveyard monitor	referral system functioning
SO 3: nutritional status improved	GAM <10% SAM U5 < 1%	- nutritional screening - nutritional surveys - foodbasket monitoring	adequate general food rations (2100kcal/day, 70g protein/day) = food security ensured
SO 4:			
sufficient and safe emergency water supply	15-20 l person/day drinkable water	- water testing results (delaqua/chlorination - water supply stats	longer term water supply system in use by 01/07/00

Figure 5.3   An example of a logical framework of an MSF Holland proposal

Explanation of acronyms: CMR: crude mortality rate = total number of deaths divided by the total population x 100.000; mortality rate = number of deaths divided by the total number of persons in the population; kCal = kilocalories; MoH = Ministry of Health; GAM = global acute malnutrition; SAM U5 = severe acute malnutrition under five year olds (acute malnutrition of children defined by the ratio of weight for height (=W/H) classified by severity using criteria of the World Health Organization).

Once a project was initiated, the head of mission was required to report on its status and progress every four months. These reporting moments – called the four monthly, eight monthly, and 12 monthly (4M, 8M and 12M) – gave the organization the flexibility to adjust the annual plan to the current situation. This meant that new projects could be planned for and adjustments to running projects could be made. The reporting was done according to a uniform reporting format (see for an example, Figure 5.4).

Project Purpose (PP):
Control of mortality and morbidity of the refugee population through adequate emergency public health services.

PP indicator (=planned result): Remark: PP indicators standard and backdated!
15.000 refugees (currently 10,000) Target reached in next 4ter.
Nutritional survey every 3 months
CMR < 1/10.000/day   U5MR < 2/10.000 day in next 4ter
TFC children < 70% W/H as from May '00
SFC   70% - <80% W/H
1/1000 population Community Health Workers integrated in Community Based Program
Water: 20l/pppd drinkable water, target reached in May. 1:20 latrines
Other PP indicators not yet identified

Current Value of PP indicator:
CMR's fluctuating but since last week of April "out of control"
Nutritional survey: 11.8% < 80%/ 3.0% <70%
Nutritional services will start next 4ter
18l/pppd drinkable water/ latrine target reached + 1:20 latrines target reached

Value the interaction between project planning and environment by discussing:
No health indicators set at the beginning of the program because of unknown (health) status and target. Program started some 8 weeks ago.

Status: **major problems**

Constraints/opportunities (Observations CM)
Difficult Refugee population in terms of organization and acceptance of outside assistance. Very demanding, difficult to approach. No sufficient, well trained health staff available (national- and refugee). Food security at stake. Agreement with partner organizations not firm. Logistic constraints and shortages in several commodities have already led to deteriorating nutritional status. Feeding programs of MSFH therefore in isolated situation. Water trucking program MSFH extremely cost-ineffective. Longer term partner incapable of implementing longer term solution (pipeline).

Response/Planning next quarter
1. sufficient and adequate PP indicators identified
2. malaria control
3. nutritional feeding program implemented, food security monitored
4. laboratory (referral) referral service identified and operational
5. referral service fully operational = rehabilitation health center completed
6. training program for national and local health staff implemented
7. MSFH to take over longer term water supply by implementing simple, adequate piping system
8. transfer of emergency water supply to longer term supply system completed

Figure 5.4   An example of a quarterly project report

Explanation of acronyms: CMR: crude mortality rate = total number of deaths divided by the total population x 100.000; U5MR = under five year mortality rate; TFC: therapeutic feeding centre: aims to reduce the mortality rate of severely malnourished people by means of specialized diets and medical treatment; SFC: supplementary feeding centre = a less intensive feeding program for less acute malnourished people (compared to TFC); W/H = weight for height index (method to calculate degree of malnutrition)

MSF Holland in the world

MSF Holland is not an organization that operates isolated from the rest of the world. First of all, the organization is part of the international MSF network. At the time of the study, this network consisted of 5 operational units and 13 delegate offices all over the world. All these 18 offices were associations and had an elected president. The other operational units beside MSF Holland were: MSF France, MSF Belgium, MSF Switzerland, and MSF Spain. There was a joint MSF secretariat and an international council of the eighteen elected presidents in Brussels, Belgium.[8]

The delegate offices assisted the operational units by taking care of the recruitment of volunteers, advocacy and lobbying, fundraising in the respective regions, and PR activities. All MSF offices based their work on a collective International Charter (see box 5.1). This charter had been re-affirmed in the so-called Chantilly document that was formulated in 1995. In this document, medical aid and witnessing of human rights abuse were defined to be inseparable elements of MSF's work in the world (Advocacy Information Kit, 2000:1).

Box 5.1   The MSF International Charter

- MSF offers assistance to populations in distress, to victims of natural or man-made disasters and to victims of armed conflict, without discrimination and irrespective of race, religion, creed or political affiliation.

- MSF observes neutrality and impartiality in the name of universal medical ethics and the right to humanitarian assistance and demands full and unhindered freedom in the exercise of its functions.

- MSF volunteers undertake to respect their professional code of ethics and to maintain complete independence from all political, economic and religious powers.

- As volunteers, members are aware of the risks and dangers of the mission they undertake, and have no right to compensation for themselves or their beneficiaries other than what MSF is able to offer them.

MSF Holland is also rooted in the Dutch society by means of an association and antennas. The association has been found in 1996 and consists of former and current employees of MSF Holland. The association elects a board which supervises the foundation MSF Holland, i.e. the operational part of MSF Holland. The association board and the board of directors are responsible for safeguarding MSF's identity, effectiveness, and efficiency. The antennas are regional networks manned by former MSF expats. The antennas aim at disseminating MSF's ideas in Dutch society. This is done by means of presentations in companies, schools, universities, etc.

Archetype of the administrative organization

From the above, we conclude that MSF Holland's formal organizational structure resembles some of the characteristics of Simon's ideal type of the administrative organization as discussed in Chapter 3. MSF Holland is an organization in which there is an emphasis on specialization and formal authority. There are a substantial number of procedural and substantive coordination mechanisms and a clear formal hierarchical line in decision-making. Experts are important actors in Operational Support Team meetings and through their advisory relationships with the field. Hence, we do not find any clues in the formal organizational structure that MSF Holland is an 'ambiguous' organization, characterized by garbage can decision-making, as assumed on the basis of existing NGO research.

Although we have only looked here at the formal organizational characteristics, we draw the preliminary conclusion that MSF Holland resembles Simon's ideal type of the administrative organization. Based on the theoretical framework of this study, it could be expected that the dominant decision-making mode within MSF Holland therefore resembles the logic of consequence. Whether this is the case or not, will be explored in Chapters 6, 7, and 8. In Chapter 6, the characteristics of MSF's dominant decision-making mode are described, while in Chapter 7 a closer look is taken at some decision-making occasions that clearly did not follow this dominant decision-making pattern. In Chapter 8, two cases of decision-making in humanitarian emergencies in Africa will be presented with the aim to give the reader a more in-depth sense of MSF decision-making in practice.

Notes

1   MSF Holland's first humanitarian aid project was in Chad in cooperation with the Belgian MSF branche.
2   This information is derived from the MSF Holland yearly reports (1996–2000).
3   For a more indepth account of the organization's early history see De Milliano, J., 1991, *Tussen Korenvelden en Puinhopen, Onderweg met Artsen zonder Grenzen,* Amsterdam: Lannoo/Balans, en De Haan, A. *et al.*, 1995, *Artsen zonder Grenzen, Tien Jaar Noodhulp Wereldwijd,* Bosch & Keuning.
4   After that, Health Net was set free. MSF provided an institutional grant in order to develop Health Net's independence. Nowadays there is no structural relationship with MSF Holland anymore.
5   In 2001, there was one operational director for East Africa and South Asia (from Burma to India); one for Central and South America, the Caribbean and the Middle East; one for West Africa, South Asia and the former Soviet Union; and one director for Southern and Central Africa, East Asia, Eastern Europe, the Balkans, the Pacific, Algeria and the Maghreb.
6   At the time of the study, the organization was preparing the merger of the humanitarian affairs department with the Context and Evaluation Unit.
7   At the time of the study, there were plans to reorganize MSF's headquarters structures once again. The plan was to give the advisory departments more say in the design of new project proposals as well as in the decision-making process of extending projects.

8   MSF Holland is linked to the delegate offices of MSF Germany, UK, and Canada. In 2000 these three offices raised almost 28 million guilders (€12,7 million) for the Amsterdam office. This structure also creates extra channels for institutional donors, such a governments and the European Union. The other delegate offices are located in the USA, Japan, Australia, Italy, Denmark, Sweden, Austria, Norway, Luxembourg, and Hong Kong (yearly report 1998).

Chapter 6

Consequentiality in Aid Provision: MSF's Dominant Decision-Making Pattern

In this chapter we will take a detailed look at MSF's daily practice of decision-making. Since the organizational features of MSF Holland show resemblance to the ideal type of Simon's administrative organization, as we concluded in the previous chapter, the theoretical framework would predict that the logic of consequence is MSF's dominant pattern in decision-making. If decision-making follows a logic of consequence, we should find sequential and prospective reasoning, maximizing behavior, and information and expert driven decision-making.

We have coded the interview material and documents. The results of this analysis are presented in this chapter. The data suggest that the logic of consequence is indeed the dominant decision-making pattern within MSF Holland. We will discuss two categories of decisions: decisions whether to start humanitarian aid interventions or not, and decisions whether to end projects or not. But first, we will present an overview of MSF's decision-making outcomes. It is these outcomes, and the processes that led to them, that are the central subject of attention in this study.

MSF selection outcomes

In the following tables, we present the humanitarian aid expenses of the organization. The focus is on the years 1996–2000, which was the casestudy period. MSF Holland has a substantial budget to spend on humanitarian aid projects. This budget has steadily increased in past years, as we can see from Table 6.1.

Table 6.1   MSF Holland expenditures per continent from 1996–2000 (in Euros × 1000)

Continent	1996	1997	1998	1999	2000
Africa	17.509	15.349	16.686	21.022	26.138
Asia	6.537	6.683	9.881	12.177	14.816
Latin America	2.117	3.198	3.727	6.166	6.178
Europe and Middle East	5.889	3.399	1.747	9.455	4.637
Totals	**32.052**	**28.629**	**32.041**	**48.820**	**51.769**

The largest part is spent on the African continent (see Table 6.2). Anually, approximately half of the budget is spent on projects in this continent, indicating that the aid flow to Africa is quite consistent. In 2004, even 75 percent of the total aid budget was spent on Africa. Asia is the second important continent for MSF Holland. The proportion of the budget devoted to this continent increased from 20 percent in 1996 to 28 percent in 2000 (but fell to 14 percent in 2004). MSF Holland spent an average of 11 to 12 percent on projects in Latin America between 1996 and 2000, indicating a fairly consistent aid pattern. Only with concern to Europe and the Middle East we find substantial fluctuations in relative expenditures with a minimum of 5,5 percent and a maximum of 19,4 percent.

Table 6.2   MSF Holland expenditures per continent in percent of total expenditure per year (1996–2000)

Continent	1996	1997	1998	1999	2000
Africa	54,6%	53,6%	52,1%	43,1%	50,5%
Asia	20,4%	23,3%	30,8%	24,9%	28,6%
Latin America	6,6%	11,2%	11,6%	12,6%	11,9%
Europe Middle East	8,4%	11,9%	5,5%	19,4%	9,0%
Totals	**100,0%**	**100,0%**	**100,0%**	**100,0%**	**100,0%**

If we compare the distribution of aid among the continents (see the following tables), we can observe some interesting developments in the years 1996–2000. Within the African continent (see Table 6.3), seven countries have received aid for five years in a row (1996–2000), consuming a minimum of 73,9 percent (1996) and a maximum of 94,8 percent (1998) of the total MSF expenditures in Africa. This implies that within the African continent MSF Holland invests most of its money in a fairly stable group of African countries.

In Asia (see Table 6.4), we observe a downward trend in relative spending by MSF Holland on countries that received continuous aid. In 1996 more than 86 percent of the Asia expenditures were spent on the six countries mentioned in table 6.4. In 2000, this percentage had dropped by 30 percent.

The expenditures on countries receiving continuous aid in the Latin American continent declined even more steeply, from 81,3 percent in 1996 to 20,9 percent in 2000 to 0 percent in 2004 (Table 6.5). In Europe and the Middle East, the Russian Federation was the only country to receive continuous aid in from 1996 to 2000. The expenditures on the Russian Federation range between 0,4 percent to 63 percent of the total aid budget spent on this continent.

In summary, MSF Holland spent most of its money on the African continent and the Asian continent from 1996 to 2000. In addition, MSF Holland spent a fairly large part of its budget on a stable group of African countries, while we observed a downward trend for the Asian continent, and a very steep decrease in concentrated spending for the Latin American continent. This money was spent on a variety of project activities. For example, the five most common MSF project components in 2000 were training, education and supervision (in 26 of the 41 project countries); exploratory missions (23 times); prevention and management of emergency situations (21 times); rehabilitation activities (20 times); and water and sanitation projects (20 times).

Table 6.3   MSF's African countries of continuous aid in 1996–2000
             (in Euros × 1000)

Country	1996	1997	1998	1999	2000
Angola	1.945	2.113	1.836	2.294	1.964
DR Congo	6.248	3.387	2.168	2.649	4.329
Ethiopia	400	286	757	1.433	2.917
Sierra Leone	786	683	731	1.534	2.135
Somalia	115	532	606	669	1.040
Sudan North*	2.731	4.236	2.832	4.422	4.159
Sudan South			5.999	4.356	2.461
Uganda	730	429	893	1.109	1.025
Total 7 countries	**12.955**	**11.666**	**15.822**	**18.466**	**20.030**
Total Africa	**17.509**	**15.349**	**16.686**	**21.022**	**26.138**
% of Africa budget	**73,9%**	**76,0%**	**94,8%**	**87,8%**	**76,6%**

* MSF had separate teams in North and South Sudan

Table 6.4   MSF's Asian countries of continuous aid in 1996–2000
             (in Euros × 1000)

Country	1996	1997	1998	1999	2000
Afghanistan	1.054	1.048	1.099	1.413	1.966
Bangladesh	513	711	1.123	1.018	1.168
Burma	444	575	1.061	1.178	1.375
Cambodia	1.157	1.049	1.644	1.578	1.685
China	2.057	254	1.812	1.031	923
Sri Lanka	403	780	845	789	895
Total 6 countries	**5.628**	**4.417**	**7.584**	**7.007**	**8.012**
Total Asia	**6.537**	**6.683**	**9.881**	**12.177**	**14.816**
% of Asia budget	**86,1%**	**66,1%**	**76,7%**	**57,5%**	**54,1%**

**Table 6.5   MSF's Latin American countries of continuous aid in 1996–2000
                 (in Euros × 1000)**

Country	1996	1997	1998	1999	2000
Brazil	910	1.492	1.223	1.014	905
Peru	811	1.042	906	776	387
Total 2 countries	**1.721**	**2.534**	**2.129**	**1.790**	**1.292**
Total LA	**2.117**	**3.198**	**3.727**	**6.166**	**6.342**
% of LA budget	**81,3%**	**79,2%**	**57,1%**	**29,0%**	**20,3%**

How can we understand and explain this pattern in selection outcomes? For example, why did the organization use to have a stable pattern in concentrated spending for the Asian and Latin American continent, and why did this change from 1997/1998 on? It is this kind of questions that we will try to answer with help of the theoretical framework of this study. First, we will discuss MSF decisions to start or reject project proposals, followed by a discussion of MFS decisions to end or extend humanitarian aid projects.

Starting humanitarian aid interventions[1]

When MSF Holland detected a country in which a humanitarian medical crisis was taking place and the organization had no team on the ground, the question arose whether to send a new country management team to prepare an intervention or not. Once MSF Holland had a presence in a country, the team members often observed new needs that required intervention as well.

The idea to start a humanitarian aid intervention originated from the field (the country management team) or from the headquarters (for example, the Emergency Desk). Most initiatives for new projects came from the field. The operational director received proposals to start interventions from his country management teams and had the authority to reject proposals without discussing them with the other Management Team members. Decisions to start humanitarian aid interventions were ultimately made within the Management Team in the Amsterdam headquarters.

To give an indication of the frequency with which these decisions were taken; the MT decided about these kinds of proposals 43 times in the period from January to July 2001. The MT rejected one of the 43 proposals and postponed another five proposal decisions due to lack of information. The fact that the MT hardly rejected any project proposals indicates that project proposals were rejected by the operational director before they came to the MT.

MSF's dominant decision-making pattern regarding the initiation of project activities was captured by an operational director who described a project as follows:

It was a natural course of events: some people went in, an assessment was done, a proposal was written that fit the Country Policy and the Mid Term Policy, the proposal made sense, it went back and forth, there were a few hick ups, and then it was approved [int OD3, 2001].

Another operational director described MSF decision-making concerning the rejection of proposed projects when referring to a particular rejection decision:

We do not have a reason to be there. This population has a medical problem, but it does not have a humanitarian problem .... It is not because of conflict, not because somebody in government has decided that these people are not worthy of care, it is just that the rural parts of this country have lousy healthcare services everywhere .... That is not a problem we can engage very effectively .... so, it is not at all targeted and not at all aggressive and that's where we want to go as an organization and more importantly, that is what we do well, it's where we can be most effective [int OD4, 2001].

These quotes indicate that MSF decisions concerning the approval or rejection of project proposals followed a specific order, in which information was collected to establish a necessity to intervene. Then, this information was connected to the organization's goals and to efficiency and effectiveness criteria. In the following sections we will see in more detail how these decision-making processes worked. The research material shows that MSF decision-making processes were characterized by information and expert driven decision-making, sequential reasoning related to the organizational objectives, prospective reasoning, and attempts to maximize.

Information and expert driven decision-making

When MSF Holland heard about a possible humanitarian need, the usual way to go was to check this information by means of exploratory and assessment missions, which contained data regarding health matters (such as morbidity and mortality figures), the food situation, the nutritional situation, and the presence of other aid agencies.[2] In addition, they contained recommendations for action. This information was the point of departure for the decision-making process that then unfolded. For example, in a case describing the decision to intervene in an Asian country, an operational director said:

The team went in .... They did an assessment in the camps and based on these findings they identified water and sanitation needs as priority needs, as well as a few medical needs. There were no other organizations. So I had a discussion with the Head of Mission (or: country manager, LH) and we decided to go ahead [int OD3, 2001].

It was important to determine the need for intervention. The recommendation to intervene was made if the data collected suggested that the target population faced a medical humanitarian crisis that was life threatening.[3] If there was no clear need to intervene, the chance for approval of a new project decreased.[4] There was one country, for example, that had been suffering from a drought for several years. In

2000, MSF Holland sent out assessment teams several times to determine whether intervention was necessary. On every occasion, MSF decided that the need to intervene was not sufficiently great and urgent enough. There were needs to address but these were beyond the mandate of the organization, such as the lack of food for cattle. In addition, other aid agencies already had stepped in. Consequently, no intervention was proposed.

The information available was sometimes used very precisely to decide whether to intervene or not. For example, in case of a disease, specific prevalence rates were used in order to determine whether an epidemic was evolving.[5] If the prevalence stayed below a certain percentage, no intervention was advised, as a health advisor illustrated:

> A team wanted to do a meningitis [sleeping sickness, LH] intervention .... I asked them if they had enough information that proved that the number of cases was increasing. There are always more cases in that season and we only want to intervene at the beginning of an epidemic because if it is already decreasing we are wasting our money, so to speak. The team collected the information...I analyzed it and concluded that there was no epidemic. At the same time the number of cases decreased, so we did not continue our plans [int HA2, 2001].

Beside assessments and exploratory missions, other information collection activities, such as surveys or focus group discussions, were important if not necessary activities in order to establish the need to intervene.[6] The role of experts in the data collection phase and the evaluation process of these data was important as well.[7] As we can see from the above-mentioned quote, medical coordinators in the field and health advisors from headquarters were involved in the decision-making process. The exploratory mission members were also experts concerning to the collection of, for example, morbidity and mortality data.

Sequential reasoning related to the organizational objectives

When the information required was available and experts had shed their light on the data collected, a sequential process of decision-making unfolded. As we pointed out before, the need to intervene had to be established and the information collected was related to the Mid Term Policy and the Country Policy. These policies stated what kind of emergencies were 'typical MSF' and what the objectives of the organization were.[8] If a country management team proposed activities that did not fall within MSF policies the chance of rejection of the proposal increased.[9] If there was a clear connection to the organization's policies, the proposal was duly approved. For example, the decision to intervene in a former Soviet republic was clearly derived from the organizational policies, according to the country manager:

> In the Country Policy the rationale for working in that country was related to a geographical area of which we had determined that the population was vulnerable because of political isolation .... It was typical MSF because we identified a vulnerable group, there were real medical needs ... and the reason for vulnerability was related to conflict [int CM5, 2001].

In addition to the fact that first information was collected and then related to the organization goals, the decision-making process was sequential in other ways as well, for example, by formulating alternatives for action.[10] One health advisor gave a clear example of this for a decision to organize an assessment mission for an Asian country:

> Now one of us will go to a country where MSF has never been before .... The assessment then comes back to the OST [Operational Support Team at the headquarters] and then we can decide several things: we can do another assessment later, or we go back with a small team for another two months to do additional research whether to open a mission or not, or we go visit an organization that is already present and see what they are doing [int HA1, 2001].

This sequential way of reasoning also translated itself to the work processes in the organization. The dominant work order was as follows: first the problem needed to be defined and factual evidence of a medical humanitarian crisis provided; then possible options for action were formulated and related to the organizational objectives of the organization; next, the proposal was sent to the experts in the organization as well as to the higher ranks in the hierarchy; eventually, a decision was taken.

If sequentiality in action was lacking, people found this difficult. For example, the same health advisor cited above also spoke about a sleeping sickness program in Africa. The project team added an objective to the project because the team had discovered that many patients also suffered from HIV/AIDs and did not have any social network for medical care. The advisor argued that this was done without a proper problem analysis. Hence, she advised the team to do a problem analysis and develop a logistical framework, before resubmitting the project proposal to the Operational Support Team and the Operational Director [int HA1, 2001].

Prospective reasoning and attempts at maximizing

The sequential reasoning mode sometimes had a prospective character, because future consequences of projects were taken into account.[11] In one case, for example, it was clear from a survey that an African country was facing a severe food crisis. The harvest had been very bad and no UN or non-governmental agency was present to bring in food. The MSF team in the field proposed to start an intervention, because of the clear need for food. However, the team proposed a seeds and tools distribution program, which is very 'un-MSF'. The Management Team in the headquarters was hesitant to approve of such a project, because of the potential future consequences of such an intervention. After lengthy discussions the project was accepted – as an exception to the rule – because there was a real need and no other organization around to do this [int OD1, 2001].

There was complementary evidence for prospective reasoning in the project proposals and assessment reports. As was pointed out in Chapter 5, every country management team needed to clarify the conditions for success for the activities they proposed. These assumptions needed to be summarized in the logical framework of a project proposal (see Chapter 5, Figure 5.3 for an example). Only for emergency proposals an exception was sometimes made. Conditions for success that were often mentioned in the proposals were: MSF should have access to the area; the situation should be safe enough; cooperation with the authorities should be possible and the staff needed for the project should be available. These logical frameworks were present in most project proposals studied for this research. Beside, alternatives for action were often specified in the assessment reports studied, and sometimes even scenarios for the future were formulated. The same goes for the country policies.[12]

Furthermore, there were attempts to maximize the organization's aims since the effectiveness and efficiency of projects was taken into account.[13] This was the case in a Latin American country in which the country management team established a clear need for cholera intervention. However,

> ... the government was not motivated to do something because of political reasons and the population was apathetic. However, there were open gutters. Then you have to weigh the costs against the benefits. We can give them the know-how but the population has to do it themselves. We had all the ingredients for a project but the population lacked the motivation [int CM3, 2001].

A cost benefit analysis was also made if other organizations were already present or the situation was considered to be less catastrophic than initially thought. Security considerations weighed into the process as well. Any of these aspects could lead to the recommendation not to intervene, such as was the case after a huge landslide in a Latin American country:

> Very rapidly, we saw that there was no space for MSF. There were a huge number of NGOs, and in this kind of situation you have to do something in the first few days and after that it is already too late. There were so many, many NGOs present that it was easy to say .... Even if we wanted to do something, we had to write a proposal, find the human resources, it was really too late [int CM4, 2001].

Project proposals were more likely to be rejected if they were 'non MSF' or if doubts existed about the effectiveness of the proposed intervention. For example, in one assessment report intervention was advised against because 'there were no (public) health or humanitarian needs at present' and 'there are no short term needs where MSF can have a major impact' (rapid assessment report, 1999).[14]

'Consequentiality' in project initiation: An example

Let us take a closer look at some MSF decision-making dynamics in one particular country that had 'typical' MSF Holland projects and in which the logic of consequence was dominant for both the approval and the rejection of project proposals.[15]

As stated in a trip report of the operational director in 1999, the need to intervene in this country was indisputable, based on the facts and figures:

Any statistics if available in the country show terrible needs, health statistics/indicators put this country at the bottom of the global list .... Presently the situation does not look promising at all and it is not expected that the situation will improve in the next years to come. On the contrary, all indicators point towards deterioration and several conflict sites in the future [OD trip report August, 1999].

The operational director deemed it necessary to intervene. However, MSF intervention was only deemed legitimate if related to the organization's expertise, policies, and chance for success [OD trip report August, 1999].

In 2000, a Country Policy (CP) was written in which an extensive analysis of the situation in the country was made concerning the general, political, and humanitarian context. The overall policy objective for MSF's presence in the country was defined as follows:

that the people .... live in dignity; that by promotion of their right to humanitarian assistance and better access to health care they enjoy improved health, physical and mental, with reduced threat from epidemics and disasters [CP 2000].

This overall objective was split up in three sub objectives for which specific groups, areas, and health and advocacy activities were defined. In addition, MSF Holland anticipated several trends in the country's political context: a continued and increased fighting between the ruling elite and opposition groups resulting either in population movements or in more oppression without population movement; a decrease in central control of the ruling elite resulting in increased security risks; or a return of refugees from neighboring countries. Based on the MTP and the CP, the country management team planned to start an emergency preparedness and response project and a mental health project in the Annual Plan of 2000. The team also decided to continue MSF's basic health care projects in the region and to employ some advocacy and assessments activities.

In March 2000, MSF Holland conducted an assessment in a city in the north west of the country to explore the health needs in that area, as was planned for in the Annual Plan. The assessment team identified four options for intervention, i.e. a TB program, a support program for the pediatrics ward in the city hospital, a support program for the gynecology ward in the city hospital, and a mother child care program. The second alternative for action was chosen because of the great medical need that was present and the fact that this project was deemed to be 'manageabble' by MSF [sitrep March/April 2000].

In August 2000, MSF Holland sent out another assessment team, this time to study the drought situation in the country. The team concluded that the country was facing a severe food crisis and recommended further monitoring and survey activities as well as nutritional activities, such as a supplementary feeding program, based on the following analysis:

From this rapid assessment, MSF concludes that the population assessed faces a food crisis .... Through a logical-frame analysis of the trends presented in the qualitative data available, the emphasis is placed on: loss of income, loss of food from home gardens and animal products, loss of reliable water resources, and predicted loss of food production capacity for the next season [drought assessment 2001].

By mid October, the team had expanded its capacity by almost 50 percent to deal with this emergency [4M health update, October 2000]. In January, the situation kept on deteriorating, and the Country Manager expected this process to continue and hence decided that MSF Holland would step up its preparedness [sitrep January 2001]. The country manager made a prognosis for the coming months and he presented various scenarios. One of those scenarios was major escalation of hostilities in the north, creating massive population movements, requiring a long term humanitarian response [situation report January 2001]. This scenario proved to be pretty reliable and the Country Manager started to plan for an expansion of the nutritional program

However, when the data regarding the nutritional situation came in by the end of the month, the team concluded that the people were able to cope with the drought themselves unexpectedly well. 'All early indicators suggested a disaster, which did not occur' [trip report 2001]. Yet the expectation was that the harvests would fail and therefore the danger of hunger had not disappeared. It was recommended to continue the existing supplementary feeding programs, but not to start any new ones, because there was no need to. Hence, new information led to a decision to stop upgrading the MSF activities.

This case shows the importance of data collection in MSF decision-making processes, as well as of the formulation of alternatives (sequential reasoning) and scenarios (prospective reasoning), and the necessity to relate the project activities to the organizational goals, for example to only intervene when there was a clear need (attempts at maximizing).

Ending humanitarian aid interventions

When MSF Holland decided to start a project, new decision moments kept on appearing. The organization faced these moments when the planned ending date of a project had arrived and a decision about a possible extension had to be taken; or when a team reported that a project was problematic and a decision had to be taken whether to end the project or not. Again, the MT had the final decision-making power with concern to the ending or extension of project activities. What did these decision-making processes look like?[16]

Sequential and prospective reasoning and maximizing behavior

The decision-making process to extend or end project activities often followed a sequential mode of reasoning.[17] Take the following example:

> For a hospital project we had committed ourselves for the longer term of three years. After the three years passed, I wanted to hear from headquarters what they wanted .... I wanted their feedback .... We did that by means of a midterm evaluation ... and described the

developments and the investments needed. We provided the MT with extra information and said: we believe there is still a lot of work to be done and we need to know whether there is still long-term commitment at headquarters. And yes, there was commitment [int CM2, 2001].

MSF Holland often closed a mission or a project down if the need to be present had disappeared.[18] This need disappeared, for example, because the context of aid provision had changed for the better. The other way around, project activities had more chance to be extended if there was a clear need to stay in a country.[19] This, for example, happened in an MSF hospital project in an African country. MSF Holland had been present in this hospital, which was located in a transition camp, for quite a while. MSF provided medical care to refugees on the way back to their home villages. MSF was preparing to close down the project and to hand the project over to the local staff, which was ready to do the job on its own because only few people entered the transit camp. However, the context of the project suddenly changed for the better. Due to sudden but realistic prospects for peace, more returnees entered the transition camp than usual, requiring MSF's continued assistance in handling this sudden influx of returnees [int HA1, 2001]. The project was therefore prolonged for another two years.

Next to newly emerging needs, another reason to extend a project was if there were problems with completing the hand-over of a project. This was the case, for example, in an Asian country:

> It was decided in August to extend the hand-over until April 2001 [instead of March 2001, LH], by which time winter will have passed and accessibility to the region will be better. In the meantime this would give us time to create a responsible hand-over partner plan [4M health update, October 2000].

In other words, the decision to end or extend MSF projects were taken in a sequentially structured process in which one anticipated on the future need and effectiveness of the project, indicating prospective and maximizing behavior.

Relating the project results to the organizational goals

MSF ended projects if the needs for intervention disappeared. Another important reason to end projects was when the objectives of the project had been met.[20] This happened in an Latin American country where MSF provided health care in a prison:

> It was clear that we had reached the objectives of the project .... We had organized a health center and a doctor of the Ministry of Health (MoH) was present two times a week to treat patients. It was all settled, there were medicines etc. provided by the prison and the MoH, and we were simply not needed anymore. So we stopped [int medco 2, 2001].

When MSF decided to close down the last MSF project in a country, MSF Holland would first explore whether there were other needs that required action. This search process was connected to the organizational goals. If there was no clear need that related to MSF's policies, the MT would request the country management team to close down the mission. The following example illustrates this point:

> Our programs went well and there was a positive development in the context. The government became more involved and the [indigenous] organizations became aware of their rights. It was easier for them to find their way to government officials. I went there in November to do a problem analysis to see which problems were still not solved and how these were related to the Country Policy (CP). The CP was old, so we looked into the Mid Term Policy and from that we concluded that MSF did not have a significant role to play there. There were needs but more developmental in character, such as capacity building, and other organizations could do that better than we do [int HA1, 2001].

Another reason for phasing out a project was when it was ineffective or too expensive.[21] An operational director illustrated how the ineffectiveness of a program led to a decision to close a project. This was the case in an Asian country where MSF's presence had become redundant because other organizations had stepped in. Many of these organizations provided their services for free, which made people shop around for medical care. This influenced the quality of care negatively. Hence, the project was ended [int OD2, 2001]. Beside this, there were examples of MSF Holland projects that were ineffective but for which an adjustment of the project was expected to lead to a more effective intervention,[22] such as the following:

> In the Northern part of the country we have a project in a city with two rivaling clans. They fight every night. We work in the city hospital. We had a problem analysis discussion about the project. The project has been extended and expanded to the rural areas because our coverage was not good enough [int HA1, 2001].

Consequential project termination: an example

The interview material touching upon various decision-making occasions indicates that MSF decision-making processes in the decision category 'ending and extending' were mainly characterized by elements of the logic of consequence. The following example illustrates how the logic of consequence dominated MSF decision-making dynamics throughout one particular case: a health care intervention in an African country.

In February 2000, MSF Holland intervened in an African country with post-emergency aid to the health facilities in the country after extensive assessments of the situation. In addition, the MSF team launched some small supplementary feeding projects. Already after a couple of months, some of the projects were ready to close down. In June 2000, for example, the country manager reported that the feeding centers in the capital city would be closed down because of a 'decline in participants' [sitrep June 2000]. One month later, it appeared that additional supplementary feeding programs were not needed anymore [sitrep August 2000].

In September, the country manager spotted a project that did not have the expected impact. This concerned a project in a hospital and some surrounding health centers, of which the facilities were underutilized [trip report September 2000]. Because of a lack of impact and the idea that the reason for underutilization was that many people relied on alternative health care facilities, the CM proposed to phase out of this project as soon as possible, but not without finding an explanation for the underutilization of the hospital [trip report September 2000]. The team therefore planned to do a study to the reasons of the underutilization and to see how MSF could better reach the population in need [sitrep November 2000].

This study was reported on in the December situation report to the MSF headquarters. Unfortunately, no clear reasons for the underutilization of the hospital services had been found, so it was impossible to formulate a proposal to improve the project [sitrep December 2000]. In January 2001, the country management team therefore sat down to review their projects and reported to headquarters that they had decided to phase out of the basic health care activities due to significant recovery regarding physical access and economic possibilities [sitrep January 2001].

In the meantime, the team had been working on an emergency preparedness and response program, because of rumors of potential emergencies. The aim was to 'investigate systems and structures in place' in case something would happen as well as 'determining whether there is a role for MSF in addressing these concerns' [sitrep February 2001]. However, 'the initial indication suggests that the need for such a program is decreasing' [sitrep February 2001]. In March, the team stopped working in a particular region, as was announced in January, because:

> Even though it is apparent that significant health needs continue to exist in the area, the reasons of isolation and marginalization that led MSF to select this population as the target for this project have been significantly relieved [sitrep March 2001].

In the same month the team also ended the emergency response program because the Ministry of Health seemed to be capable to assure a minimum level of care and because there was general access to health care [sitrep March 2001].[23]

This case demonstrates how MSF decision-making processes were characterized by consequential decision-making dimensions such as information collection as a tool for decision-making in the case of the underutilization of the hospital, as well as decisions to stop interventions because the need for intervention had disappeared, as was the case in the emergency preparedness project.

Archetype of the administrative organization?

In this chapter we have looked at the daily decision-making practices within MSF Holland. Based on the theoretical framework of this study we formulated the hypothesis that since MSF Holland's formal organizational structure resembled Simon's administrative organization to a large extent, we expected to find the consequential decision-making mode to be dominant. The interview material, the documents studied, and the observations made, together with more detailed case descriptions concerning particular humanitarian interventions, showed how 'consequential' the decision-making process within MSF Holland was in reality.[24]

The logic of consequence seemed to be in close harmony with MSF Holland's features of the administrative organization. We saw how the emphasis on information and specialization was a real asset of MSF Holland, not just in the formal structure, but by means of exploratory and assessment missions, reporting mechanisms, the Operational Support Teams, and individual advisors and experts. We observed how MSF's procedural and substantive coordination mechanisms, such as the Mid Term Policy, the Annual Plan, and the Country Policy, carried weight in the decision-making process. The four monthly reports and the project proposal format, including the logical framework, were also important procedural coordination mechanisms in the decision-making process. The hierarchical line in the organization, from the CMT, the Country manager to the OD and the MT, was the line in which important decisions regarding the initiation, rejection, extension, and termination of project activities were ultimately made.

In addition, we see that the choice of project locations, activities, and target groups was related to the consequential decision-making mode. MSF Holland initiated projects when proposals fitted the Mid Term Policy and Country Policies. For example, the decrease in concentrated spending can be understood as a response to the new Mid Term Policy which pleaded for focusing on those emergencies with both a humanitarian *and* a medical component. Less concentrated spending points to fewer projects with long-term, and therefore, developmental elements. In addition, effectiveness and efficiency arguments dominated decision-making processes regarding questions whether or not to intervene. Projects ended if project objectives had been achieved, needs to intervene had disappeared, or problematic implementation hampered the effectiveness of projects. Hence, the logic of consequence helps us to understand the outcomes of MSF's decision-making processes. However, the data also suggest that the logic of consequence is less dominant with regard to the termination of projects when compared to the initiation of projects (see note 24 for the details).

The picture one gets from this analysis is that we are dealing with an administrative organization in which all processes were structured, ordered, and clear. Hence, we could argue that the evidence presented in this chapter leads to the confirmation of the hypothesis as formulated in the beginning of this chapter, i.e. that MSF's resemblance to the ideal type of the administrative organization is connected to a specific decision-making mode, namely the logic of consequence. This conclusion leads us to refute the assumption often formulated in NGO research that NGOs are predominantly loosely structured and therefore characterized by garbage can decision-making.

Although MSF employees might recognize part of the description presented in this chapter, they would add that there is more to MSF Holland's decision-making processes than solely policies, procedures, facts, and calculations. Therefore, we need to have a closer look at those examples of MSF decision-making that were clearly non-consequential in character before we can confirm the hypothesis presented in this chapter. To this we will turn in the next chapter. In Chapter 8, we will see once again how real and dominant this consequential decision-making mode is within MSF Holland by means of an extensive case description of MSF aid provision in an African country that experienced a refugee influx. This case description is followed by another decision-making case concerning a post-war intervention in Africa, which represents a mix of consequential and non-consequential characteristics.

Notes

1   This section is based on a study of 32 interview examples concerning the initiation of project activities and 21 interview examples about rejected proposals.

2   In 17 out of 32 cases concerning the decision whether to launch an intervention or not, the importance of assessments and other information gathering instruments was mentioned.

3   In 24 out of 32 initiation interview cases respondents mentioned the importance of establishing a need for intervention.

4   In 6 out of 21 project rejection cases the absence of a clear need was mentioned as a reason not to intervene.

5   Prevalence rate are very disease specific.

6   In 22 out of 32 initiation cases fact finding activities other than assessments and exploratory missions were deemed important.

7   In 18 of the 32 cases on initiating projects, the respondents mentioned that they had asked for advise from one of the supporting departments in the headquarters, or were involved as an expert themselves.

8   In 22 out of 32 project initiation interview cases the proposed project activities were explicitly related to the organizational objectives.

9   In 11 of the 21 rejection cases this was a reason mentioned for rejecting a project proposal.

10   We could establish a sequential reasoning pattern in 22 of the 32 initiation cases.

11   Only in 9 out of 32 project initiation cases and in 8 out of 21 rejection cases did we establish prospective reasoning.

12   An analysis of 16 project proposals showed that there were 11 regular proposals with a logical framework in which these assumptions were described and 5 emergency proposals in which no assumptions were formulated. In addition, a study of 13 assessment reports led to the conclusion that all 13 reports either made recommendations for specific intervention or formulated various alternatives for action. In 6 of these assessments scenarios or forecasts were elaborated on as well. In country policies scenarios can also be found. In a study of 9 CPs, a prognosis of expected developments was found in 6 CPs.

13   In 11 of the 21 rejection cases a cost benefit argument was made.

14   In 6 out of 21 rejection cases project proposals were considered to be "bad alternatives for action" because they were believed to be ineffective or because the expertise in MSF was missing.

15   A 'typical' MSF country is a country in which MSF's presence is legitimate according to the organization's own policies and plans.

16   This section is based on the analysis of 15 extension interview cases and 26 ending interview cases in these two decision categories. Of the extension cases, 6 interview cases

were extensions in time only and 9 interview cases were extensions in time together with an adjustment of the project in terms of contents. Five of the 26 termination cases dealt with evacuations as a result of security constraints. The other terminations contained formal decisions to end the project.

17 In 17 out of 41 interview cases we could establish a sequential reasoning mode in which a specific decision-making order was used to reach a decision to extend the project.

18 In half of the 26 ending interview cases the absence of a (new) need to intervene was mentioned as a reason for closing down the project.

19 In 7 out of 15 extension cases the presence of a clear need to stay was mentioned to be of importance.

20 This was in 12 out of 26 cases.

21 This was in 9 out of 26 ending cases.

22 Three out of fifteen cases were extended because the organization wanted to make the intervention more effective

23 Although these projects ended, the MSF mission in this country did not close down, because the team identified other needs for which it organized interventions.

24 In the figures below, a summary of the results of the interview analysis concerning project initiation cases is given. We conclude from this that the interview material along with the results of an analysis of project proposals and assessment reports indicate that MSF Holland decision-making processes are characterized by information driven processes of sequential and sometimes prospective reasoning, in which the reason to intervene is clearly connected to establishing a need to intervene and the proposed project activities are related to the organizational goals.

Table 6.6   An overview of 'start' interview cases in relation to the logic of consequence

The number of cases in which	No
A clear need for intervention was mentioned	24
The decision-making process was described in terms of sequentiality	22
The proposed activities were related to the organizational policies	22
The importance of information collection other than assessments was stressed	22
The involvement of experts was mentioned	18
Assessments were mentioned as an information gathering instrument	17
Prospective reasoning was established	9
There were attempts to maximize the organizational goals	7
Alternatives for action were formulated	5
Total number of cases = 32	

From the next figure we learn that in most rejection cases the reason to reject a project proposal was that the proposal did not match organization goals; a cost benefit analysis was made and therefore another project proposal prioritized; and the need to intervene had disappeared.

Table 6.7   An overview of 'rejection' interview cases related to the LoC

The number of cases in which	No
The proposed activities were not related to the organizational goals	11
A cost benefit analysis was made and this activity was not prioritized	11
Problematic consequences were expected (prospective reasoning)	8
Absence of a clear need was a reason to reject	6
The proposed activity was not considered to be the best alternative for action (not effective enough or expertise was lacking)	6
Assessments were mentioned as an information gathering instrument	5
Experts advised against the proposed activities	4
A lack of info was mentioned as a reason to reject	3
There was a wrong, or lack of, sequentiality: no or wrong use of procedures	1
Total number of cases = 21	

The following figure shows how often the above mentioned dimensions of the logic of consequence appeared in the interview cases. In 27 (more than half of the) cases, we found four or more consequential decision-making elements.

Table 6.8   An overview of the no. of LoC dimensions present in the interview cases

No. of LoC dimensions mentioned in interviews→	0	1	2	3	4	5	6	7	8
No. of initiation interview cases →		1	1	2	6	5	4	9	3	1
No. of rejection interview cases →	0	4	6	6	4	1	0	0	0
Total = 53	**1**	**5**	**8**	**12**	**9**	**5**	**9**	**3**	**1**

Tables 6.9 and 6.10 present the results of the interview cases regarding the analysis of 'ending' and 'extending' cases. The most important consequential decision-making elements concerning the extension of projects are a prospective, sequential reasoning pattern in which it is necessary to identify a clear need to stay with an eye on the organizational goals, based on assessments or evaluations.

For the interview cases concerning the ending of project activities we can conclude that decision-making processes were consequential in the sense that we could establish sequential reasoning patterns in which projects were closed down if the need to intervene had disappeared; if the project objectives had been met; or if a project had become too expensive or ineffective.

As we can deduce from Table 6.11, in 24 out of a total of 41 interview cases one or two of the dimensions of consequential decision-making could be established. In addition, another 15 cases resembled three or four of these dimensions. Compared to the previous decision-making categories – approving and rejecting proposals to intervene – the logic of consequence less clearly dominates decision-making processes within MSF if it concerns the decision categories ending and extending. For example, we established 27 initiation cases with four LoC elements, while we only found 8 cases with the same number of LoC elements in the category of terminating project activities.

Table 6.9   An overview of interview cases about extending projects related to the LoC

The number of cases in which	No
A clear need for extension was mentioned	7
The decision-making process was described in terms of sequentiality	6
It was mentioned that the proposed activities were related to the organizational policies	4
Prospective reasoning could be established	4
a) assessments were mentioned as an information gathering instrument (2)	
b) evaluations were mentioned as an information gathering instrument (2)	4
Attempts of maximizing the organizational goals were mentioned (cost benefit analysis – create a more effective intervention)	3
The importance of fact finding/information collection is mentioned	2
The involvement of experts were mentioned	0
Alternatives for action were formulated/reported on	0
Total number of cases = 15	

Table 6.10   An overview of interview cases about ending projects in relation to the LoC

The number of cases in which	No
There is no clear need to intervene anymore	13
The activities were not related to the organizational goals anymore, objectives have been met	12
A sequential reasoning mode could be established	11
A cost benefit analysis was made and this activity was not prioritized	
- project is too expensive	
- project does not have enough impact/is not effective enough	
- others can take over	9
Assessments and/or evaluations were mentioned as an information gathering instrument	6
Prospective reasoning	4
Experts advised to end the project	1
The extension would not to be the best alternative for action (not effective enough or expertise was lacking)	0
Total number of cases = 26	

Table 6.11   An overview of the no. of LoC dimensions mentioned in the interview cases

No. of LoC dimensions mentioned in interviews→	0	1	2	3	4	5	6	7	8	9
No. of extension interview cases →	2	4	4	2	2	1	0	0	0	0
No. of termination interview cases →	1	8	8	4	4	1	0	0	0	0
Total = 41	**3**	**12**	**12**	**7**	**6**	**2**	**0**	**0**	**0**	**0**

Chapter 7

Disagreement, Commitment, and Constraints: MSF's Secondary Decision-Making Patterns

Why should we do water and sanitation activities [watsan] or not in the context of this country? It is quite hard to answer this question, mainly because although we know why we should be in this country, we don't know yet how our activities can be relevant. As this applies to all MSF H activities, it also applies to water and sanitation. My reading of the situation is that within this context, we have difficulties finding our track: the humanitarian crisis is quite clear but the medical crisis is not that clear, and to find the overlap between these two as suggested by the MTP is even more difficult. The conclusion is that we have not yet found a relevant thing to do beside medical brigades [trip report water and sanitation advisor, February 2001].

The project the water and sanitation advisor referred to in this quote did not match MSF policies. The advisor claimed that the relevance of the project activities was dubious. Still, the project continued to exist, something we would not expect if the dominant decision-making mode was consequential, such as was argued in the previous chapter. In this chapter, those decisions that clearly deviated from the dominant, consequential decision-making mode, such as the one above, will be discussed.

Again, we will discuss decisions concerning the initiation, termination, and extension of projects and missions, as well as rejections of project proposals. Three categories of 'deviant' cases came to the fore in the analysis: cases in which consequential reasoning was part of the decision-making dynamics but not related to the hypothesized organizational features of the administrative organization; cases in which appropriateness was part of the decision-making process; and cases in which garbage can decision-making elements were part of the process.

The cases presented in this chapter represent practically all deviant cases found in the material collected for this study, contrary to Chapter 6 which contains a limited number of examples, which serve as illustration of the results of a larger study of the material (94 interview cases).

Stretching the boundaries of the administrative organization

In the previous chapter we saw how the logic of consequence worked in accordance with an organizational structure that resembles the 'administrative organization'. However, the research material entailed evidence of a more 'creative use' of the logic of consequence which sometimes conflicted with the formal organizational structure. This creative use of the logic of consequence became apparent when MSF employees did not agree on the interpretation of the organization's formal rules, procedures, and policies.

Bypassing the formal structure

MSF Holland employees sometimes bypassed the organization's formal structure when there was disagreement between headquarters and field, or between headquarter departments. One former medical coordinator captured this as follows:

> If you are a medco, you can turn to your health advisor and he can help you to find the right arguments that the country manager cannot ignore. You could also turn to the operational director and tell him that you do not share the opinion of the country manager [CM]. A CM might have a very good reason to ignore somebody else's views and if that is the case, you will accept that, but if that is not the case, then you go to the OD or the health advisor [int HA1, 2001].

Another example of this occurred in a weekly MT meeting, in which the four Operational Directors and the two general directors discussed policy issues and new project proposals. One operational director told his colleagues about an expected water shortage in one of his project countries. The country management team wanted to apply a temporary solution for the water shortage by organizing water provision by trucks. This solution would be sufficient because it was expected that rain would soon fill up the rivers. The OD asked his colleagues if an approval for this idea, including the budget, could be given in advance, before the country management team started writing a proposal. The MT agreed with this idea. The formal procedure of first writing a proposal before asking approval of the MT was bypassed.

Consequential reasoning as a persuasion strategy

Even if MSF employees were going by the formal rules, they sometimes exploited the formal structure to persuade others in the organization to get a project proposal approved. MSF Holland employees knew that speaking the language of the logic of consequence raised the chances for approval of their project proposals.

In a Latin American country, for example, the country management team faced a dengue outbreak. The organization had no experience with treating this disease but nevertheless the country management team thought MSF had to initiate a dengue project:

> We looked for information on the Internet ... and we made a proposal with a focus on vector control (i.e. killing the insects with insecticides and lavacides (= egg killers, LH)). I didn't put in the proposal any treatment for the patients ... I forgot to put this in because everything I was reading emphasized vector control .... They (=headquarters) said the proposal would be accepted if there was a medical part in the program. That means early diagnosis, case management, and treatment, which is very simple [int CM4, 2001].

In the end, the country management team left the case management part out of the project and focused solely on vector control. The country manager ended his description of this decision-making example with the following words: 'Our project responded to major needs .... MSF is a learning organization, I played with this wording ... "we can learn from this"' [int CM4, 2001].

In another case, an MSF employee told me about the proposal of her country management team for a sleeping sickness program:

> If you propose activities that have a flavor of development, and our sleeping sickness did have such a flavor, then they are reluctant. But if you say: there is an epidemic, they are OK with it [int CM6, 2001].

Here we see that members of a country management team used logic of consequence language - in which numbers and organizational goals are crucial – to make their proposals more convincing for the headquarters. As one respondent said:

> It also has to do with salesmanship ... The MT has to decide and fortune favors the bold if the MT is in doubt .... It is important to know the right people and what they are susceptible for. In addition, it is good to know the jargon, if you know how to stress the humanitarian aspect and the crisis aspect [int CM3, 2001].

Consequential reasoning to legitimize decisions already taken

MSF Holland employees sometimes also went beyond the logic of consequence as a persuasion strategy by using a consequential argumentation strategy to legitimize decisions that already had been taken or to 'hide' the real reasons to initiate a project.

For example, in an Operational Support Team meeting, a project proposal was subject of discussion. It concerned an African country in which many people were fleeing and the food situation was deteriorating. The country management team proposed to start a measles vaccination campaign for 50.000 people in order to get access to this area. This would enable the team to monitor the refugee and food situation in the area. The measles campaign could then be followed by a feeding program, if needed.

In the internal project proposal the team indicated the aim for a vaccination coverage rate of 80 percent, although they knew that a coverage rate of 95 percent is required to really prevent an epidemic from happening. A coverage rate of 80 percent would be ineffective, so why start such a vaccination campaign? Some OST members commented on this, also because the main objective of the project proposal was explicitly formulated as the prevention of a measles epidemic. Others responded to this criticism by stating that in formal proposals the coverage percentage of 95 percent should be mentioned, however, for an internal MSF proposal it should be sufficient that the reason to launch this intervention is to get access to a specific area. The Emergency Desk was not satisfied with this argument and commented that MSF

Holland is not an organization that intervenes to prevent epidemics from happening. Instead, MSF Holland intervenes if the epidemic is already there. The health advisor and the representative of Humanitarian Affairs protested against this interpretation of the MSF mandate and argued for a direct food intervention instead of a measles campaign. This plan was opposed because MSF only implements supplementary feeding programs for mothers and children and no general food distribution programs. In addition, the logistics experts informed the other OST members that food could only be delivered through the air, which is very expensive, and that he expected additional difficulties concerning visa, government consent, and communication [OST notes, May 2001].

Here we see how a discourse of coverage rates, efficiency, and policy was used by some MSF employees as a cover up for the 'real' motivation for intervening in a specific area, namely getting access to monitor the food situation. This motivation might have had a consequential character, however, it was not a 'sincere' use of consequential decision-making elements to come to a decision. Instead, the decision to intervene had already been taken and the consequential decision-making language was used to rationalize this intervention afterwards, while everybody knew that the proposal would not create the desired effect. Such a project proposal would have been rejected if the organization had applied a 'pure' form of consequential decision-making, because ineffective results of this intervention could be expected beforehand. In this case, however, the project went along.

A second example of consequentiality as a legitimization strategy came from an MT meeting in which the four monthly reports from the field were discussed and the planning was adjusted accordingly. One of the four Operational Directors presented the project status of his portfolio. For one African country it appeared from the financial overviews that the one project left to be done in that country cost less than the coordination costs of the country management team. The other MT members asked the OD for an explanation: how can a country management team cost more than the project activities it implements? The OD stated that these costs were so high because the members of the country management team were also responsible for monitoring the situation in a neighboring country. A colleague asked him why this was the case. In addition, he asked for a justification for these high coordination costs. The OD responded by saying: 'OK, then we will find a justification' [4M notes, May 2001].

These examples show that there were incidences within MSF Holland in which activities were initiated for which a justification was not given beforehand – as one might expect if the 'pure' form of consequential decision-making was applied – but after the activities had been approved or initiated.

Noblesse oblige

In some instances, MSF decision-making processes had a non-consequential character. This seemed to be the case when the organization had to deal with legacies of the past that created a commitment to the population in need or when outside or inside pressures were so high that the organization felt an obligation to live up to these expectations. These are both indicators of appropriate decision-making (see Figure 3.3 in Chapter 3).

When the past catches up with the present

MSF Holland had been working with the current MTP since 1999/2000. Before that year, the organization was less focused on pure medical humanitarian emergencies than it is nowadays. The organization worked in countries of which some MSF employees wondered whether these were 'real' humanitarian crises. The organization initiated projects that sometimes had more of a medical and developmental than a humanitarian character. The MT had to deal with this heritage of the past and tried to phase out of these kinds of projects and missions. However, this did not happen without any struggle.

In an Asian country, for example, the country management team was convinced that a project was needed, but the Operational Director (OD) was not. The OD anticipated the new Mid Term Policy that would be formalized soon. He rejected the initiation of a combined HIV/STD (sexually transmitted disease) project. This project would fall within the current MTP but outside the new MTP. The country management team pleaded for initiation because it believed there was a clear need for action. In the end the project was approved since expectations of approval had been raised with the local government in the meantime. The country manager felt it was simply too late to cancel the plan:

> As head of mission I thought we had taken one step too many in the discussion how we should implement the program ... and not so much about whether we were going to do it at all. The moment to call it off had passed in my eyes. So I supported the medical coordinator and said: we have to do it, because not doing anything is not an option .... In the end the OD gave the green light to proceed [int CM8, 2001].

Another example comes from an Asian country for which the MT in Amsterdam had decided to close down the mission by the end of 2002. Not all projects could easily be handed over or phased out. MSF Holland had a long presence in this country and this had created feelings of commitment towards the Ministry of Health and the local population. One operational director said about all this:

> We had a lot of discussion about this country in which we have invested for 20 years. I share the feelings in the field that we should leave there in a proper way. Since it has been quiet for a while, some people in Amsterdam get a bit nervous about it, they want it to close because it uses a lot of resources, and we have to show that we are able to close down countries. But this is a country in which we have invested so much and in which things are finally changing for the better and there is a nice project which could serve as an exit strategy, but it will take a little bit longer than expected, then you have to fight for it to leave it in a proper way [int OD2, 2001].

The health advisor concluded the same one year before and pleaded for a special status of this project country. He proposed to get temporarily involved in more developmental activities as an exit strategy [trip report health advisor, August 2000]. The health advisor thought this special status was especially applicable to a hospital and health center project in one of the country's districts. This project was problematic because of the low salaries of health personnel, which made them either leave the hospital or very unmotivated to do the work properly. In addition, the AIDS problem was growing in the district. The idea was launched to organize a health financing scheme, so that health personnel would earn more and therefore would stay working in the hospital with a higher morale than before, also after MSF had left. The health advisor supported this idea in the light of the planned exit of MSF from the country.

One would have expected MSF Holland to phase out of this project if the dominant consequential decision-making mode had been followed, because the project did not have the expected impact and the intervention did not match MSF's MTP anymore. Here we see how MSF Holland felt an obligation to ensure a successful handover, although that would take a considerable amount of time. Exit was guaranteed by means of a new project, which was developmental in character and therefore very 'un-MSF' to initiate. In other words, MSF's obligatory behavior followed from past commitments which could not be ignored, as the operational director mentioned earlier stated:

> In the more difficult cases we try to phase out. That does not always work ... sometimes the exit strategy destroys what you have accomplished with your presence ... or we have to admit that the exit strategy we came up with is not realistic at all. Then you are struggling with the question how to end those projects, and then you extend reluctantly with a strong emphasis on the idea that the purpose is to close [int OD2, 2001].

Living up to expectations

Next to a heritage from the past, MSF decision-making was sometimes influenced by another dimension of appropriate decision-making, i.e. when it responded to outside or inside expectations about the organization's behavior. In such instances, the absence of a need to intervene or doubts about the effectiveness of a proposed intervention did not longer provide the basis for rejecting project proposals.

For example, MSF Holland had to decide whether to intervene in an Asian country that had been flooded. One journalist portrayed the floods as a disaster. The country manager told the headquarters that not much was going on and an intervention was not needed. In the end, MSF initiated a project although the country manager was right. However,

> CMs do not always realize that people expect things from us, that we have to take the outside world into account as well .... and although the CM had told us that not much was going on, we can't do much with that information if there is a lot of pressure within Holland or from our own network to do something [int 1, 2001].

Apparently, MSF Holland felt that it was not acceptable not to go, although we could have expected – based on the dominance of the consequential decision-making mode – that the organization would not intervene because there was no clear need. Instead, MSF responded to pressures from within its own network and from outside, coming from the general public.

In another situation, MSF acted on feelings of commitment towards the population in need, although there was a real danger that the organization could not initiate the most effective intervention. This concerned an African country in which the country manager faced floods in an area of which headquarters had decided that it was too dangerous to work in:

> We had heated discussions whether we could intervene there or not, also because we did not want to use too many of our resources which could cause internal fighting among the local people .... In the end, we intervened because we felt a responsibility, the situation was so serious that we could not stay away, so we tried to minimize the security risks [int CM2, 2001].

A shrinking operational space: solutions start looking for a problem

A third deviation from the consequential decision-making mode was observed when the operational space for MSF action shrunk due to contextual constraints, such as security reasons, the presence of other aid agencies, lack of access to the areas that needed aid most, or the absence of needs that fit MSF's mandate. In these cases, MSF Holland started a search for needs and potential project activities that sufficiently met the organization's mandate. This search process was characterized by a process in which 'solutions started looking for a problem', indicating the presence of garbage can decision-making elements within the organization (see Figure 3.3 in Chapter 3). Two cases in which such garbage can elements were clearly present were a health care intervention in Africa and a water and sanitation ('watsan') intervention after a tropical storm in Latin America.

Looking for a needle in the haystack

In January 2000, MSF Holland decided to send an exploratory assessment team to an African country which had just opened up for international aid agencies after years of war.[1] MSF France was already present but MSF Holland was not sure whether their presence would be sufficient to cover the needs in the country.

In February, the exploratory team concluded that the Dutch branch had come too late to initiate humanitarian emergency aid activities in and around the capital, since other organizations had already started nutritional, watsan, and medical programs [explo report, February 2000]. Those areas in which the population was in clear need of aid appeared to be too dangerous to access (yet). Although the mission expected that these areas would soon open up, they argued that:

we are probably too late to produce an effective operation. All our partners have well established offices with adequate logistic means, with expatriate and local human resources that can be very quickly deployed in these regions, with stocks of all the necessary material and with a network of contacts and relations ... so probably, it is wiser to look for another type of intervention [explo report February 2000].

The report continued with an assessment of the humanitarian rehabilitation needs and a proposal to reconstruct the medical infrastructure, followed by an evaluation of positive and negative points of such an intervention. Other options of action explored were: rehabilitation of and support to the national sanitary network; support to a district (which was labeled as 'not a strategic nor philosophic option for MSF H'); the creation of an emergency pool ('relatively expensive and you run the risk of loosing your entire stock during looting, war, etc.'); and endemic diseases, especially sleeping sickness.

One month later, the head of mission concluded that immediate emergency aid was not required because other agencies were already in place and on stand-by for the final closed areas to open up [sitrep, 4 March 2000]. Instead, the head of mission proposed to start a post emergency intervention [sitrep, 4 March 2000]. An additional assessment of surrounding areas, however, did not result in the conclusion that there were many other serious needs, except for one specific region where MSF thought emergency rehabilitation needs could be addressed. However, this region was difficult to acces yet [sitrep 4 March 2000]. The team asked Amsterdam for advice about which direction to take, either to aim for a post emergency intervention or 'if there is not a will to start such a program then we propose that the explo stops now to prevent raising any false expectations' [sitrep 4 March 2000]. It was decided to opt for the post emergency intervention.

A week later the team identified a city that could become the MSF base in the designated area, because it was easy to access by plane and train [sitrep 10 March 2000]. However, finding a potential effective alternative for action was not easy. A couple of days later the team reported that a possible intervention for refugees in the border area proved to be unnecessary because:

> everything is fine and .... UNHCR is covering their health needs. I also called UNHCR in the capital and got the same response – no need for MSF [sitrep 15/3/2000].

In addition, MSF France reported for another area that there was no need to launch a refugee intervention because there were 'no signs of malnutrition or epidemics' [sitrep 19/3/2000]. The options for actions seemed limited. By the end of the month the team proposed to initiate a project in a southern area assessed earlier by the French MSF section, although there was no urgent humanitarian emergency. Nevertheless, it was deemed wise to start an intervention :

> There is sufficient justification for MSF H to start a program in the upper N region .... I recommend that we move fast while the window of opportunity is open and allows access .... There is no urgent humanitarian emergency, however, the basic health care system

has totally collapsed and there is no access to basic health care for the general population [sitrep 29/3/2000].

By June, the team had several projects up and running in that area: health centers were supported, drugs provided, while at the same time an emergency preparedness and sleeping sickness proposal were being prepared.

Nothing to do

In November 1998, a tropical storm hit a Latin American country extremely hard. MSF did not have a team in this country, but was able to send some of its team members of the neighboring MSF Holland mission to check out the situation. After three days MSF decided, in coordination with the Ministry of Health, to start immediate drug distribution to '30 health units, the 5 most affected health posts and to intervene in 10 communities' [sitrep 9/11/1998]. A couple of days later, MSF decided to provide these communities with shelter, water, and latrines as well. In the meantime the first reports of cholera became public and MSF kept an eye on this by monitoring the situation.

While the first aid activities were implemented, the medical coordinator did some needs assessments. After a couple of days she reported that the medical assessment in a particular department showed no need for an MSF intervention at this moment, because of good coverage of the Ministry of Health and the presence of other NGOs [sitrep 12/11/1998]. Another two days later, other assessment teams returned from the countryside and shared their impressions with the headquarters in Amsterdam. They also concluded that the needs were not as enormous as had been expected:

> Our first impression is that even the most remote areas are covered by personnel of the Ministry of Health. They also have means of transport. Possible MSF interventions could be in the field of cold chain material, material for vector control, and material for wells and latrines [sitrep 14/11/1998].

The team started to look around for other international aid agencies and tried to coordinate a concerted effort. The team decided to wait for a coordination meeting before defining MSF's future role in this country. In the meantime the team kept on reporting about the number of cholera cases, which was still not very worrying. MSF promised the Ministry to assist in the treatment of wells and latrines as well as in a preparedness plan for a cholera epidemic, since the Ministry was facing a lack of capacity and resources to take care of this itself.

On 21 November the teams announced that all MSF medical material sent to the field had arrived in good condition. There was enough personnel, medicines, and medical material at that moment. The team observed a continued need for water and sanitation activities, as well as health care needs in other regions in the country [sitrep 21/11/1998]. The team therefore decided to focus on the coastal regions of two departments in the country. In addition, they planned a second visit to a region which was hit by floods and received little support. The team visited this region within a couple of days and concluded that this area needed extra attention since it was much affected by floodings, a lack of health personnel, health risks in the region, and low coverage of the area by MoH [sitrep 25/11/1998]. Water and sanitation activities were judged to be most needed.

In the beginning of December the country management team provided an account of the activities of their colleague organizations. They reported that CARE was planning to start a well cleaning and improvement program in two of the regions where MSF had aimed to do the same work. MSF decided therefore to look for other regions "equally affected by the tropical storm, which are not receiving any support" [sitrep 5/12/1998]. Besides, the organization performed another assessment in two other regions and reported that they could set up water and sanitation activities there. MSF decided to return to one of the villages in these two regions to assess the need for a pipe system due to slowly drying wells. However, they soon discovered that a Baptist church organization had already begun to implement the construction of a piped system, without having consulted the Ministry of Health [sitrep 11/12/1998]. Once again, another agency had already picked up the work. The operational space was small, since many aid organizations had come to the country and started projects with hardly any effort to coordinate their operations with their colleague organizations. This hampered MSF action:

> Due to the fact that MSF has had to focus on other regions after the commitment made between CARE and MoH at the central level for U and SV, we face delays in the presentation of a project proposal. It is necessary to investigate the situation very well to avoid duplication of activities, which can happen easily because of the number of organizations present and the lack of communication among them [sitrep 11/12/1998].[2]

A lack of alternatives for action: garbage can decision-making

These two cases illustrate how a limited operational space constrained MSF Holland in its humanitarian aid provision and in its ambition to apply a strictly consequential decision-making mode. There was a clear willingness to intervene, but based on consequential decision-making tools, such as data collection and exploratory missions, the MSF teams on the ground reported that intervention in various areas was not needed, did not match MSF's Mid Term Policy, or needs were sufficiently covered by other aid agencies.

Instead of deciding that intervention might therefore not be as needed as was anticipated – something that could have been the outcome of a strictly consequential mode of deciding – the teams kept on looking for possibilities for action until they found an area in which an intervention was needed that sufficiently matched MSF's policies and mandate so that an MSF intervention could be justified. The way this decision-making process unfolded represents a process of 'solutions looking for a problem', which is an aspect of garbage can decision-making.

From the examples described above we learn that MSF sometimes decided to intervene in a country without knowing whether such an intervention was really needed or feasible. This then created situations in which the reason for MSF presence had to be found after the intervention had started, which is a form of 'inversed' prospective reasoning. At times, these reasons could be found and the logic of consequence helped to justify MSF intervention after the intervention had been launched, such as was the case with the health care intervention in Africa. Every now and then, however, this was not possible and that left the MSF team on the ground with a substantial problem.

The following example illustrates this point. MSF was present in a Latin American country that suffered from severe violence for years. MSF wanted to be present to show solidarity, but it was hard to find relevant project activities related to the MTP. When a water and sanitation advisor visited the country management team, he reported problems concerning the project portfolio:

> But the major constraint, especially at field level, is to define what to do. Our presence is clearly justified but this is not the only reason for a medical/humanitarian organization to be in this country. So what else? Unfortunately, the medical reason has not yet been found to be The Reason: needs are not that big [trip report watsan advisor, February 2001].

The advisor questioned MSF's presence in a village to cover water and sanitation needs because the emergency phase was solved a long time ago. He suspected that the needs in this village were not much different from other people [trip report watsan advisor, February 2001]. In addition, the watsan advisor thought that water and sanitation activities in general were not the proper activities to employ:

> Watsan is not a major need to address, it is always there and beside medical brigade and non food item distribution, it might be a way to pay attention to affected people's problem, give them some dignity and finally strengthen their community structure [trip report watsan advisor, February 2001].

A combination of a humanitarian and medical emergency could not be found. Additional security constraints even made it more difficult to find proper project options. Here we see how the process of solutions looking for problems comes to an end, leaving the team on the ground with a difficult situation to work in.

In situations in which solutions start looking for a problem, the individual, such as a watsan advisor, had more room to define the organization's activities than in consequentially structured decision-making processes. Policies and procedures no longer offered enough guidance to the decision makers. Persuasion then became important. If MSF employees – and especially headquarters and the MT members - could be persuaded that MSF had a legitimate reason to be present somewhere, a project had more chance to continue to exist. If people could not be persuaded, it was more likely that a project would be terminated.

The impact of disagreement, commitment, and constraints

In this chapter, we have looked into the deviant cases of MSF Holland's dominant decision-making mode, i.e. the logic of consequence. Three types of deviant cases were presented. First, examples of consequential decision-making were presented that did not match the features of the administrative organization; these were cases in which the formal structure was bypassed, or the logic of consequence was used more as a persuasion or legitimizing strategy than a work method to arrive at decisions. Second, we described examples in which commitments due to legacies of the past and inside or outside pressures changed the process into appropriate decision-making. Third, we presented examples in which the operational space was so limited that due to a lack of alternatives for action garbage can decision-making dynamics emerged. However, these garbage can decision-making dynamics were constrained by the organization's structure: reasons for intervention and presence still needed to be related to the organization's goals, and the hierarchy in decision-making still needed to be followed.

The examples described in the previous chapter indicated that MSF Holland's preferred decision-making mode is the logic of consequence. However, this chapter shows that the possibilities to apply the logic of consequence are limited in occasions where disagreement, commitment, and constraints come into play. Disagreement seemed to lead to a bypassing of the formal structures or to the application of logic of consequence language to convince headquarters that a proposal should be approved. If the decision to intervene had already been made, but not through a 'pure' consequential decision-making mode, the reason for MSF presence sometimes remained unclear until the decision could be legitimized afterwards with help of the logic of consequence. This seemed to be the case if there was a strong commitment in headquarters to intervene, even though a medical humanitarian emergency, or aspects of it, were absent. The time factor could be of influence as well; the pressure to go might have been so strong that there was no time to apply consequentiality in decision-making. Finding a post-decision justification for an intervention might take quite some time, leading to a search process of solutions looking for problems. The decision-making process then offered more room for persuasion and negotiation, since the existing rules and policy guidelines in the organization did not provide sufficient guidance. Hence, individual entrepreneurship and group dynamics became more influential in the decision-making process. It was not so much the need to intervene as defined in the organization's policies that determined the organization's activities, but the craftmanship to formulate justifiable reasons for action. Sometimes this worked out well, but the more limited the operational space, the fewer options for action remained, leaving the team on the ground with empty hands. In such circumstances, MSF presence seemed to be more symbolic than substantial.

More an ambiguous than an administrative organization?

We hypothesized in the theoretical framework of this study that the characteristics of organizational decision-making processes were connected to the features of the organizational structure. In Chapter 5, we concluded that the formal organization of MSF Holland resembled Simon's administrative organization to a large extent and therefore consequential decision-making processes could be expected. This expectation proved to be valid for a substantial part of the decision-making processes studied.

In this chapter we looked into the exceptions to the non-consequential decision-making dynamics. We conclude that non-consequential decision-making processes emerged in times of disagreement, commitment, and constraints. One could wonder why these non-consequential elements were present, if the theoretical framework does not allow much room for this to happen. Two answers to this question are possible.

First, the theoretical framework does not allow much space for contextual factors outside the organization which could influence the character of decision-making processes. From this chapter we learn that it is exactly the contextual constraints that obstruct the logic of consequence to function properly. Hence, the organizational structure might allow a certain decision-making mode to become dominant – such as was the case within MSF – but contextual factors might explain those cases in which the organization did not follow the dominant, preferred decision-making mode.

Second, we could wonder to what extent the formal organizational features within MSF Holland had an influence on the daily practice of decision-making. In other words, did MSF's organizational structure in action resemble March and Olsen's ambiguous organization – the type of organization that we connected to the logic of the garbage can - more than we expected in Chapter 5? This chapter shows that MSF Holland was not a complete archetype of the administrative organization. We saw that group interests played a role in decision-making. This sometimes led to disagreement about the organization's activities. Persuasion, alliance building, and entrepreneurial behavior then became important mechanisms to come to a decision. Formal structures and policies did not matter as much anymore. This has to do with the mere fact that policies and guidelines never contain answers to all questions concerning organizational activities. Policies and procedures always meet a 'grey zone' with little prescribed direction, especially in such a complex context of humanitarian crises. Hence, the organization's technology was not as clear as it seemed to be in Chapter 5. Discussion and disagreement could also be the result of the fact that some of MSF's organizational features resembled other features of the ambiguous organization as well. For example, MSF Holland was characterized by fluid participation: many employees only had short-term contracts and positions in the field changed every 6 to 12 months. Most employees do not work a life-time for the organization; they do this work a couple of years and then leave the organization. High-rank positions changed often too. This makes it hard for the organization to create a shared outlook on work processes, decision-making procedures, and organizational goals. In such circumstances, preferences can become problematic and induce discussion, debate, and garbage can decision-making dynamics. Hence, MSF Holland is not a complete archetype of the administrative organization and resembles more elements of the ambiguous organization than expected, just as is claimed in NGO literature. Here we see how the formal organization can differ from the organization 'in action'.

Nevertheless, we should not forget that this chapter discussed the exceptions to the rule. Since garbage can decision-making is more of an exception than a rule within MSF Holland and the elements of the ambiguous organization do not seem to dominate the organizational structure (because the administrative organization keeps on providing boundaries to the decision-making process), the theoretical framework still seems to hold to a large extent.

Notes

1   This is the same example that is mentioned in Chapter 6 as a typical case of consequential decision-making concerning the ending of projects. Interesting in this regard is the fact that different decision-making modes can be present in one decision-making case, for different phases in the decision-making process. The consequential mode was present concerning decisions to end project activities, while the garbage can decision-making mode was present concerning the initiation of project activities in this country.

2   To limit the length of the case description, the story ends here. However, this was not the end of the MSF intervention. MSF still saw needs that could be addressed, such as rehabilitation of wells, upgrading of wells, and water quality control. The team also observed a need for monitoring the general health situation with concern to malnutrition and the spread of infectious diseases. By mid December the team finalized a project proposal for water and sanitation activities [sitrep 18/12/1998]. In consultation with the MoH, MSF decided to start working in four departments.

After a while, the team launched the idea to expand the watsan project [sitrep 5/1/1999]. In February, the emergency was not over yet. Cholera became a real problem. The number of monthly cases rose from 7 tot 74 in one month. In addition, the WFP and FAO warned that the food and nutritional situation was deteriorating due to failed harvests and a lack of food aid. The country had only received 6,6 percent of the identified needs in food provision [sitrep February 1999]. In the meantime, the team had cleaned half of the wells it planned to clean. In addition, the health education component was started and MSF assisted the MoH to counter the cholera problem in the country. A proposal for these cholera activities was submitted to the OD in Amsterdam.

In March, the country was struck by two earthquakes but MSF's projects were not hit. MSF visited the sites hit by the earthquake and donated tents to the Emergency Committee. A cholera epidemic did not materialize and in April the number of cases decreased significantly. The CM planned to write a Country Policy [sitrep March/April 1999].

In the sitrep of May and June the country manager reported that the danger of a cholera epidemic had definitely disappeared. However, the team felt a need to extend the preventive activities for four months. In addition, HQ was asked to extend the well cleaning program because the educational component took more time than expected. During these months, some regions were struck by heavy rains and floods. MSF visited the area but saw no need to intervene. MSF started to identify communities prone to new flooding that were unattended by the authorities or other organizations. The team announced that a proposal for flood prevention activities would be sent to the headquarters soon. Beside this, the country management started to explore the need for a HIV/AIDS intervention [sitrep May/June 1999]. This intervention started in 2000, together with a dengue intervention.

Chapter 8

From Consequential to Garbage Can Decision-Making: Two Examples of MSF Aid Provision to Africa

The previous two chapters have given us insight into MSF's daily decision-making practices. We concluded that MSF's dominant decision-making pattern followed the logic of consequence, while MSF's secondary decision-making patterns varied from stretching the boundaries of the administrative organization to appropriate and garbage can decision-making.

In this chapter, we will present two cases concerning MSF's humanitarian aid provision in Africa in order to illustrate how all three decision-making logics – the logic of consequence, the logic of appropriateness, and the logic of the garbage can – can become part of MSF's daily decision-making dynamics. The two examples chosen clearly differ in character: the first case represents an example of consequential decision-making, while the second case depicts completely different decision-making dynamics, in which garbage can decision-making eventually becomes dominant. By describing these two cases next to each other, we hope to show the differences between the three decision-making modes and how they influence the outcomes of decision-making.

MSF's consequentiality in action: A refugee influx

In March 1999, the MSF Holland office in Amsterdam received the following email from an employee, who happened to be in an African country for personal affairs:

> Following renewed military activities, thousands of refugees have entered the Northern province. Preliminary indications are that the refugees sought protection from rebel advances, which reportedly (source UNHCR) resulted in indiscriminate attacks against civilian and military targets alike (email from an MSF employee to headquarters, 15 March 1999).

This information created an occasion for decision-making within the organization: a decision could be taken whether to go to this country – where MSF Holland did not have a presence yet – or not. MSF Holland decided to launch an intervention in a transit camp for refugees, due to the refugee influx into the country. In order to do this, the MSF Holland team made decisions about the location and activities of its interventions. Later, it had to decide whether to end or extend the project. This case represents the typical consequential way of working of MSF Holland; it shows how the decision-making process concerning one particular intervention is full of sequential and prospective reasoning, maximizing and anticipatory behavior, and information and expert driven decision-making.

Starting the intervention: what to do and where?

It was fairly clear from the beginning for MSF Holland that it should have a presence in the area. There was a clear medical and humanitarian need: many people had left their homes and were entering a village not capable of taking (medical) care of its visitors. A situation very suited for MSF action, since this situation required an intervention as described for in the Mid Term Policy. In addition, UNHCR had requested MSF Holland to become an implementing partner.

Nevertheless, the members of the Emergency Desk asked the employee to visit the area for an exploratory mission to see what was going on and what MSF action was needed. The employer started exploring possibilities for action rightaway. He stated that it was important to start an intervention on two specific locations where refugees needed to be assisted. He proposed to focus on health, water and sanitation, and the planning of a refugee camp with the UNHCR [email 16 March, 1999].

On 21 March, the Red Cross counted more than 12.000 refugees in the region. Because the MSF/UNHCR camp was not functioning yet, a transit camp was set up, near the border where the refugees were coming from. MSF decided to help other international aid organizations in the transit camp with organizing a water and sanitation system. In addition, MSF started cooperating with an Irish relief agency in a water supply enterprise. Another concern was the health situation; there was the danger of a measles epidemic because one was running out of vaccines [email 21 March, 1999].

MSF continued to assist with the water supply and decided to monitor the measles situation, as well as to look into other alternatives for action, such as the 'cold chain' (medicine distribution). In the meantime it appeared that the site chosen for the MSF/UNHCR camp was not an ideal site to establish a camp. The roads to the camp site were in very bad condition. The MSF employee, now acting as the MSF country manager, heard about a possible second site for a camp, which would be much easier to access [email 23 March, 1999]. MSF discussed the plan regarding the new campsite with UNHCR. Its representative agreed with the plan. In the meantime, the first aid materials entered the region.

The country manager (CM) communicated with the Amsterdam office about the next steps to be taken. The Emergency Desk, consulted as an expert in these matters, expressed an interest in a health and water/sanitation component on both camp sites. Camp management and food distribution were not considered to be good alternatives for action.

Getting things started in difficult circumstances

On the 28 March, twelve days after the first email to the Amsterdam office, the country manager reported that an MSF logistician and nurse had opened a clinic in the transit camp, 24 hours after the aid materials for it had arrived. The nurse had organized medical teams; these were up and running in shifts of ten hours each. After one and a half days of work in the clinic, the team presented the first morbidity statistics to the Amsterdam headquarters: 232 admissions to the hospital, of which most patients suffered from diarrhea and malaria.

At that point in time, 500 persons crossed the border into the country every day. The food distribution was hampered. The country manager reported that they were almost out of stock and no new food had arrived. In the meantime, the camp site preference had shifted again back to the original area, though to a slightly different location. MSF negotiated with the local authorities that preparations for the camp construction would start.

However, on 5 April not much had changed: all refugees were still in the transit camp; there were still refugees entering the country regularly; food stocks had still not come in due to broken bridges; and the clinic was treating 200 to 250 patients per day. Six people had died in the meantime. The preparations for a measles vaccination campaign had come to a halt as a result of transportation problems and the fact that the wrong material had been sent to the transit camp. In addition, there were reports of a cholera outbreak in the transit camp. Six cases had been confirmed. The CM feared for a spread of the disease and anticipated a cholera epidemic. Therefore

> an isolation site was set up by MSF the same day and the treatment started. On 2 April a cholera kit arrived from our warehouse [....] The UNHCR has stopped transferring the refugees from the last two sites to the transit camp because of the outbreak [...] Everybody is on full alert [email 5 April, 1999].

An MSF visit made earlier to the site near the camp location originally planned for made clear that practically nothing had been done to make the site ready for construction. Therefore MSF took the lead and designed the refugee camp. The MSF watsan engineer started to develop the site, assisted by Red Cross volunteers. An MSF water treatment plant was set up and the site for the MSF clinic cleared in order to facilitate the construction of the clinic [email 5 April 1999]. Other sites, for food distribution and shelter, were also cleared. The Emergency Desk in Amsterdam sent two more expats to this site and a doctor and a nurse were expected to arrive soon.

On 19 April, the first 325 refugees arrived in this camp. It took more than a day to travel from the border to the camp, due to bad road conditions and difficulties with crossing a river. A second transport of another 400 refugees was postponed because of these problems. At the same time, old ideas were abandoned and new alternatives for action arose, aiming to overcome some practical problems of aid provision:

Yesterday I spoke to Y, he had met with the site planner of CARE who had visited new proposed sites in the west, among others, our second site. In his opinion this site cannot be used as digging latrines is not possible ... He expressed that he would be very interested in cooperating with MSF-H on ... new sites for emergency water and health .... [email 19 April 1999].

By the middle of May, the transit camp was practically empty due to the transportation of refugees by the UNHCR. MSF-H therefore decided to end their project in the transit camp. The team handed over the field dispensary and the cholera isolation site to the National Red Cross and the Ministry of Health. In the meantime, the construction of the refugee camp continued. More than ten thousand refugees had arrived. MSF Holland had taken the lead in this and cooperated with many other international NGOs. MSF was involved in the water supply and the medical care in the camp and attempted to closely co-operate with the Ministry of Health regarding these matters.

The refugee camp clinic presented its statistics for the period of 17 April to 7 May. A total of 1313 patients were treated in that period, of whom most suffered from malaria and acute respiratory infection. The mortality rates were low. Each medical officer treated almost 70 patients per day, which was considered to be too many. The team asked for more staff.

Changing scenarios while anticipating future developments

On 14 May, the MSF team had to leave the camp due to a security incident. This disrupted the recently started nutritional survey which the MSF nutritionist had organized. The CM anticipated that the outcome of the survey would lead MSF to start a nutritional program in the camp, mainly because of the fact that the arriving newcomers would be in a worse shape than those who were in the transit camp much longer. The preparations for a possible nutritional program and the ordering of materials and kits had already been done [email 15 May 1999].

At the same time, the fighting in the neighboring country continued and even intensified close to the border. The CM also anticipated that an attack would very likely cause an influx of refugees into the country once again. MSF therefore joined other organizations on a site planning trip and a new potential transit site as well as a refugee camp site was identified. Contingency plans were developed with the organizations involved and MSF placed an international order for contingency planning to be able to react immediately on a large influx. In the meantime, the developments were closely monitored [email 15 May, 1999].

By the end of May, more than 11.000 refugees were in the camp. MSF heard that another 10 to 15.000 refugees were staying in the border areas, refusing to leave the border. However, MSF decided to hand over the watsan component to Oxfam and made plans to hand over the clinic by the end of July, if the situation remained stable.

The extra transit camp site chosen earlier appeared to be totally unsuited due to the proximity of a swamp and "zillions of mosquitoes". Oxfam chose another site and while this was being prepared, the former site was used. The MSF contingency order had arrived and was stored in a warehouse close to the sites. The team made plans to prepare a proposal for a small nutritional project. In the beginning of June the results of the nutritional survey were available:

A nutritional survey was carried out in M refugee camp between 21 and 25 May 1999 on a sample of 512 children aged 6 to 59 months. Global acute malnutrition (weight-for-height less than 2 standard deviations or presence of oedema) was: 8.6 percent ± 2.4 percent. Severe acute malnutrition (weight-for-height less then 3 standard deviations or presence of oedema) was: 2.0 percent ± 1.4 percent.

Based on a population of 11,000 (average at the time of the survey), an estimated 146 children are therefore moderately malnourished and 44 children are severely malnourished. Malnutrition rates appeared higher among new arrivals (in the new blocks). Measles vaccination coverage was high (93.4 percent – most children were vaccinated in K). At this stage a nutritional intervention is not warranted given the overall health situation (under control- see MSF Health Report) [report on nutritional survey, May 1999].

Based on this information, which indicated that the nutrition levels were still acceptable, MSF Holland decided not to launch a nutritional intervention. Instead, MSF recommended that WFP would do something to vary the food basket. The MSF team decided that the only thing they would do was to encourage the refugees to start growing their own vegetables in order to get a more varied diet.

By the end of June the second transit camp became operational, with only a very small number of refugees crossing the border on a daily basis. The situation was becoming stable and MSF started to prepare the hand over of her activities. MSF Holland's activities were not needed any longer since the project objectives had been met. MSF decided that one expatriate staff member would stay in the capital of the country until the end of that year in order to closely monitor the situation, since new fighting, and therefore a new influx of refugees, was expected. In the meantime the refugee camp was included in the National Immunization Days, so the children had finally all been vaccinated.

A visitor from Amsterdam advises

By the end of June, a Health Advisor from the Amsterdam office Public Health Department visited the refugee camp and reported an effective operation. He agreed with the plans for handover and with the decision not to implement a nutrition project. Instead, he pointed to a possible need of mental care for the traumatized refugees. In his trip report, the Health Advisor recommended not to get involved in the upgrading of the clinic, but he approved of the plan to organize a seminar on cholera with the Ministry of Health.

The health advisor reported about the interest of the Dutch embassy to have MSF Holland make an assessment of the country's preparedness to deal with the almost annual outbreaks of cholera. This would mean that MSF Holland was to stay in the country to start a project in the north where cholera is endemic. But the health advisor saw no reason to do that because the Ministry was able to cope with an outbreak but simply lacked the material [trip report July 1999]. The health advisor saw no urgent need to initiate such a project, also because other actors were able to cope with this problem on their own. Nevertheless, he still thought it was too early to leave the country completely because the situation could change for the worse. [trip report July 1999].

History repeats itself

In the last weeks of June nobody in the clinic died and the morbidity rates were extremely low. MSF Holland saw no clear need to extend its stay and therefore decided to terminate the project in the refugee camp, as was advised by the health advisor. After consultation with the health advisor, the team was getting ready to hand over the clinic to the Red Cross. One MSF employee would stay behind for another month to give advice and monitor the situation [email 28 June 1999]. However, the situation changed once again.

In the beginning of July the team had to be evacuated from the refugee camp as a result of security incidents caused by ex-combatants. It lasted a week before all international organizations could return, after a delayed food distribution had come through. The organizations met to discuss a security plan. Another 1000 new refugees arrived in the camp unexpectedly, bringing the total of refugees to 12,337, while another 3000 refugees remained in the second transit camp waiting to be transported to the camp.

MSF heard about suspected cholera cases and took care of extra screening of new refugees [email 13 July 1999]. The number of refugees crossing the border rose again to about 300 persons per day. This was the result of decreasing security and food supplies. The CM expressed his concerns about possible future developments; he expected the camp population to rise from 13.000 to 22.000 people. He proposed to defer the handover of the project because the Red Cross was not ready to take over and to consider additional health care facilities for the increasing refugee population[email 17 July 1999].

By the end of July, the refugee population had grown to 13,543. The Red Cross could not agree with the hand over at the end of September, so a compromise was reached and a new hand-over date was set for mid August. MSF would stay behind with an advisor and promised that a stock of drugs for 20,000 refugees would be in place before MSF would leave the camp definitively.

In the meantime, the mortality rate rose again [email 26 July 1999]. The team revised its budget to cover its extended stay in the camp and submitted it to headquarters. At the same time, the team wrote a proposal for the whole province, in case the worst happened, so that the proposal could be immediately submitted to donors. The refugee population kept growing to 14,353 in mid August. The statistics, however, showed that the health situation was under control [medical report August 1999, see Figure 8.1].

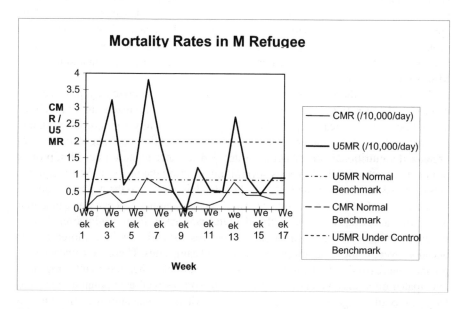

Figure 8.1   MSF medical report, June 1999
(See for an explanation of the acronyms Chapter 5, Figure 5.3)

The number of consultations in the clinic had increased from 734 at the beginning of July to 974 at mid August. Malaria (30 percent), acute respiratory infections (15 percent) and diarrhea (8 percent) were the main causes of illness. In addition, there was a rise in "minor complaints" to 50 percent of all patients.

In the end, the hand-over date of the clinic was postponed to 31 August, when MSF was finally able to leave the clinic in the hands of the Red Cross. After a month, the CM organized a trip to the area in order to monitor the situation and set out a strategy for future decision-making moments:

> In order to update scenarios and anticipate changes, MSF will visit above mentioned areas on a regular basis. Together with changes in forecasts and scenario's, findings of these fieldtrips will form the basis for ongoing discussions between CM and HQ of how the exit strategy of MSF Holland in this country can best be executed [trip report October 1999].

At the time of the trip more than 17.000 refugees lived in the refugee camp. The government had decided to transport all refugees in the border area (9.000 to 16.000 refugees) to this camp. The Red Cross became responsible for all activities in the camp.[1]

Consequential decision-making as the order of the day

This case about a refugee influx in an African country represents an average MSF Holland humanitarian intervention in which a business-as-usual decision-making process unfolded. All decision categories discussed in Chapter 6 made their appearance: the decision whether or not to intervene, the idea to initiate a nutrititional project that was rejected based on the results of a nutritional survey, the decision to end the project in the transition camp, and the decision to first extend and later end MSF's presence in the refugee camp.

We saw how the decision-making process was characterized by information-driven decision-making, for example because MSF organized an exploratory mission; because the team reported regularly about mortality and morbidity figures as a means to measure the effectiveness of the intervention; and because the team organized a nutritional survey before it decided whether to start a nutrition project or not. The team consulted experts several times during the process: the Emergency Desk was asked for advice and later the health advisor came to the country to advise on the future of MSF in this country. The decision-making process was sequential in that first an explo was organized and advice was asked from headquarters before the intervention was launched. Also, alternatives for action were explored before decisions were made about project activities and camp sites. There were instances of prospective reasoning in the project period, for example when the country manager anticipated on a possible cholera epidemic in April as well as a potential new and large influx of refugees in May and July; and when the decision was made not to initiate a nutrition project since the research data made clear there was no real need to intervene. In addition, the team members acted in accordance with the MSF policies by starting to prepare for a handover once the situation stabilized and the project objectives seemed to be met. The other way around, the team decided to extend its activities as soon as it was clear that the situation was deteriorating and the handover partner was not able to do the job alone.

There were also some non-consequential elements in the decision-making process, especially in the beginning of the intervention. For example, the fact that MSF heard of the refugee influx was not a result of purposeful information collection, but of a coincidence: the MSF employee who alarmed headquarters happened to be in the country to renew his passport. Nevertheless, there were substantially less non-consequential decision-making elements present in this case than the consequential elements touched upon above. In short, this case shows proof of how "consequentialized" MSF's daily decision-making processes can be.

The law of diminishing alternatives: A postwar intervention

In Chapter 7, examples of 'deviant' decision-making occasions were presented, indicating that MSF Holland decision-making processes were not always neat and tidy consequential processes in which the formal structure determined the order of decision-making. In the following case, concerning one particular MSF Holland intervention in an African country after a war, we will see how the non-consequential aspects of decision-making – especially the process of solutions looking for a problem – go together with consequential decision-making dimensions, either in harmony with features of the administrative organization or in dissonance with the formal structure. At the same time we see that the logic of consequence decision-making mode is abandoned as a result of contextual constraints, such as the limited operational space and security concerns. This induced what we will call 'the law of diminishing alternatives for action', meaning that the fewer options for actions existed, the more the decision-making process became characterized by garbage can dynamics.

Planning assessments but without gaining access

Since 1997, MSF Holland was interested in working in the African country in this example. In December 1997, MSF Holland organized an exploratory mission to assess the prevalence of a disease called kala azar (sleeping sickness, LH). MSF Holland had received information from MSF teams in two neighboring countries which indicated that the disease was becoming epidemic in the border areas between the three countries. A kala azar intervention by MSFH might therefore be an option for action in this country. However, the government was not much in favor of this assessment. The authorities claimed that there was no epidemic and that the data MSFH wanted to collect were already available. MSFH was not allowed in.

In 1998, the relationship between this country and its neighbor became tense as a result of various hostilities. The neighboring country invaded parts of the country in which MSFH aimed to intervene. The people living in the border areas fled from the violence and moved up north to settle in camps for internally displaced people (IDPs).

In January 1999, MSFH returned to this country to assess whether MSFH could assist in IDP camps. MSFH had a desire to work on both sides of the conflict and since the team already had a presence in the neighboring country, the organization aimed at working in the other country as well. However, the government refused their offer once again, claiming it could handle the situation by itself.

Access is achieved, the mission is started

In the beginning of 2000, MSF did another assessment. This time, the government allowed MSFH to start working in the area due to the huge number of internally displaced people. This was the result of new tensions between the two countries in 1999. The government could not completely handle the situation on its own anymore and allowed international aid organizations to come in and assist in the aid provision.

An MSFH assessment team traveled to the country and reported a lack of adequate staff and supplies in the medical facilities of the IDP camps, as well as lack of proper storage facilities and poor sanitation. The assessment team proposed to focus on these issues and formulated a project proposal for IDP camps which included activities such as the provision of medicines (including vaccines) and medical equipment, and expat presence for 'the purpose of solidarity, monitoring, and outreach training' [policy paper, 16/02/01].

The Emergency Desk asked the assessment team some critical questions as to why this situation was a medical humanitarian emergency. Since it is MSF Holland policy only to intervene in situations that are both a medical and a humanitarian emergency, this was a relevant question to ask, especially because this country had been in this situation for almost two years already. The main argument of the assessment team was that the coping mechanisms of the population were deteriorating and that extra assistance was therefore needed soon. However, it was also reported that the basic needs were already covered by other governmental or non-governmental agencies.

Nevertheless, MSF approved the proposal and opened a mission in the country. In a position paper of March 2000, the main reasons mentioned for MSF's presence in the country were that there was a fragile situation with a lot of IDPs; that MSF wanted to work on both sides of the conflict; that this situation offered possibilities to learn from the 'un-African' approach this country had in dealing with the conflict; and that it would enable the team to perform emergency preparedness activities.

In consultation with the Ministry of Health, six camp sites were identified for MSF activities. However, by the time MSF was ready to start its activities, new hostilities broke out in May 2000. Some IDP camps moved further up north. MSF therefore changed its plans and got involved in three major IDP camps: two camps in the mid-eastern part of the country and one camp in the south west of the country. In addition, the organization did some work in the smaller camps. The teams focused on water and sanitation activities, such as building latrines, cleaning and repairing wells, and providing access to clean water. MSF did not provide any medical aid, because this was covered pretty well by the government or other international aid organizations.

Assessing opportunities for work: a small operational space

Since the United Nations was preparing to establish a special UN zone in the former war zones of this country, MSFH anticipated that a lot of work would be necessary as soon as the zone was open and free of landmines. However, the opening of this zone took more time than expected. After a couple of months, the MSF team had completed most of its water and sanitation activities in the IDP camps outside this UN zone. The team had to wait for the zone to open up.

Since there was as not much to do as had been expected, the team initiated various assessments throughout the country to be sure other needs were not neglected. While traveling around, the team members did small repairs of water systems when needed. First, the western and north eastern parts of the country were assessed extensively. The team established needs in the western part of the country, but the Ministry of Health had already invited another medical agency to cover this area [assessment report 1/8/00]. MSFH did some watsan work in a camp in the same area, but stopped working there at the end of July 2001. In the north eastern part of the country, thought to be a risk area because of a long-lasting drought, no urgent needs were found as well. Overall, the team concluded that there did not seem to be urgent medical humanitarian – and therefore typically MSF – needs in the country that the team could cover:

> Bottom-line – there are many watsan things we can be doing; medically – as in the whole country – we are struggling. I would like to look at mental health, which has been on the cards sometime and is overdue .... We really need to discuss our complete programs in [the country] on the medical side and try to decide what our role is to be here. We can do watsan until the cows come home but so can Oxfam [assessment report 1/8/00 – HoM].

In November the team started to discuss whether to phase out of the camps or not. The head of mission asked the health advisor in Amsterdam for advice about some small feeding programs the organization had developed in the IDP camps. It was argued that the general malnutrition rate was low and that the general food pipeline functioned well [email HoM to HA, 7/11/00]. The health advisor agreed with the idea to stop the feeding programs and so the programs were terminated.

By the end of November the head of mission once again approached a health advisor in Amsterdam to discuss the 1997 idea of conducting a kala azar prevalence study in the country. The head of mission was anticipating a possible request from the Ministry of Health (MoH) to assist: 'It is not certain when this survey will be done but in case the MoH asks for assistance, should we offer?' [email HoM to HA, 28/11/00]. The health advisor wondered how kala azar was related to the country policy and argued that previous studies showed that the disease itself was not so dominant that one could speak of a humanitarian crisis. He doubted whether MSF had a role to play, but he did not object to a re-assessment of the situation because:

- Who knows what new information might come out of an assessment (KA is a dynamic disease which may flare up like a bushfire);
- With the IDP activities slowly fading out (as I understand), support to KA may provide an opportunity to have a continued strategic presence for some time in order to monitor the unstable situation even after the IDP problems have been resolved;
- MSF has a lot of relevant expertise to offer.

He therefore advised to do such an assessment and to wait with making commitments to the Ministry until it would be clear what MSF's strategic future in the country would be [email HA to HoM, 28/11/00].

In the beginning of January 2001, the team assessed another area in the north of the country for possible intervention. The watsan expert of the MSF Holland headquarters responded to the assessment report by stating that he did not see a need to intervene because there was no direct link with the MTP to be found [email watsan expert to HoM, 20/2/01]. After discussing the assessment report in the Operational

Support Team in Amsterdam, the logistics expert expressed the general feeling in the OST about the proposed activities:

> The medical department and the watsan advisors both found that the medical and environmental health issues that came up through the assessment are not critical in the sense that they constitute a reason for MSF to intervene. This combines with rather unspecific humanitarian issues (refugees, neglected populations). What this leaves is a proposal to go there for four months to find out if a solid justification for further MSF engagement exists. The general finding was that this is not substantial enough to go ahead [email logistics expert to HoM, 26/02/01].

In the beginning of April, the team formulated a plan of action in case the UN security zone would open up. The team proposed to follow the people from a camp in the east of the country to their home area in the south of the country. The idea was to help this population to rehabilitate their water and sanitation and medical facilities, because the living conditions in the home area would be worse than the living conditions in the IDP camps. The plan was ready but the UN security zone remained closed.

Since the team could not identify other needs that would legitimize an MSF intervention, a discussion was started with the Amsterdam headquarters whether to close the mission or not, or to at least minimize MSF's presence in the country. Some people in the Amsterdam headquarters felt that there was a need to stay in the country, especially the Operational Director [email OST member to HoM, 10/4/01]. However, the country manager felt differently and anticipated the termination of the programs: "The team feels that objectives have been reached (more or less). A proper evaluation should be done before pulling out of the camps" [email 16/4/01].

The UN zone opens up: new opportunities for action arise

Two days after the email in which the country manager proposed to stop working in this country, the UN zone opened up. The plan of action to follow the population of one camp to their home area came into the picture again. A discussion emerged whether to follow up on this plan and to send an expat to the area to start a project:

> However, we have made certain commitments (ref. Plan of Action) and should stay to see these through to ensure our good reputation stays in tact. On the other hand, if we are not prepared to do what MoH actually wants us to do in the UN zone (rehabilitation and reconstruction, i.e. the shopping list principle) then it may be better to cut and run before we lose our good reputation [email HoM 12/5/01].

In the same month, the country manager and the operational director discussed the option of closing or downsizing the mission. The country manager argued that closing down the mission after a possible intervention in the south was the only option:

> To be honest, we feel this is likely to be the picture all the way down the lines. In other words, not much for MSFH to do in health terms. We can even do this with just national staff.[...] Because the MoH is very capable, there is no clear role for MSFH in terms of health.

[....] In terms of monitoring, the PC is not convinced there is a viable reason for MSFH to remain, and to a very large extent I agree. This is what we have been doing for the last nine months and the results are extremely small. For the most part, we are fooling ourselves if we think we can influence things in [this country]. There is a need for continued monitoring for a short while at least (see if movement of IDPs from camps and repatriation from neighboring countries goes well, etc), but we should not forget there are also other agencies present who are capable of doing this monitoring [email HoM 14/5/01].

The operational director (OD) shared this analysis. However, in the beginning of June the OD sent an email to the head of mission in which he proposed to do the project in the south together with monitoring activities in the country as a whole. Somebody of the CMT had written in the margins of the email: 'No, there is nothing to do! Maybe, we'll see ....' By the end of June this project in the south was up and running, although the country manager acknowledged that it was not a 'typical MSF project':

For [this project] we are doing quite a bit more than we committed to the government; now we're seeing first hand how things are working on the ground (did not want to overcommit in advance, just in case) ... it is all a bit 'borderline' from an MSF (and MTP) point of view, but 'creativity' is coming to the fore!!! [email HoM, 26/6/01].

In the eyes of the project manager, this project was the only thing left to do. With concern to working in other areas in the country, she replied: 'MSFH is struggling even to find a few scraps of work without getting in the way of other organizations' [email HoM, 27/6/01].

For a moment it looked like MSF could become more involved in a camp in the west of the country after an unexpected influx of 24.000 IDPs. Nevertheless, the country manager saw no need to intervene: 'In short, the situation seems to be well covered by others for now, so we don't think our input will be needed' [email HoM 18/7/01]. It seemed that MSF was ready to pull out of the country once the rehabilitation of watsan and medical facilities was finished.

Postponing the project before leaving the country

By mid July, something unexpected happened: the Ministry of Health formally requested MSF Holland to stay in the south to assist the Ministry in combating malaria in the region. Malaria was an endemic disease in the south and the Ministry feared an epidemic since the population MSF had been assisting had been living in a malaria-free area for almost two years. It was very likely that a lot of people had lost their immunity against the disease. The medical coordinator in the CMT very much favored this intervention. The OD was also open to discuss the extension of the project for malaria activities

The malaria option is technically more restricted and needs negotiation and clarifications. If what we have is a more open request for support that includes malaria as one of the aspects, I think it is technically less problematic and hence we should start thinking about it [email 24/7/01].

One day later, the operational assistant of the operational director responded to her boss's email by formulating the clarification and justification the operational director asked for:

> So, a vulnerable population, a weak MoH, potential outbreaks (peak of malaria to be expected in Sept/Oct) combined with a request from MoH to help, leads to feelings of most CMT members and the HA and me that continuation of MSF's help is justified [email OA 25/7/01].

Two days later, there was a project outline that proposed to accept the request because MSF Holland was the only NGO present in the south. This area was the proper area to work in because there was a vulnerable group of people that faced the risk of a malaria outbreak, due to decreased immunity, lack of shelter, watsan damage, food aid dependence, a weak health system, and lack of staff. It was proposed to do some training, to finally do the kala azar assessment, and to monitor the peace process. The proposal also mentioned potential constraints for the project, such as lack of access due to the rainy season; increased security risks; a danger to be dragged into larger watsan activities; MoH substitution; how to find a local labtechnician, as required by the government?; external/partner funding difficulties; and a lack of UN/military rescue options. On the 27 July, the OD responded to the issue of government substitution:

> If it is clear this is the aim and it does not damage anything in itself, no major problems. Since MSF's humanitarian mandate is more concerned with survival and alleviating suffering (more than sustainability or the creation of long-lasting systems) the fact of doing substitution is not such a terrible problem. Like sustainability, we have nothing against it, but it is not our first priority. In some occasions we are very happy to get it as an added benefit, but is definitely not what we are after [email OD, 27/7/01].

On 31 July, the operational director and the operational support team in the Amsterdam headquarters approved the proposal. A week later the operational director informed the CMT that the MT had approved the project [email OD, 6/8/01]. The project would run until the end of November to cover the malaria season. MSF Holland formulated the condition that the local government should do everything in its power to prevent the epidemic from happening. The local government initiated activities to fill all the water pools in order to prevent mosquitoes from hatching in the water. Since the governmental malaria prevention plan was very effective, no malaria epidemic emerged. The MSF team decided to end the project in the south and started preparing to close down the mission. By the end of 2001 the MSF team had left the country.

The limits of consequential decision-making

The case described above shows how consequential decision-making dynamics were part of a process which also had features of appropriate and garbage can decision-making. MSF Holland apparently felt a strong commitment to be present in this country, although it was difficult to find options for actions which matched MSF policies. Therefore, a search process was launched with a series of assessment missions. These assessments led to the conclusion that MSF intervention was not needed, taking MSF policies into account. The team continued its search for suitable options for action and this brought the organization to the people of a camp in the east of the country and finally to their home area in the south. For this project, the CMT was able to find legitimate arguments to launch it.

The country management team often expressed their doubts about the need for MSF intervention. In April, the team started discussions with headquarters. Headquarters, however, had a different opinion and urged the CMT to be patient. It took until November before it was decided to close down the mission. The OD decided that the team should stay in the country without downsizing it, also because the UN zone opened up and MSF felt a commitment towards the government to implement the Plan of Action it had formulated earlier in the year. Although the hierarchical line in the organization was followed, there was disagreement at the headquarters about this decision and the country management team did not obey without protest and debate.

This example illustrates what a non-sequential decision-making process within MSF Holland looks like. Interesting to note is that non-sequential decision-making elements coincided with consequential decision-making dynamics. In effect, it is the results of this consequential work method that led the team to conclude that certain proposed interventions were not needed or already covered by other aid agencies. Therefore, MSF decided not to launch such interventions. The organization then had two options: either to leave the country or to continue the search for potential projects. In this case, the organization chose the latter option and it is here that the consequential decision-making mode was partly replaced by garbage can decision-making dynamics until the organization found options for action that could be justified by the MSF mandate. The MSF mandate was thus not completely disregarded and kept on providing the framework for acceptable interventions.

Certain individuals played a substantial role in the process of finding justifiable actions, since there was disagreement about what MSF should do. The operational assistant helped the medical coordinator in the field to formulate reasons to intervene in the spirit of the Mid Term Policy. The operational director argued for the initiation of a project in the south. The MSF employees used persuasion strategies to convince each other which action should be taken. In addition, we see how the formal structures were bypassed when the operational assistant became involved in the decision-making process.

Furthermore, the 2000 intervention had a history of its own, which leaves the impression that the 1999 hostilities and the government's willingness to let MSF enter the country provided MSF with a window of opportunity to finally gain a foothold after various attempts to get access to this country. The kala azar survey had a prominent position on MSF's 'to do' list for a long time, until MSF decided to skip this activity in the summer of 2001.

The reasons why MSF Holland could not work consequentially consistently also became clear in this case: we saw how limited the operational space was, due to the massive presence of other aid agencies, the delays in opening the UN security zone, security reasons, and a strong local government. This induced the law of diminishing alternatives and of garbage can decision-making dynamics. In addition, the commitment to be present in this country defined the decision-making process, despite evidence – collected by means of consequential data-gathering instruments – that MSF presence was not needed as much as one might have expected. This all led to a process of solutions looking for problems.

From consequential to garbage can decision-making

The two cases discussed above are illustrative for MSF's daily decision-making processes. The first case represents an example of the preferred decision-making mode, i.e. the logic of consequence, although non-consequential elements were also present in the decision-making processes described. This case exemplifies the dominant decision-making pattern in the organization, as was argued in Chapter 6.

The second case shows us an example of a less dominant decision-making mode within MSF. The case describes attempts to decide consequentially on the field level without finding alternatives for action that match the organization's mandate and policies. This led to the conclusion of the MSF country management team that MSF intervention was not needed as much as was expected. From a consequential decision-making perspective it is surprising to see that the MT did not decide to end its presence at that point.[2] As a consequence, garbage can decision-making dynamics replaced the dominant consequential decision-making mode on the field level until suitable options for action were found. A limited operational space restricted MSF's alternatives for action which added to the garbage can decision-making dynamics.

Notes

1   For the purpose of the length of the argument, the description of this case ends here. However, this was not the end of MSF Holland's presence in the country. In 2000, one MSF expat monitored the situation and after a couple of months a new influx of refugees from the same neighboring country and another neighboring country required MSF Holland to intervene once again, also on other locations.
2   MSF adds to this that the MT decision to go to this country was taken consequentionally. We did not have access to this level of decision-making at the time of the field research to determine this myself. We argue here that garbage can decision-making could be observed on the *field* level.

PART III
ACT Netherlands' Decision-Making in Practice

Chapter 9

The Opposite of the Administrative Organization: ACT Netherlands' Organizational Features

A brief history of the organization

Action by Churches Together Netherlands (ACT Netherlands) originates from the oldest ecumenical aid organization in The Netherlands. This organization was founded under the name 'Dutch Interchurch Aid' in 1952. Its roots go back to World War II when an ecumenical committee for the rehabilitation of the Dutch protestant churches – named 'Interchurch Reconstruction Committee - was established under the umbrella of the World Council of Churches.

After a big flood hit the south-west of The Netherlands in 1952, this committee received aid. This led to the decision to do something in return for the help the committee received in that year. The committee therefore started to help people who returned from Indonesia and Australia in the years after World War II. Later, Vietnamese refugees also received aid from the committee. In the same year, the committee became a foundation and was named Dutch Interchurch Aid (DIA).

In 1966, DIA organized its first substantial fundraising campaign for a famine in India (Van Capelleveen, 1997:34). The organization raised 26 million guilders (almost €12 million) in one night. Two years later, the organization was a participating actor in the organization of a major aid airlift to Biafra. In 1969, DIA launched another huge fundraising campaign, this time for overseas protestant churches, and raised 29 million guilders (more than €13 million). The campaign was such a success that DIA decided to make it a regular two-year campaign.

In the seventies, the European Community faced major food surpluses. DIA became one of the aid agencies responsible for the redistribution of the Dutch surpluses. This responsibility was shared with Mensen in Nood (Caritas Holland) and Novib (Oxfam Holland). This resulted in a DIA food security program and the creation of the DIA food department. From 1972 on, DIA cooperated with the catholic relief NGO Mensen in Nood (Caritas Holland). The first collective fundraising campaign – together with all major Dutch humanitarian aid NGOs – was organized for the Sahel in 1974 ('S.O.S. Sahel'). After that, many more collective fundraising efforts followed, among which the well known fundraising campaign for Ethiopia called 'Africa Now' (Van Capelleveen, 1997:38–40).

In 1986/1987 the organization faced a huge reorganization within the Dutch protestant churches. Since the protestant churches were members of the board of Dutch Interchurch Aid, Dutch Interchurch Aid had to follow these changes. The result was that the organization had to focus its work more specifically on relief and food aid.

A decade later, DIA faced organizational changes once again. In 1997, a cooperation agreement was signed between Dutch Interchurch Aid and two other NGOs, namely ICCO and DOG (Dienst over Grenzen).[1] This was meant to end in a merger between the three organizations in the coming years. The reason behind this merger was that the Dutch protestant churches had decided that there should be a clearer division between government money and private (church) money within DIA. Because the food aid department of Dutch Interchurch Aid was largely dependent upon government money, it needed to have more distance from the protestant churches. In January 2000, the Dutch protestant churches therefore decided that the relief aid department of DIA should merge with the missionary and diaconal department of the protestant churches. The merger was concluded on 22 March 2000. The relief aid department continued under the name of 'ACT Netherlands'.

In the beginning of May 2000, the employees of the relief aid department of Dutch Interchurch Aid moved to the central office of the Dutch protestant churches in Utrecht. The merger involved only those activities that were funded by the churches. The part of Dutch Interchurch Aid that was funded by institutional donors, such as the EU or the Dutch government, – this especially concerned the former DIA food aid department – was merged with the two other NGOs ICCO and Dienst over Grenzen.

We studied ACT Netherlands decision-making processes in 1999 and 2000, before and after the merger with the Dutch churches. In October 2002, ACT Netherlands ceased to exist as a specialized emergency unit and merged with the regional desks of the Protestant churches and ICCO.

The opposite of the administrative organization

In order to establish what the organizational features of ACT Netherlands were at the time of the study and to what extent these features resemble one of the three ideal types of organizational settings presented in Chapter 3, we will take a closer look at ACT's organizational structures, work methods, policies, and decision-making procedures.

The organizational structure before and after the merger

Until the merger in March 2000, Dutch Interchurch Aid was a foundation. The board consisted of representatives of fifteen protestant denominations. The board appointed the executive board. The executive board was responsible for policy formulation and approvals of projects above 50,000 guilders (approximately €23,000). In addition to a general secretariat, there were three departments within the organization: 1) the Disasters and Refugees department; 2) the Food Aid department; and 3) the Finance and Organization department. In total, 32 people worked for Dutch Interchurch Aid.

The Disasters and Refugees department was divided into regional sections. For Europe, a special desk was set up in 1995 by the Dutch Protestant Church, ICCO, and Dutch Interchurch Aid (yearly report 1995:20). Aside from these departments, three other sections had headquarters within Dutch Interchurch Aid, i.e., *Kerken in Actie*, *Kinderen in de Knel*, and *Bureau Beleidsvorming Ontwikkelingssamenwerking*. These three sections each had their own board and published their own annual report.

Nowadays, ACT Netherlands is a sub-department of the Foreign Department within the National Service Center of the Dutch protestant churches. ACT Netherlands is considered to be an expert sub-department, because of its expertise concerning humanitarian aid issues (see Figure 9.1). ACT Netherlands consists of eight project officers who each manage a project portfolio that is divided regionally. There is a project officer for Asia, East and North Africa, South and West Africa, Latin America and for Central Asia. In addition, there are special project officers for the Great Lakes region, the Balkan special program, and the Turkey special program. The head of department is in charge of these project officers. In addition, there is a secretariat of three administrative staff members.

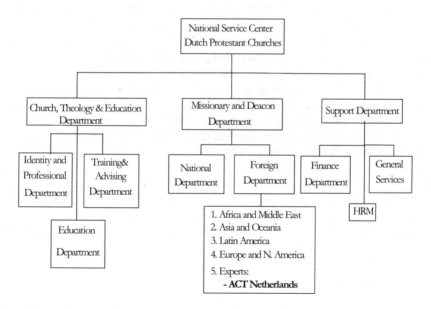

Figure 9.1   ACT Netherlands' position within the National Service Center

The ACT policy paper: A broad range of activities

Until the beginning of 2001, the policy of the organization was based on one single policy paper, dated May 1998. In this paper, the following themes were discussed: the definition of crisis situations; the instruments to use and the activities to employ in order to handle these situations; the networks the organization works in; and funding activities.

ACT Netherlands works in emergency situations. These were defined in the policy paper as 'the interactions of a natural or human crisis and a vulnerable population. Poverty and the lack of protection are the major determining factors why so many people are more vulnerable than others' (Policy paper, 1998:4). The lack of protection did not only refer to disasters and conflicts, but also to situations in which certain groups are marginalized or neglected economically and politically.

At the time of the study, prevention and preparedness were major components in the aid activities of the organization, as these are means to reduce vulnerability. The organization was also interested in human rights issues, conflict management, conflict prevention, and lobbying. The organization therefore described its work as 'crisis management in conflict areas based on a developmental approach' (Policy paper 1998:5, our translation). On a more concrete level, the project activities focused on: crisis management, human rights activities, relief aid, rehabilitation, taking care of basic facilities, organizational development, and supporting civil society.

The organization works with local partner organizations. The paper described some criteria for ending working relationships with local organizations. First, relationships should be ended when the local partner is able to continue working on its own, because it has developed enough capacity to handle crises on its own. This is the case if the organization is able to develop a vision of the future; if it has enough capacity to implement programs well; and if it has the capacity to raise funds independently. Second, the relationship can be ended whenever a crisis has diminished and/or the organization is capable of working on its own again.

In the paper, the organization stressed the importance of diversity in funding. Governmental money could be used to finance 'normal' project activities, while private funding could be used to finance more controversial projects. The organization estimated that it needed 10 to 15 million guilders (€4,5 to €6,8 million) to spend on the latter category of projects. The international ACT network was deemed to be useful because it helped Dutch Interchurch Aid to work more effectively. The network also provided the opportunity to make 'gestures of solidarity' to groups that the organization is not in touch with directly.

Regional policy purposes

The policy paper also described various regional policies. In Central Asia, Dutch Interchurch Aid aimed at training, income generating activities, and south-south exchange programs.[2] In addition, attention was paid to growing tensions between various groups in the area, as well as to the possibility that people could become displaced. The geographical focus was on Kirgizstan and Kazachstan, where the organization fulfilled a leading role. The organization also supported projects in Tadjikistan and Chechnya. The budget aimed for was 2,5 million guilders (€1,1 million) per year.

The African continent was divided into four areas of attention: West Africa, Southern Africa, the Great Lake area, and the Horn and east Africa. Table 9.1 presents the regional focus per area, and the activities that the organization planned to implement. The budget aimed for was about seven million guilders (€3,2 million).

Table 9.1   Regional policy purposes in Africa (Policy paper 1998)

Countries	Activities aimed for
Angola	- rehabilitation consortium
Burundi	- peace and reconciliation
Congo	- supporting local capacity
	- search for more network partners
Eritrea	- humanitarian support for the Beja
Ethiopia	- capacity building
	- lobbying (ethnic tensions)
Ghana	- conflict management
Guinea	- new partners
	- rehabilitation aid
	- building civil society
Kenya	- peace and reconciliation program
Liberia	- rehabilitation and reintegration aid to returning refugees
	- building civil society
	- attention to human rights
Nigeria	- new partners
	- human rights issues
Rwanda	- work will be handed over to other organizations
	- conflict prevention
Sierra Leone	- new partners
	- rehabilitation aid
	- building civil society
Somalia	- search for new activities with one remaining small partner
South Africa	- conflict areas
	- less involvement planned because of fewer refugee and food problems and the large presence of the humanitarian aid community in the country

In Asia, the organization focused on Afghanistan and various refugee situations in Thailand, Nepal, South India, and Kashmir. The organization also worked with partner organizations in Nepal concerning disaster preparedness. In India, they paid attention to conflict prevention. In the past years, the organization ended some partnerships with local organizations in Cambodia, the Philippines, Bangladesh, Pakistan, and some parts in India. One hoped to spend two or three million (€1 tot €1,4 million) per year on these areas.

In Latin America, Dutch Interchurch Aid worked in a local network called Project Counseling Service. Guatemala would receive attention because of returning refugees. Peru and Colombia were also of importance, because of internal tensions and narco-crime. The organization hoped to start working with internally displaced people in Mexico. Partnerships with organizations in Nicaragua and El Salvador would be ended. The budget aimed for eight million guilders (€3,6 million).

The organization established a special desk for the European continent in cooperation with other Dutch humanitarian aid NGOs. In the Middle East, ACT worked in Kurdistan in the so-called Dutch Consortium. There were also some activities in Lebanon. The budget for Europe was a million guilders (€454.000), and the budget for the Middle East was half a million guilders (€227.000).

Work methods and decision-making procedures

ACT Netherlands is an organization that co-operates with partner organizations in developing countries. The organization does not implement its own projects but transfers money to the partner organizations that implement project activities. The partner organizations apply for money by submitting project proposals. Aside from that ACT Netherlands sometimes approaches these organizations and offers them help.

At the time of the study, ACT Netherlands worked with three networks of partner organizations. The first is called *Action by Churches Together* (ACT). This is a network of protestant churches and aid organizations from all over the world (related to the World Council of Churches) that combine there efforts. The network maintains a secretariat in Geneva where member organizations hand in so-called ACT appeals describing humanitarian aid projects. These ACT appeals are sent to every member of the network. The second network is located in Latin America and is called *Project Counseling Service*. This network was established in 1975 by the Danish Refugee Council, the Norwegian Refugee Council, Christian Aid (UK), HEKS (Switzerland), and Dutch Interchurch Aid. The aim of the network was to support local resistance organizations after the outbreak of crises on the Latin American continent in 1975. At the time of the study, this network was the single distribution channel for all ACT Netherlands' funds in Latin America. A third network was being established in Central Asia. This network should be able to counterbalance the dominant Central Asian authorities and should lead to the creation of civil society. Beside these three networks, the organization had close ties with the World Council of Churches. In addition, the organization had liaison offices in Eritrea, Kazachstan, and Macedonia. These offices made a first selection of project proposals from partners in the region.

The ACT Netherlands' project officers and the head of the sub-department met once every week to discuss the work process and activities within the department. All project proposals had to be discussed in this weekly departmental meeting. Every member in the departmental meeting received the project proposal before the meeting was held. If proposals exceeded the amount of 50,000 guilders (approximately €23,000), the head of the Foreign department had a say as well. In case of an emergency, there was a special procedure that enabled the head of the Foreign department to approve a project. The head of ACT Netherlands was the person who decided whether to initiate this emergency procedure or not.

Each project proposal considered to be a relevant and serious proposal was described in a so-called intake form. This form described the location, organization, target group, budget, funding, and activities in the proposal. It was followed by space for the other members of the department to write down their comments and questions. The form ended with a brief statement on the decision taken: an approval with the approved budget, or a rejection.

Anything but the logic of consequence

From the above, we conclude that ACT Netherlands is not as tightly structured formally as MSF Holland is. On the one hand, this makes sense, because ACT Netherlands is comprised of a significantly smaller number of employees. On the other hand, it can be argued that even for such a small organization, ACT Netherlands hardly has any specialization, except for the regional division of labor. All employees have a formal say in the decision-making process, indicating there is no clear line of authority. Expert decision-making, specialization, and formal authority are not very dominant characteristics of the organizational setting. There are hardly any substantive or procedural coordination mechanisms in the organization, except for the project format, the one policy paper described earlier, and the emergency decision-making procedure. In the policy paper, we find some elements of maximizing – and therefore consequential – behavior in the criteria for ending relationships with partner organizations. We also read about 'expressions of solidarity', referring to an element of the logic of appropriateness.

If we compare the decision-making outcomes to the policy paper contents, we see that the financial targets formulated in the policy paper are not strictly adhered to. For example, the aim was to spend one and a half million guilders on Europe and the Middle East (€682,000), while ACT spent more than 17 million guilders (€7,7 million) on this region in 1999. The project activities implemented do show resemblance to the activities described in the policy paper. Most of the countries targeted in the policy paper received substantial amounts of money. This leads to a somewhat fuzzy picture about the relationship between the policy paper and the actual decision-making outcomes. The aid locations resemble the policy aims – which might be an indicator of the administrative organization - whereas the expenditures do not match the policy targets at all.

From this, we conclude that ACT Netherlands does not show much resemblance to Simon's idealtype of the administrative organization. There is a clear absence of structures, procedures, guidelines, and experts. We therefore expect that ACT Netherlands' dominant decision-making mode does not resemble the logic of consequence. The information does not tell us whether we could expect to find a logic of appropriateness decision-making mode or a garbage can decision-making mode to dominate the organization. Based on the NGO literature, we might expect the latter.

In the next chapter, we will try to establish what the dominant decision-making mode in ACT Netherlands is and to what extent this fits the hypothesis of the absence of consequential decision-making.

Notes

1   ICCO is a development aid NGO that is predominantly funded by the Dutch government through the so-called 'co-financing program'. Dienst over Grenzen is an NGO that fulfills the function of a job agency for Dutch expats who want to work for governments in developing countries.
2   This involves exchanges of well-trained and experienced experts from one developing country to another developing country for educational reasons.

Chapter 10

Working With 'The Family':
ACT's Dominant Decision-Making
Pattern

Now we have gained more understanding of MSF Holland's decision-making processes, we proceed to the decision-making dynamics of the second organization studied for this research: ACT Netherlands. In the previous chapter, we concluded that ACT Netherlands' organizational features differ from MSF Holland's organizational features. The theoretical framework that guides this study would predict that ACT Netherlands' decision-making processes will therefore also differ from MSF Holland's decision-making dynamics.

Since the organizational features of ACT Netherlands did not show much resemblance to the administrative organization, we formulated the hypothesis that the dominant decision-making mode in ACT Netherlands would not resemble the logic of consequence. The information available about the formal structure of ACT was not detailed enough to formulate specific hypotheses about the expected dominant decision-making mode within ACT. In this chapter, we will nevertheless attempt to establish the dominant decision-making mode in ACT Netherlands.

We ended the previous chapter with the conclusion that both the logic of appropriateness and garbage can decision-making could be present in ACT Netherlands. If decision-making follows the logic of appropriateness, we should find instant and retrospective reasoning, obligatory and rule-based behavior and decision-making by analogy (see also Figure 3.3 in Chapter 3). The defining characteristics of garbage can decision-making are simultaneous and individually prospective reasoning, entrepreneurial behavior and decision-making by coupling (Figure 3.4 in Chapter 3). But first, let us take a closer look at the outcomes of decision-making within ACT in the years 1996 to 2000.

ACT selection outcomes

ACT Netherlands has an interesting pattern in its decision-making outcomes regarding the project locations and activities chosen. In terms of the volume of total expenditures, we can see that the organization's aid budget fluctuated substantially from 14,3 million guilders (€6,5 million) in 1996 to 40,2 million guilders (€18,3 million) in 1999 (Table 10.1).

Table 10. 1   ACT Netherlands expenditures per continent in Euros × 1000 (1996–2000)

Continent	1996	1997	1998	1999	2000
Africa	4.839	2.867	3.242	4.411	2.720
Asia	897	1.651	2.430	3.839	2.977
Latin America	658	1.963	1.287	1.958	743
Europe and Middle East	128	681	846	8.045	4.973
Totals	**6.522**	**7.162**	**7.805**	**18.253**	**11.413**

The organization also has shifting regional priorities in terms of expenditures, as can be deduced from Table 10.1 and 10.2. For example, the organization spent 23,8 percent of the total aid budget on the African continent in 2000, while in 1996 the organization spent almost 75 percent of its budget on this continent. Europe and the Middle East form regions for which the aid expenditures fluctuated substantially in between 1996 and 1999, from 1,9 percent in 1996 to 44,1 percent in 1999. For the Asian continent there is less fluctuation in aid expenditures, while for Latin America we can establish a decline in spending since 1998.[1]

Table 10.2   ACT Netherlands expenditures per continent in percent of total expenditure per year (1996–2000)

Continent	1996	1997	1998	1999	2000
Africa	74,2%	40,0%	41,5%	24,2%	23,8%
Asia	13,8%	23,1%	31,1%	21,0%	26,1%
Latin America	10,1%	27,4%	16,5%	10,7%	6,5%
Europe and Middle East	1,9%	9,5%	10,9%	44,1%	43,6%
Totals	**100%**	**100%**	**100%**	**100%**	**100%**

However, we observe quite consistent patterns regarding the distribution patterns of the aid activities in three continents (see Table 10.3 to 10.5). Europe is the only exception to this rule. In Africa, there are 26 countries that received humanitarian aid from 1996 to 2000. Nine of these countries received aid every year (1996–2000) using 64 to 83,8 percent of the total budget for the continent.

In Central and East Asia, 22 countries received aid through these five years. Eight countries received aid during all these five years, taking 75,3 to 91,9 percent of the total budget for the continent. The fluctuation in expenditure is smaller than for the African continent, but the maximum variance is still 16 percent.

Table 10.3   ACT's African countries of continuous aid in 1996–2000 (in Euros × 1000)

Country	1996	1997	1998	1999	2000
Burundi	90.909	22.727	25.000	50.000	70.269
Eritrea	41.728	58.826	288.441	64.782	221.105
Guinea	45.909	45.455	62.273	63.636	163.636
Kenya	2.046.893	31.197	847.889	2.326.451	232.555
Liberia	434.915	1.042.076	622.030	377.326	847.305
Nigeria	19.545	40.909	40.328	34.091	21.364
Sierra Leone	263.463	27.273	224.676	475.065	161.818
Sudan	17.818	557.711	479.421	234.324	77.272
Somalia	135.107	203.445	4.507	72.727	54.454
Total 9 countries	**3.096.287**	**2.029.619**	**2.594.565**	**3.698.402**	**1.849.778**
Total Africa	**4.838.939**	**2.867.124**	**3.242.060**	**4.411.139**	**2.720.490**
% of Africa budget	**64,0%**	**70,8%**	**80,0%**	**83,8%**	**70,0%**

Table 10.4   ACT's Central and East Asian countries of continuous aid in 1996–2000 (in Euros × 1000)

Country	1996	1997	1998	1999	2000
Afghanistan	22.727	116.374	413.939	513.435	1.267.839
India	13.636	56.818	181.678	238.636	235.227
Indonesia	11.364	34.091	52.273	401.364	278.997
Iran	2.273	57.181	30.000	118.295	68.498
Kazakhstan	95.857	479.932	374.793	521.749	411.523
Kirgistan	261.449	178.047	336.314	618.918	216.573
Nepal	12.273	40.909	22.364	22.727	68.181
Thailand	272.727	428.357	454.545	454.545	190.909
Total 8 countries	**692.306**	**1.391.709**	**1.865.906**	**2.889.669**	**2.737.747**
Total Asia	**896.595**	**1.651.413**	**2.430.496**	**3.839.479**	**2.977.213**
% of Asia budget	**77,2%**	**84,3%**	**76,8%**	**75,3%**	**91,9%**

On the Latin American continent, eleven countries received aid between 1996 and 2000. Four of them received aid for all five years, receiving 91,2 to 51,1 percent of the total budget for the continent. This, again, is a substantial fluctuation in expenditures.

Table 10.5 ACT's Latin American countries of continuousing aid in 1996–2000 (in Euros × 1000)

Country	1996	1997	1998	1999	2000
Colombia	48.151	111.618	153.364	158.181	238.455
Mexico	14.545	15.227	22.727	32.395	22.682
Nicaragua	15.909	7.273	741.818	651.254	92.568
Peru	415.906	1.657.114	119.455	159.200	100.909
Total 4 countries	**494.511**	**1.791.232**	**1.037.364**	**1.001.030**	**454.614**
Total LA	**657.693**	**1.963.172**	**1.287.412**	**1.957.804**	**743.250**
% of LA budget	**75,2%**	**91,2%**	**80,6%**	**51,1%**	**61,2%**

From a study of aid activities of the organization through the years it can be concluded that the organization supports a wide variety of aid activities. The 'top five' of aid activities for 1995–1999 were (out of a total of 591 projects counted): organizational development projects; emergency aid projects; rehabilitation projects; human rights projects; and training and education projects. These five activities made up more than 70 percent of all aid activities (see Table 10.6).

Table 10.6 Nature of ACT Netherlands project activities (1995–1999)

Nature of the projects	No. of projects	% of projects
1. Organizational development	121	20,5
2. Emergency aid	99	16,8
3. Rehabilitation	84	14,2
4. Human rights	61	10,3
5. Training and education	49	8,3
Total	**414**	**70,1**

From the comparison among the continents (Table 10.7), one can see that especially in Latin America and Asia the project activities are fairly concentrated. In Latin America, mostly rehabilitation and reintegration projects and organizational development projects are supported, whereas in Asia, over half of the projects deal with emergency aid and organizational development. In Africa and Europe, the project activities are more diverse. In Africa, mostly human rights and peace projects are being supported, next to organizational development projects, and training and education projects. In Europe, most projects deal with organizational development and emergency aid.

**Table 10.7   An overview of the nature of ACT Netherlands' project activities
per continent**

	Org. dev.		Emerg. Aid		Rehab.		Human R.		Educ.	
	No.	*%*	*No.*	*%*	*No.*	*%*	*No.*	*%*	*No.*	*%*
Af 244	33	13,5	27	11,1	18	7,4	43	17,6	29	11,8
As 148	37	25,0	47	31,7	14	9,5	6	4,1	10	6,8
LA 88	23	26,3	6	6,8	40	45,5	6	6,8	2	2,3
E 111	28	25,2	19	17,1	12	10,8	6	5,4	8	7,2

In conclusion, ACT Netherlands' activities are characterized by shifting total expenditures and shifting preferences for continents throughout the years; consistency in aid locations per continent, except for Europe and the Middle East; and a wide variety in aid activities, of which organizational development, emergency aid, and rehabilitation aid were the most important. Interesting to note is that, although there is a vast group of countries that receive aid continuously, the expenditures on these countries fluctuates substantially. How have these selection outcomes come about? The next sections attempt to answer this question.

Working with the family

At the time of the study, ACT Netherlands had seven project officers who each had the responsibility for a certain region in the world. These project officers were the 'gatekeepers' of the organization. They received requests for funding and they had the decision-making authority to make a first selection of project proposals. Once a project officer decided to process a request for help, he/she would write a project proposal and submitted it as an 'intake' to a decision-making forum called the staff meeting. The other project officers then had some time to read the proposals in advance. They could write questions or comments on a separate page in the proposal. How was the first selection of requests made?

The project officers of ACT had a network of long-standing partner organizations, which I refer to as 'the family'.[2] Of the project officers interviewed, there were four project officers whose project portfolio involved mostly 'members of the family'. This network of family members influenced the first selection of requests for funding that reach the organization, as one project officer clarified:

> We work with partners ... when you make a choice to work with a partner, you are not tied to it forever...However, you only have a limited amount of time and money, so you have to make it a bit continuous. So, if I have been working with organization A ... then I won't work with organization F anymore and not because organization F is not as good as organization A, but it simply stops somewhere [int3, 1999].

The importance of past experiences: Retrospective reasoning

Decisions to approve and extend project proposals were often linked directly to the fact that the partner organization had been funded by ACT Netherlands before.[3] For example, a project in Eastern Europe was duly approved for this reason, as the project officer responsible for this region explained:

> We supported this program last year, so it was not difficult to decide, it fits our policies ... and the program had been proven to work well last year [int5 2000].

The program involved the provision of seeds and since these were needed soon, the program was approved before a formal project document had been written. This quote also demonstrates that the decision to approve or extend projects was often related to the argument that these partners had proven to be effective implementing partners in the past.[4] Although the effectiveness argument could be seen as a consequential decision-making feature, in these cases it was a form of retrospective reasoning, since the decision to approve or extend projects was related to an evaluation of *past* performance of the partner, not to a prospective evaluation of *expected* performance.

In the staff meetings, we observed retrospective reasoning as well. For example, in a meeting in which the ACT officers discussed an ACT appeal regarding a Latin American country, the project officer responsible explained that this proposal was the successor of an emergency appeal right after some heavy floods. Since that project went fairly well, despite some coordination problems, there was no reason to reject the new project proposal. The proposal was approved without discussion. Another project proposal discussed in this meeting concerned a peace initiative in an African country. The project officer argued that the organizing group had been successfully involved in such activities before and so the proposal was approved [notes staff meeting 28/9/2000].

In addition, it is interesting to note that from the twelve interview cases concerning the initiation of project activities with new partner organizations, five of these partner organizations had been accepted by ACT because other partner organizations had recommended these organizations to ACT. This is another indication that past experiences – this time of trustworthy partners – are a determining factor in ACT Netherlands' decision-making process. As one project officer explained:

> This Dutch partner organization, which is a very good partner of us, asked us to provide some additional funding. That's what we did, because I know that they know what the situation looks like, so then I simply follow their request. But then I won't read a lot of information anymore about what the situation looks like .... They have a field office there, and the person who asked it has a lot of expertise regarding the region, so then you make an estimate of this person and the project and then I thought: it looks alright [int1 2000].

Rule-based decision-making: Categorizing partner organizations

Connected to the issue of past experiences, a sense of trust is important in ACT decision-making processes. Once a partner organization was trusted, the decision-making process unfolded almost automatically: few questions about the project proposal were asked, and approval followed almost instantly. So, whenever a familiar partner organization submitted a project proposal to ACT, it was seriously considered, because, as one project officer said:

> If it concerns real projects that I want to spent time on, then it is a process, a dialogue, of which you know from the start that something will come out of it. It is not clear yet what will come out of it, but clarity will come by means of email, etc. We therefore hardly reject anything ... that is also how the system works [int1 2000].

In the staff meetings, the 'intakes' (i.e. the project proposals) were often approved without discussion. If there was any discussion at all, it focused on project proposals from unknown partner organizations. Sometimes questions were asked and these were answered by the project officers, but these questions rarely led to rejection or delay. The mere fact that a project proposal had made it to the intake meeting indicated that the applicant was trustworthy, and approval followed almost automatically. Rejecting an 'intake' was therefore a very unusual thing to do. For example, in one project proposal a refugee organization asked 25.000 guilders (approximately €11.500) for organizational support. This proposal did not have any financial or project information from the partner organization attached to it, although there was a one page intake form written by the project officer. The organization was referred to as 'our organization for refugees in the region' and the only comment made by one of the project officers was: 'It would be nice if we received a project program proposal. Are we're gonna get that?' [project file]. The proposal was approved without further discussion. In another intake meeting, someone said; 'Just look at the comments in the proposal, and if they are not there, the proposal is approved' [observation notes].

A study of meeting notes of 1999 and part of 2000 showed that only three project proposals were rejected in the staff meeting in more than a year's time. Sometimes the decision-making process was postponed because project officers asked for additional information. In 1999, the staff meeting approved a total of 162 project proposals and postponed the decision concerning 15 proposal approvals because of lack of information. There was only one proposal that was ignored and not responded to because 'nobody trusted this partner organization to implement the activities in a fair way' as the minutes said [minutes 23/11/1999]. From January to April 2000, 35 proposals were approved, two were postponed, and two other projects never returned to the staff meeting as an intake and can therefore be regarded as a rejection.

There seemed to be two categories of applicants. First, there was a category of known, and therefore trusted organizations and second, there was a category of unknown organizations.[5] This categorization of applicants is an example of rule-based decision-making, since these categories determined the decision-making process and outcomes to a large extent. As one respondent made clear:

> We receive hundreds of requests which you cannot take seriously and then we write a standard letter with a rejection for reasons of budget and mandate .... Hence, there are different categories of project proposals .... Then you have the ACT appeals that we should support officially ... but we don't do that, because we cannot follow upon all these requests .... The third category consists of familiar partners that we will take seriously ... They contact you and tell you: 'we want to do this or that', in five brief lines and then you

say yes or no. If you say yes, then they will come with more. And then you have to come up with very good arguments if you want to reject it, otherwise you'll have them do the work for nothing [int1 2000].

Once an applicant fits the first category according to a project officer, the decision-making process unfolds quite instantly and automatically:

We just have a planning of the partners we know, the partners we trust and the things we want to do, and that is a restriction we impose on ourselves and then you seldom reject a proposal ... [int4 1999].

As soon as the applicant fits the category of 'unknown organizations', an almost automatic rejection of the project proposal followed, because the partner did not have the same 'blood type' [int5, 2000]. Or as the same respondent said:

... we do not just work with unknown groups, we cannot afford to do that, even though we have a lot of money .... What we sometimes do when we receive a request and you know somebody who is working in that area who says: we know these guys and they are OK, then we sometimes go and take a look if we can do something with them. But most of the time we have to limit our work instead of expand it [int4 1999].

From a study of rejection letters sent to organizations that requested support from ACT in 1998 (see the top five countries receiving rejections in Table 10.8), we can see how this categorization of applicant organizations defined the decision-making process.

Those project proposals submitted by unknown organizations from countries where ACT already has a partner network – such as South Africa, DR Congo, Nigeria and Sierra Leone – were rejected because ACT already had a network there, even though some of the project activities proposed fit the ACT mandate (such as organizational development, refugee assistance, human rights, and training and education).

Other activities, such as building churches, schools etc., and the request for individual grants, were clearly outside the ACT mandate and therefore rejected. Project proposals coming from countries where ACT did not have a presence, such as Cameroon, were rejected as well because the existing network took up all ACT's time and energy, leaving hardly any room for newcomers to the network.

Instant decision-making and obligatory action

The staff meeting was not a forum in which project proposals were discussed extensively and where decisions were really taken. The interviews showed that the approval and rejection of project proposals was decided upon by the individual project officer. These project officers almost seemed to know immediately whether a project proposal was of interest to the organization or not. This is because the organization's mandate provided rules of action, rules about appropriate participants, and rules of appropriate behavior that guided the project officers in their actions. As one project officer said:

Many things are not taken into consideration. They are thrown away within three minutes after you have seen them, because you know that it won't suit [int1 1999].

Table 10.8   The top five of countries receiving most rejection letters (1998)

Country	Nature of the projects proposed	Reasons for rejecting
South Africa (15 rej)	• refugee assistance • org development • buying material • building church, hospital etc • (mental) health care • human rights • income generation • children • disabled • individual grants • education	• limited mandate • already a network present • no possibilities to extend • ACT only works with organized groups
DR Congo (14 rej)	• org development • building church, hospital etc • education/seminars/training • refugees • social work • medical care • children	• no mandate to do this • already a network present • no possibilities to extend • no focus on that specific area
Nigeria (11 rej)	• human rights • refugees • org. development • food • clothes • education	• tight/limited budget • other financial obligations • already a network present • no possibilities to extend • limited mandate
Sierra Leone (10 rej)	• reconciliation • displaced women • human rights • poverty alleviation • agriculture • education • shipment of goods • human rights	• budget too high • already network present • no possibilities to extend • no budget
Cameroon (10 rej)	• rehabilitation • water project • reconciliation • refugees • building orphanage • children • church support • education	• lack of personnel • no/limited mandate • ACT does not work in this country • lack of financial means to expand

An important element of the mandate is that it told the project officers what kind of projects were the organization's business of interest. The organization's focus was on organizational development. The project officers were convinced that the right way to provide aid was by supporting and strengthening the local structures in a development country. The organization aimed to help these local organizations to enhance their organizational capacity to deal with disaster, hunger, or conflicts. From this a certain code of conduct towards the partner organizations followed, as one project officer described:

> I think it is important to give people the opportunity to organize themselves. And we want to support such a process by sharing the risks associated with the process, we let them make their mistakes and won't walk away immediately; if mistakes are made, we will offer training when needed [int1 1999].

The project officers' actions therefore not so much focused on project activities; instead, one focused on the organizations that implement these activities. The mandate also contained principles of behavior towards the partner organization. The above quote indicates that the organizational development approach required project officers to give partner organizations time to develop themselves and to learn from past mistakes.

The commitment towards the partner organizations was therefore strong within ACT. Project officers would never decide to suddenly stop working with an old family member nor would they easily reject proposals of a known and trusted partner either, even when there were (potential) effectiveness and efficiency problems.

The relationship with a partner cost time, energy, and money. It was part of ACT's vision to make a sincere effort to empower these organizations. The next case illustrates this point. Somewhere in Africa, ACT worked with a local protestant partner organization for several years. At a certain point in time this organization was in serious problems, since the financial and project reports did not meet the required standards. Then the audit report of 1997 never reached the project officer. First, the officer and the other donor organizations held back the money for the 1998 program and the partner was told to organize financial assistance. As soon as this was promised, the ACT officer decided to continue the funding, because:

> otherwise the whole thing would collapse and we can't let that happen, so we let them know that we are watching them closely ... and now I am working on the 1999 project proposal, because their own proposals are sometimes quite vague ... but I will simply let it be approved under the condition that the missing financial reports will be sent to us as soon as possible [int4, 1999].

When this project officer was asked why he kept on working with this organization, the answer was: 'This is kind of a natural partner for us ... and if that works a bit, you will try to keep on working with them' [int4, 1999].

Feelings of commitment especially played up when the project officers talked about the ending of partner organization relationships. This was a painful and slow process which the project officers preferred to avoid, as was the case in the following example: ACT had an Asian family member which had been ACT's partner for many years. At a certain point in time, there had been severe floods in this Asian country. ACT's partner organization submitted a project proposal for approximately €50.000 in order to provide emergency aid to the people in need. However, some project officers found the partner's reputation problematic. Everybody who knew the organization seemed convinced this organization was corrupt. However, corruption had never been proven and so the project officer responsible for this partner argued that as long as there was no proof of corruption, ACT could not legitimately end the partner relationship. The project officer argued:

> This organization is a stable partner in the ACT network, they have been receiving millions of emergency aid for years already ... I said: it could be a bad proposal, but if you have been working with a partner for such a long time, you cannot say 'we don't like you anymore, so we'll stop ...' ... This gave a lot of internal discussion .... This is quite sensitive, we were one of the first to help them, we are very old partners. It is a clear sign to the rest of the network if we withdraw our support ... [int1, 2000].

On the one hand, all other project officers doubted in the staff meeting whether it was a wise thing to fund this organization. The project officer responsible, on the other hand, argued that this organization had worked in this area before and therefore knew the people. The project officer won this argument and the proposal was approved [notes staff meeting 9/10/2000]. The project officer suggested organizing a value-for-money audit to see whether corruption could be proven.

A couple of months earlier, the head of the department had approved another proposal of this organization through an emergency procedure. When the proposal was discussed in a staff meeting after the emergency procedure, one project officer protested against this decision. She commented on the proposal: 'After all these problems with [this partner organization] I do not understand this decision.' Another project officer asked for more information and motivation concerning this decision. Still, the project went ahead. Here we see how an organization whose reputation is dubious received the trust and commitment of a project officer until it would be proven that the organization is indeed corrupt. The guiding rule was here 'innocent, unless proven guilty'.

From the above examples, it has become clear how the mandate defined commitment to be important in the relationship between project officers and partner organizations. This led to obligatory action, since there were clear rules within ACT as to what is proper behavior and what is not, resulting in reasoning mechanisms such as in the following case. This concerned a discussion whether to end the relationship with an old family member or not. This old family member had been running a training and education program for years with the help of ACT. Nevertheless, some project officers argued that this program did not fit ACT's mandate anymore, since it had become a long term development project. The project officer responsible pleaded for prolonging the relationship because:

[This organization] has survived a difficult year .... The team handled the situation quite well and is very motivated to work. It will be very stimulating for the whole team if we do not further complicate things for them by refusing to contribute to their budget [intake form, 10 February 1999].

In other words, the ending of relationships with old family members is only acceptable within ACT Netherlands as a last resort in a long process of investing in the partner organization. In addition, the rejection of a project proposal of an unknown partner is much more acceptable than the rejection of a project proposal from a known partner. One would not easily start working with a new partner organization; instead one rather would extend projects from known partner organizations.

An example of appropriate decision-making

Let us take a closer look at one particular example of appropriate and obligatory decision-making to see how defining commitment is in the relationship between ACT and its partners. One project officer mentioned an example of the termination of a partner relationship. ACT had supported this organization for four years, however, without the expected success. The organization suffered from internal problems and the quality of the work was low. The project officer exerted a lot of effort to help the partner organization improve itself. First, the project officer asked for an external evaluation of the organization, which was quite negative in tone. Then, the project officer made a plan with this organization to improve the quality of the work. He invited a consultant to investigate possibilities of improvement. The consultant was not very enthusiastic about the organization's capacity:

The core problem, being the troublesome relationship between staff and director, has to be solved as soon as possible, as it takes too much energy from all the parties involved. This hinders the organizational change process ... [The organization] even faces the risk of loosing credibility if this is not solved. This is, however, more easily said than done [support mission report, November 1999].

Finally, it was suggested that an interim manager be installed, a very expensive solution. However, the project officer could not find a suitable person for this job and then finally decided to end the project after consulting the other donors of the organization. The project officer explained:

It was an impossible situation ... We realized that it would take us another three years to invest time and money to change that situation, and then we came to the conclusion that it wasn't worth that any longer .... It was a long-lasting process, because we put in external expertise but also because we thought it was quite embarrassing: it is 'not done' in our circles to do such a thing .... We had already told them that we would continue our support. But ultimately there was no chance that it would bring us anywhere, and that became very clear. Then there is no other possibility [int4 2000].

The project officer referred to the fact that he started to doubt the partner organization's capacity quite soon after the first project was approved but that he continued to work with the organization because he 'did not want to 'kill' a local support organization... and that is what you do if the main donors announce they are terminating their funding' [int4, 2000]. He tried to help the organization for another two years, before the decision was taken to stop working with this partner. In a letter, ACT and its donor partners expressed their regret for the painful situation:

> In the course of the meeting it has become evident that we have lost confidence in the capacities of [your organization] to solve its internal difficulties and genuinely improve its weaknesses .... We realize that this decision deviates from earlier moral commitments .... We are most willing to look for decent ways to finalize our cooperation ... On behalf of the Dutch donors I express our sincere regrets for how things have turned out. It is far from what we had expected, when we started our partnership. I think these feelings of disappointment and regret are mutual [email 27/7/2000].

A report of the messenger of this bad news said: 'The meeting in which this decision was taken was difficult, because [the donors] did not want to drop these people just like that' [report, July 2000, p.8]. This messenger, a consultant whose visit was planned anyway, stayed for a couple of days after the message had been conveyed. She helped the employees to think over the consequences of this decision and to explore opportunities for the future. The donors paid this consultant and also promised to find a way to compensate for the damage caused by the termination of the donor relationship, which in the end was the payment of a couple of months of salary.

The commitment towards this organization was extraordinary. It took two years of trying before the donors decided to end the relationship. They were willing to pay an expensive consultant to convey the message in person and to provide 'aftercare' for a couple of days. Even after the relationship was terminated ACT still felt a commitment to take care of this local NGO by finding 'decent' ways to compensate for the damage done.

The older the ties, the more one relies ...

From the above, we conclude that ACT decision-making processes concerning old and well-known family members at the time of the study had characteristics of appropriate decision-making.[6] The decision-making process was characterized by retrospective reasoning, categorization, and obligatory behavior. Instant decision-making and reasoning by analogy, however, were less present in the interviews.[7]

In one interview, all these dimensions of appropriate decision-making came together, illustrating how the logic of appropriateness worked within ACT Netherlands. One project officer talked about a partner organization on the Asian continent which was not connected to the ACT network. After violent conflict broke out in the area, this partner organization, which ACT had been financing for the last four years, asked for additional funding. The project officer concerned described the decision-making process regarding this request as follows:

> They have organized a good emergency aid program before .... This is a partner with technical quality ... and as a rule we work with them ... we have spent about a million guilders on their projects...We have a good relationship with them, discussions go well ... the only thing is that their reporting is extremely detailed with lots of information ... but then they forget to mention things we want to know ... they regularly forget to compare their activities with their original plan ... But there is no doubt that these are very motivated, good people, although its management could be improved .... They are an old partner ...you don't wonder anymore whether this is a trustworthy partner [int1 2000].

Hence, when a new project proposal arrived:

> I had little time so I read the proposal only once ... I also had to estimate the risk ... sometimes I have little time to read things ... I saw there was little risk involved ... I put the proposal in the format and asked them some questions, but these were marginal, because they are a good partner ... the proposal came in, it contained a good analysis, and they are real experts ... so that was not problematic [int1 2000].

This project officer did not need a lot of detailed information before he decided. He seemed to have based his decision on the fact that he knew the organization and had good experiences with it, indicating retrospective reasoning. Although there were some problems with the reporting capacity and the management of the partner organization, the project officer decided to extend the project of this partner without carefully reading their project proposal, indicating instant decision-making on the basis of trust and commitment. His supervisor agreed with this approach; he stated that proposals for the following projects did not have to be very detailed; a one page proposal would be sufficient for ACT in order to commit to funding in the future [fieldwork notes].

At the same time, however, ACT decision-making processes concerning the family also showed aspects of consequential decision-making. In three of the six initiation cases, for example, a form of prospective reasoning regarding the expected effectiveness of the proposed projects could be established. In five of the eight ending cases the main reason to stop working with a partner was a failure to produce the required results. The two interview cases in which proposals were rejected were also considered to be ineffective interventions. This indicates that consequential decision-making was also characteristic for ACT's decision-making processes. As one project officer pointed out:

> Of course there are also proposals of familiar partner organizations that you don't approve because you think they are too ambitious, or because you know they are not able to handle such a project since they do not have the capacity [int3, 1999].

Nevertheless, one should keep in mind that the effectiveness argument was not only used prospectively. It was also a retrospective evaluation of past performance.

In addition, in some cases the logic of consequence was used more as a means to legitimize certain decisions afterwards than as a 'sincere' reasoning mode to come to a decision. One respondent, for example, stated:

> I always reject proposals for long term projects .... If it is really an emergency project then you have to dig a little deeper but then you have the excuse that your mandate does not allow you to do that ... before you make the effort to go into detail and to find out if they have the right partners and how they work and function, that simply takes too much time [int5, 1999].

The research material implies that the longer the relationship with ACT Netherlands was the more appropriate the decision-making process became. For example, of the two rejection cases, one case involved a relatively new partner organization that had been funded only once before and the other one was an appeal from the ACT network, for an intervention that ACT did not have any familiar partners participating in. No rejection examples were mentioned that concerned old members of the family. In the ending cases, the appropriateness became more visible when the ending concerned the termination of a long-lasting relationship with an old member of the family.[8]

In conclusion, ACT decision-making processes concerning the family can be characterized as both appropriate and consequential. The longer ACT knows its partners, the more appropriate the decision-making process becomes, and the younger the relationship, the more consequential reasoning modes are applied.[9] The appropriate decision-making style makes ACT's decision-making outcomes more understandable. It helps explain the relatively large number of countries that received continuous aid. This was a result of obligatory behavior, based on a shared value and rule system which emphasized that ending relationships with old partners is not the correct way to go. It is only a last resort, after a long process of investing in the partner. We also saw that it is very hard for new partners to enter ACT's family, since decision-making is based on the categorization of partners into 'known' and 'not known' partners. Once you are in the family, you will stay in the family, but when you are out, it is very hard to get back in.

Traces of Selznick's institution

Based on the above, we conclude that the logic of appropriateness was the preferred decision-making mode within ACT Netherlands. Although the theoretical framework predicted that we should find anything but consequential decision-making processes within ACT, this chapter shows that consequential decision-making elements could be found anyway. Nevertheless, ACT Netherlands organizational structure did not resemble any of the characteristics of the administrative organization. We did not find evidence that policies and procedures influenced the decision-making outcomes to a large extent, nor that decision-making was related to information gathering, consulting experts, or specialization.

Besides, we found hardly any evidence of the presence of features of 'the ambiguous organization'. There was little conflict over project proposals. We could not establish the presence of group interests resulting in heated debates. If there was discussion, it concerned the ending of long-lasting relationships in which arguments referring to long-term commitments often won over effectiveness and efficiency arguments. Persuasion and compromising were not the defining decision-making mechanisms. Hence, once again, the hypothesis in NGO research that NGOs are predominantly loosely structured is refuted.

It therefore seems fair to conclude that ACT Netherlands mostly resembles Selznick's idea of the institution. We saw that a shared value system guided the behavior of the project officers to a large extent. In addition, the decision-making forum of the staff meeting exemplified more symbolic than substantial decision-making processes. Hardly any formal coordination mechanisms were present. The only policy paper that existed, was more a reflection of the daily work practices, than a document formulated with an eye to the future. In a sense, it could be argued that ACT even resembles the 'overinstitutionalized' organization, meaning that the organization seemed quite autonomous and did not need to take into account the concerns of its environment.

The fact that ACT resembles the features of Selznick's institution most, compared to the two other organizational forms described, fits the conclusion that ACT's preferred mode of decision-making is the logic of appropriateness. This does not answer, however, the question why we found consequential elements in ACT's decision-making processes. In Chapter 11, when we will look into the secondary patterns in ACT decision-making, we will see how and why not only consequential but also garbage can decision-making elements sometimes came into play.

Notes

1   One reason for this lack of consistency has to do with the fact that ACT also receives money for its projects through national fund raising campaigns. The organization receives 13,5 percent of the total funds raised. Because these campaigns depend on the occurrence of humanitarian crises, the total income of the organization can vary per year, depending on the organization and results of a national fund raising campaign. For example, ACT received funds from national campaigns for emergency aid regarding Hurricane Mitch, the Kosovo crisis, and the earthquake in Turkey. MSF Holland also participates in these campaigns, but sometimes decides not to claim the percentage reserved for them if they are not involved in the activities for which the funds are raised (for example, large food distributions).

2   A total of 21 interview cases dealt with decision-making processes about project proposals submitted by – what I considered to be – members of the family.

3   In 12 out of 21 interview cases, we noted this form of retrospective reasoning.

4   This was the case in 3 out of 6 cases.

5   In the interview cases, this type of categorization was present 8 times.

6   The results of the analysis are presented in the Table 10.9 and Table 10.10.

7 An explanation for the limited presence of instant reasoning in the interviews might be found in the method applied in this study. If people make instant decisions, this is very hard to analyze from interview data. Instant reasoning can therefore only be established indirectly, for example, because clear categorizations seem to lead to a swift selection process of applicant organizations. The absence of analogous reasoning can be explained because it was always connected to retrospective reasoning in this case. The ACT project officers did not use analogies other than the past performance of the partner organizations.

8 This was noted in 3 out of 8 cases.

9 The results of the analysis are presented in the following:

Table 10. 9   LoA dimensions in interview cases concerning 'the family'

The number of cases in which	start (5)	reject (2)	end (8)	extend (6)	Total
Retrospective reasoning was apparent	5	0	3	4	12
situations were categorized	4	1	3	1	8
feelings of commitment were present	1	0	5	2	7
Instant reasoning was present	1	0	0	1	2
reasoning by analogy was apparent	0	0	0	0	0
Total number of cases = 21					

Table 10.10   LoC dimensions in interview cases concerning 'the family'

The number of cases in which	N
There were attempts to maximize the organizational goals: effectiveness and efficiency criteria were mentioned (either retrospective or prospective)	17
The importance of information collection other than assessments was stressed	5
The involvement of experts was mentioned	2
A clear need for intervention was mentioned/there was no reason to intervene (anymore)	2
The proposed activities were related to the organizational policies	2
Assessments were mentioned as an information gathering instrument	2
Prospective reasoning was apparent	2
The decision-making process was described in terms of sequentiality	0
Alternatives for action were formulated	0
Total number of cases= 21	

Chapter 11

Working Outside 'The Family': ACT's Secondary Decision-making Patterns

The logic of appropriateness reflected the dominant decision-making mode for ACT Netherlands when it concerned 'old family members', as was established in the previous chapter. However, not all decision-making processes within ACT Netherlands were related to old family members and were therefore appropriate in character. The data collected for this study also pointed to secondary patterns in ACT's decision-making processes, just as it did in the case of MSF Holland. This chapter describes these secondary patterns in more detail. These are divided into two categories: working with strangers and working without alternatives for action.

Working with strangers

Although ACT project officers preferred to work through 'the family', the organization sometimes considered proposals of new potential partner organizations. This happened when the project officers believed that ACT's presence in a specific area was needed and no (trustworthy) partner organization was available. This was the case, for example, in Central Asia. In the only policy paper of the organization, Central Asia was foreseen to be an area of future conflict. It was therefore deemed necessary to develop a reliable network of partner organizations before humanitarian intervention would become necessary.

For all these cases, project officers could not apply the appropriate decision-making mode, since these organizations had no reputation ACT could rely on.[1] How did the ACT project officers decide when unknown organizations submitted proposals? As the following project officer said:

> Sometimes you can take the risk, if I have spoken with a person for only one day, but I have the impression he is an OK person, then I can approve a project of $5,000 ....and then you see how things proceed. Then you visit them, you read their reports, and you ask around. But you cannot rely on a nice proposal and a good conversation. The ACT network plays an important role in this; it is a form of organized balloting: you are in until you make a mistake and then you're out [int1, 2000].

In addition, there were emergencies where potential partner organizations were lacking altogether. For these cases, ACT took its mandate – which aims to support organizational development – a step further by establishing so-called liaison offices, which pro-actively looked around for potential new partners. These liaison offices became the gatekeepers on the spot for the project officers and searched for potential small initiatives that could become trustworthy 'family members'.

Information driven decision-making and maximizing behavior

When project officers received a project proposal of an unknown organization, they tried to find out as much as they could about the organization's reputation and performance, in order to establish whether the organization had the capacity to implement the project effectively.[2]

In addition, it was important to find out whether the intervention was really necessary.[3] A clear example of this was described by a project officer who received a project proposal of an unknown organization that worked in an African country:

> At a certain point in time I received this proposal of this organization, and I thought that it looked nice. It focused on a very isolated area, where the donors do not like to go ... It is a political hot potato and therefore a very good reason to support such an organization [int3, 1999].

The project officer was convinced there was a clear need to intervene. However, she did not know whether this organization would be able to implement the proposed project. She therefore applied another consequential decision-making instrument:

> However, you have to check whether it is a good organization, and if you can trust them ... so that it what I checked, I had a lot of references I felt I could trust, I asked Amnesty International, for example [int3, 1999].

Since reliable information about the implementation capacity of unfamiliar organizations was not always available, assessment missions were important information-gathering instruments through which ACT project officers determined whether to approve a proposal or not.[4] One project officer, for example, described how she received a request for help from an ethnic group of refugees in an African country. She could not decide what to do because 'there was simply too little information, so we had a team standby to go there ... to see what the situation was and what aid was needed most' [int5,1999]. After the project started, the project officer read the quarterly reports very carefully to make sure everything was working out as expected.

Besides information gathering activities, experts were also involved in the decision-making process.[5] If the project officers or experts found a project proposal of a new organization to be of low quality or not in line with the organization's mandate, a rejection followed.[6] For example, one project officer – who had recently started working for ACT Netherlands – presented a micro credit scheme project to the staff meeting. The staff meeting was not in favor of this project proposal because the work method proposed was problematic. Some days later, the project officer heard that this organization had the reputation of being a 'mini-dictatorship'. There was no room for discussion and democratic decision-making. The project officer therefore decided to ask the micro credit specialists within the missionary and deacon department for advice. They thought the proposal was not good enough, since a clear marketing plan was missing. These experts also thought this organization was somewhat suspicious. They recommended an alternative – less ambitious – plan of action, which the potential new partner organization rejected. Hence, the project officer decided to reject the proposal as a whole [int3, 2000]. Here we see how experts were used to determine the need to intervene and the capacity of the implementing organization. In addition, we see how an evaluation of the expected (in)effectiveness of an intervention determined the decision to intervene.

Trial and error financing

If the data collection confirmed that the applicant organization had the implementation capacity and there was a need to intervene, the project officers started to fund this organization with a small amount of money. As one project officer said:

> What to do with new areas and activities? Ask more questions ... if it looks serious, then you can start with a small amount of money and see how they handle that .... If everything goes well, you give more [int2, 2000].

The same modus operandi could be found in the liaison offices. These liaison offices operated in countries where ACT had decided to work, but where trustworthy partner organizations were not available. At the time of the study, ACT had liaison offices in Europe, Central Asia, and Africa. These liaison offices had been established with the idea of establishing a local non-governmental organization that, in the end, should be able to stand on its own feet. The establishment of such an office takes a long time and a lot of work.

One project officer had been deeply involved in the establishment of such an office. He explained how he had gone about doing this. ACT wanted to work in an African country that suffered from a severe civil war. Although the urge to provide aid to this country was clear, it was difficult to find trustworthy organizations that could implement projects. The project officer visited the country and met a minister who was in charge of a group of community workers. This minister pointed out to the project officer that all attention of the western world was focused on the population in the camps, whereas the groups living around the camps were completely neglected. This had created a glaring contrast in the standards of living within the camp – where all needs were taken care of – and outside the camp, where people were struggling to survive. The project officer took a look for himself and concluded this minister was right. The minister seemed to be an intelligent man, capable of leading a group of people. From this visit, the idea evolved to make this man the director of a small liaison office that would select project proposals submitted by local organizations. Before this plan was realized, several formulation missions were organized to explore the situation and to develop a work plan. The members of the formulation missions recommended that the office should not be given any operational authority. The office should focus on the selection of project proposals and the support of the local organizations in terms of training and reporting. The liaison office was established half a year later and the first selection round of project proposals could be initiated [int4, 1999]. From this, we see how consequential decision-making dynamics unfolded in the establishment of this office, by means of information-gathering instruments, and the use of experts to weigh the need to intervene as well as the capacity of this minister.

All liaison offices had the same selection function. They had taken over part of the gatekeeper function of the ACT project officer. Once such a liaison office was up and running it fulfilled the function of a trial and error process manager: small local organizations were given the chance to implement small projects and if they did well, this increased their chances of becoming a permanent member of the family. As one project officer said:

> We have a small project fund there ... and one of the most important goals of the office is to test groups and NGOs ....They get in touch with a group and receive a proposal. For the groups that get some money, the liaison office looks how the people deal with the money and if they have a good relationship with their target population and if they work transparently, if the financial side is OK [int1, 1999].

The liaison offices checked the trustworthiness of the organizations through trial and error financing. If an organization submitted a proposal that looked promising – and for which the office expected a positive result – the applicant would receive a small fund. The performance of the organization then would become an evaluation criterion for future funding. As one project officer said:

> They interview the applicants and then decide if they will fund a small activity from the small project fund, which is a test fund ....The liaison office decides on that. It is not a lot of paper work, but you have to make a lot of visits and talk to the people .... Then they keep an eye on the project and the organization implementing it .... It is the perfect way to see how people act if they finally get some resources .... If it looks promising...the liaison office comes to us and then we try to get a donor involved in it [int4, 2000].

For ACT, this was the only way to go about when there were no other possibilities to check upon the trustworthiness of potential partner organizations.

An example of secondary decision-making patterns

In order to see how ACT Netherlands worked if potential partners were lacking, the following case is interesting to study in more detail. This concerned a country in which ACT Netherlands did not have partner organizations when an earthquake hit the country in 1999. ACT was interested in working in this country, because this country lacked a powerful civil society. The earthquake of 1999 provided a 'window of opportunity' to get access to the country, since the national and local government were not able to handle the emergency situation on their own. First, ACT decided to donate money to a general ACT appeal that had been launched by the local churches via the World Council of Churches. However, the local churches did not have the capacity to implement an extensive emergency aid program on their own. Hence, ACT decided to send out an assessment mission – a typical consequential work method - together with some organizations from within and outside the ACT network. The aim of the mission was to identify potential new partner organizations that would be capable of effective humanitarian aid provision.

The earthquake had proven that the potential for civil initiative was available in the country. Many spontaneous and voluntary initiatives had been undertaken and ACT was convinced that these should be encouraged and supported by ACT. The assessment mission concluded this was possible:

> The post-earthquake situation presents NGOs with an extremely important opportunity to influence the rehabilitation and reconstruction process and to act as facilitators and catalysts of community organization in the affected areas .... Moreover, the post-earthquake context presents ample opportunities to introduce bottom-up and participatory methodologies and to build local capacities in the affected areas [p. 5, report of assessment mission, October 1999].

The missions identified various pros and cons in case ACT decided to work in this country. The political situation could become especially problematic, since the government was not in favor of outside support for local initiatives. With those pros and cons in mind, the assessment mission identified various activities that ACT Netherlands could support. In addition, the team searched for local organizations that had the capacity to implement them. The team assessed the following needs: reconstruction of damaged infrastructure, temporary shelter, assistance to rural communities, psychological trauma, earthquake disaster preparedness, and support for people willing to organize themselves [Mission report, October 1999: 8–10].

The mission members also formulated a framework for assessing potential partner organizations. Three types of organizations were selected and studied. The most important group of organizations was the so-called 'first-level organizations', which were 'those potential partners judged by the mission as those having good projects, and, in the light of their organizational mission/vision and approach, are also suitable as longer term partners' [p. 12].

Second level organizations were organizations that either had good projects or a potential to become a longer term partner and third level organizations were contacts that needed follow-up in the future. Of all the organizations visited an overview of organizational strengths and weaknesses was made. Their proposals were classified in class A projects (ready for implementation), class B proposals (good projects, but some revision required) and class C projects (project proposals that were only discussed verbally). From the list of first level organizations, three organizations were invited to send in a proposal. From the second level organizations, proposals of another five organizations were approved. The project officer – who was hired later to manage the growing project portfolio for this specific country – said about that process:

> The mission members had spoken to organizations, whether they had a project ready or not. There were projects available and those were used to get started with. You cannot afford to wait for months, so you take some risk and start to work with the first organization that seems alright [int3, 2000].

Within a year, the project officer initiated fifteen projects in the country, ranging from prefabricated housing to capacity building (see Table 11.1). One project had been under consideration for quite some time, but was rejected in the end. Of the fifteen approved projects, one project was the ACT appeal, four proposals concerned organizations that had not been identified in the mission report, and the remaining ten proposals were derived from the mission report.

Table 11.1   Overview of projects in 1999–2000

Description of the project	Mentioned in report?	Budget (NLG)	Date of approval
ACT appeal	regular partner network	320.000	9/9/ 1999
Fire safety	via Dutch organization	350.000	Oct 1999
Shelter and emergency aid	yes	1.500.000	Nov 1999
Prefab housing	yes	942.000	15/11/1999
Institution building/ capacity development	yes	1.358.469	1/12/1999
Child friendly space in tent cities	yes	98.250 23.293	4/1/2000 22/2/2000
Institution building/ capacity development	Yes	155.000	9/2/2000
Primary school	no	200.000	28/22000
Photography album project	yes	51.230	3/7/July 2000
Income generation	yes	500.000	10/7/2000
Women project	yes	335.924	4/9/2000
Psycho social support	no	200.000	7/9/2000
Institution building and capacity development	yes	323.642	28/9/2000
Institutional training social service specialists	no	515.768	Oct 2000
Bridge construction	yes	90.000	2/10/2000

EEC[7] was one of these organizations that was selected by the assessment mission. This organization was established to support small local emergency aid initiatives after the earthquake. The first project funded by ACT was an institution building and capacity development project, in which EEC aimed to help local emergency committees that had been established spontaneously right after the earthquake to organize themselves. The motivation to support this organization was, among others:

> This proposal is ambitious but promising .... EEC seems to be trustworthy and has a network on different levels in society .... EEC is well connected to local authorities ... and has experience in managing donor funds .... EEC can be considered to be a serious partner who could give assistance to [these local committees] and other organizations [project proposal, December 1999].

The project was approved although a detailed budget still had to be provided by EEC. Nevertheless, the project went well and hence other projects followed, such as an income generation project, a bridge construction project, and another institution building project, because, as was argued by the project officer:

> EEC is our best partner in the country. In the past, they have proven to be a trustworthy and efficient organization, in terms of reporting, work method, etc [project proposal, 7 July 2000].

The approval of the other projects was based on an evaluation of the applicant organization capacities and the expected effectiveness of the intervention, derived from the quality of the project proposal. Another reason to approve projects was a clear need for specific interventions. In a project proposal for child facilities in tent cities, for example, the motivation for approval was that 'there is an enormous need for psycho-social care among the youth and their parents, especially among the very young children' [project proposal, 9 February 2000]. Along the same line of reasoning, a shelter and emergency aid project was approved

> because of the cold weather (it is minus ten degree Celsius) and the rain in this area. It is very hard for the victims of the recent earthquake to survive the winter. That is why [this organization] made an urgent appeal on us to give them the financial means to provide shelter for these people. This involves thousands of people that have to live outside in the winter. ...We should respond to their appeal, also because [this organization] is a trustworthy organization; it has proven to be an organization that is able to achieve something. We also need [this organization] for other projects with regard to the reconstruction of the affected area [project proposal, November 1999].

If there were any doubts about the capacity of the organization, the approved budget was transferred in small amounts of money. This provided ACT the opportunity to see how the organization would handle the first small amount of money, before the rest of the budget was transferred. This happened, for instance, with a local organization that had requested money for a project to train and educate emergency aid volunteers. Project proposals that were problematic or expected to be ineffective, such as the micro credit proposal discussed earlier in this chapter, were rejected.

From the above, it becomes clear that both consequential and garbage can decision-making elements helped ACT Netherlands to find new partner organizations in this country. The exploratory mission was used as an information-gathering instrument. The team members tried to establish what projects and organizations would be most effective when taking ACT's organizational mission and goals into account, indicating prospective reasoning and maximizing behavior. With help of this consequential work method, ACT selected those organizations that seemed to have the most potential of being effective, trustworthy and efficient. Reasons to approve project proposals were related to the need to intervene and the capacity of the implementing partner. ACT rejected proposals if the project officers found the proposal or the partner problematic and ineffective. The consequential work method helped ACT to select new partners. Once these had proven to work effectively and efficiently, appropriate decision-making dynamics came into play again, as for example happened in the case of EEC.

This case also contained elements of garbage can decision-making, especially right after the earthquake had happened. ACT had been waiting for a 'window of opportunity' to enter this country for years; the earthquake provided this window, so that ACT could introduce its work method as a solution to the problems at hand. In addition, the project officer said that they started working with the first organizations that matched ACT's mandate. In other words, as soon as a problem was found which fitted ACT's solution, ACT proceeded to give this organization small amounts of money to test the organizations' capabilities. Although the exploratory mission report indicates that the mission formulated various alternatives for action, the project officer's statements refer to the logic of 'solutions looking for a problem', i.e. garbage can decision-making dynamics. However, consequential decision-making criteria limited the room to maneuver in terms of effectiveness and efficiency, just as was the case with MSF Holland. Hence, this example shows us how consequential and garbage can decision-making dynamics coincided.

Selecting new family members

The analysis of the interview cases concerning unknown partner organizations leads to the conclusion that the logic of consequence dominates the decision-making processes to a large extent.[8] Expected effectiveness of projects and implementing organizations was an important factor in the decision-making process, indicating attempts to maximize the organizational goals. Information gathering instruments were often used to decide upon the capacity of applicant organizations and whether there was a need to intervene. Experts were also involved in the process.

Although the logic of consequence was dominant in these interview cases, there were also a few traces of appropriate and garbage can decision-making. As said before, of the twelve interview cases, there were five initiation cases for which the decision to approve the proposal was made with help of retrospective reasoning, i.e. the past experiences of other partner organizations. In another case, concerning the establishment of a liaison office somewhere in Eastern Europe, the project officer tried to work according to the rules by first trying the regular ACT network. Only when the local partner organizations were not able to manage the tremendous demand for aid themselves, the officer joined an initiative of five other western ACT members, which resulted in the liaison office [int5, 2000].

In a second case, a project officer described a decision to reject a project proposal [int4,2002]. From his story, we learn that the commitment towards new organizations can also be quite significant. This project officer had approached a human rights organization in Central Asia because this organization was focusing on activities ACT Netherlands was interested in. First, he visited this organization and talked to the director and his staff. Then, the project officer helped this organization to formulate a project proposal. This took him more than a year, because there were some communication difficulties. In the meantime, he kept in touch with the director and tried to find out more about the management of the organization. It appeared that this organization was not the kind of NGO ACT would like to work with, because they were profit-oriented and not prepared to change anything about that. The project officer then decided to stop working on a proposal after almost a year of attempts to make it work.

Except for the examples mentioned above, the traces of appropriate and garbage can decision-making were scarce. In general, we therefore conclude that consequential decision-making dynamics dominated the larger part of the selection process of new potential partner organizations.

Working without alternatives for action

When ACT Netherlands decided to start working in a country where there was no family to rely on, it first started a search for promising new family members. However, these promising new members were not always present or difficult to find. In the following case, we will see how ACT Netherlands dealt with these kinds of situations. This case involved the operation of a liaison office somewhere in the world. This case shows first how ACT Netherlands tried to follow her dominant decision-making pattern by focusing on old family members. However, this limited ACT's possibilities for providing aid in such a manner that the organization decided to allow unknown organizations to apply for funds. Then the organization shifted to consequential decision-making and we already see some elements of garbage can decision-making come into play. Finally, the decision-making dynamics completely changed to garbage can decision-making when the alternatives for action became even more limited due to a lack of known and even unknown organizations to work with.

A liaison office and its past

ACT Netherlands had been active within this country since 1982, when the country was at war with its neighbor. First, ACT was a participant in a joint initiative for humanitarian aid. In 1995, when peace had come, the organization became involved in a food aid program. One year later, ACT opened a field office in the country. The reason for opening a field office was that ACT could not work through local NGOs, since these were hardly present at that moment. The agency therefore decided to work with the government, also because the government was operating quite effectively at that moment. ACT focused its activities on the rehabilitation and reconstruction of technical schools. In addition, the field office monitored and advised on a cross border aid operation to an ethnic group fighting against another neighboring government.

In 1997, the government asked all international organizations to leave the country. ACT was one of the few organizations allowed to stay. In the following years, hostilities broke out between this country and its neighbor once again. This resulted in an invasion in May 2000. This caused many people to flee to the highlands. The government could not handle this situation and therefore changed its NGO policy. Many international organizations were suddenly invited to come in and help organize IDP camps and food distribution programs. At the same time, UN troops came into the country to secure a demilitarized zone in between the parties at war. ACT got extensively involved in the provision of humanitarian food aid, mainly funded through the EU and distributed through the governmental relief agency.

In the summer of 2000, a new ACT field office representative started to work in this country. This new representative inherited projects that were partly characterized by the special relationship the ACT head office had developed with this country through the years. First, there were food aid projects funded by the EU. Second, there was a group of humanitarian aid projects financed by the protestant churches, and several other projects, such as a peace initiative project, an institutional support project involving a local NGO, a project for women in the camps, a food project, and a school supply project. These projects can be divided into two categories: projects within the family and projects with (sometimes dubious) strangers (see Table 11.2).

Table 11.2 Two categories in ACT humanitarian aid projects

Project category	Description of aid activity/partner
Projects within the family	Food aid to ethnic group in the West
Projects with (dubious) strangers	Project with Ministry of Education
	Sanitary project with women's organization
	Food aid funded by EU and distributed through governmental agency
	Institutional support to one-man NGO
	Conference on human rights
	Food and medical aid to nomads through one-man NGO

Working with 'the family'

The decision-making processes concerning the 'projects with a past' and the 'projects without a past' - those that had been initiated relatively recently – differed substantially. One project concerning an ethnic group in the north west of the country was a typical example of a 'project with a past', since this ethnic group was a member of the family. The decision-making processes regarding this family member were comparable to the decision-making processes as described for the ACT head office; it was an example of decision-making according to the logic of appropriateness.

Due to the long lasting relationship with this group, almost all proposals were approved almost automatically, even though the current and former ACT representative in the country expressed serious doubts about the quality of the work of this group. The project was clearly not running smoothly: there was a lack of regular reporting, monitoring was hardly possible (ACT had been denied access to their area regularly due to fighting), and food, radios, and vehicles disappeared. Nevertheless, the head office approved three new small project proposals after the field representative submitted new proposals. The ACT head office agreed to fund a graining mill, well drilling, and school materials.

In the past, the head office had asked the ACT representative whether it was still worthwhile to continue funding this group, since the representative reported all these problems with the organization. The representative, however, did not have proof of purposeful misdirection of the aid, because he had not had the chance or the time to go on an extensive monitoring trip. He did not want to stop working with the group before he had in-depth insight in the way this organization worked, especially because he was convinced that these people needed aid desperately. These decision-making dynamics show proof of retrospective reasoning and obligatory behavior.

Working with strangers

The relatively recent projects were not decided on according to this logic of appropriateness. The ACT representative wished to apply this appropriate decision-making style, as he recognized this to be typical of ACT. However, the local circumstances simply restrained him from doing that.

The usual way of working within ACT was through local NGOs. The specifics of the local context made that there were few NGOs and little capacity to work with. The lack of NGOs led to 'underspending' of the ACT head office budget and put an extra pressure on the field office to find ways to spend this budget. This explains why projects with the Ministry of Education and the women organization (which is also closely linked to the government) were approved. From this perspective, we can also understand the EU funded food aid projects. The ACT office had no alternatives for action in terms of local NGOs and therefore decided to work through the government with EU money.

Nevertheless, the ACT representative tried to spend some of the budget in the spirit of ACT's traditional way of working by supporting small individual initiatives. That is why the representative decided to help a man to establish his own NGO. Before making this commitment, the representative asked the ACT head office whether they knew this man. He was well-known at the ACT head office and was also recommended by another ACT partner. The representative also funded another one-man NGO which requested food and medical aid for a nomad group in the west of the country. Third, the representative financially supported a conference on human rights that was organized by a third small NGO.

Whenever there seemed to be a suitable alternative for action available, the representative started a trial and error financing process, funding the local NGO with small amounts of money to see how the organization dealt with it. Before this decision was made, ACT tried to get insight in the needs of the target population by means of field visits, needs assessments or surveys, indicating a consequential work method. If the local organization proved to be able to handle a first small project well - meaning that the organization worked effectively and efficiently (good, regular reporting, open attitude, good accounting) – then the organization had a chance to receive more funding. This is what happened to the one-man local NGO that focused on institutional support to other small civil society initiatives.

Nevertheless, if the contrary happened, i.e. the organization did not spend the money well, the funding was stopped. This was the case with a women's organization. ACT funded a small sanitary/hygiene project of this organization in the IDP camps. Soon it appeared that half of the sanitary material was never distributed, reports were late or absent, and the organization did not respond to ACT's persistent phone calls for information. When ACT made a monitoring visit, they discovered that the material was distributed unequally: only members of the women's organization received the sanitary products. This led the representative to decide to stop funding this organization in the future. The women's organization was closely tied to the government and therefore not a very attractive partner for ACT anyway. The representative gave this organization the opportunity to prove itself, but as soon as it failed, ACT's support was terminated. This way of working, through trial and error, and through close monitoring of effectiveness and efficiency, is typically consequential in nature.

Interestingly enough, the representative did not decide the same for a peace initiative project, which had not yet sent a financial report of the conference costs as of September 2001, while the conference was organized at the beginning of that year. The representative argued that this was an interesting organization for ACT because it aimed at politically important goals in his eyes, namely the spread of democratic principles throughout the country. Since this is a project that nicely fitted the ACT mandate, the representative gave this organization the benefit of the doubt, indicating an inclination towards appropriateness.

Working with dubious strangers: A case

However, it was not always possible for the ACT representative to determine whether an organization was effective and efficient. The information needed to determine this was sometimes inaccessible, contradicting, or lacking. This constrained the ambition to work according to a logic of consequence. An example of this is one of the one-man NGOs the field office supported. This NGO provided aid and care to a nomad group, travelling around in the border area in the west of the country.

The beginning of a project: A note left in the mailbox

The man behind this NGO approached ACT for help even before the current representative had started his job. The representative found a handwritten note in his mailbox from this doctor upon arrival. In the beginning, the representative was not very interested in this one man NGO and he put the letter aside. After a couple of months, however, the representative came to the conclusion that it was hard to find local NGOs to work with. The representative remembered the hand written letter, found it in his files, and wrote a letter to the doctor. A correspondence between them developed, in which ACT tried to find out more about his NGO. ACT also made inquiries with other organizations, but nobody seemed to know this doctor and the nomad group he was taking care of. After a couple of months the ACT representative decided to visit the nomads to see for himself what this NGO was doing and whether there was a need for aid. In the trip report the following was mentioned:

> The common opinion about the [nomads] is that they acquire money as traders/smugglers. Our visit did not contradict this, as we saw at least 10 pickups around the 15 houses we could distinguish. On the other hand, housing conditions, schooling and health services definitely needed support. F and the [political leader] are very strong promoters of their case, and clearly have distinct views: one political, one humanitarian. We might try a first food distribution and build up a relation during that, to assess future collaboration (trip report 2000).

ACT decided to give the doctor 50.000 Dutch guilders (approximately €22.500) to spend on food aid and supplementary feeding. The doctor would distribute the food himself. After half a year, ACT went back to the region in order to monitor what had happened with the money. In addition, the representative used this trip to determine what the future relationship between ACT and the one-man NGO would be.

Contradicting evidence of needs

Upon arrival in the nomad area, ACT heard that a majority of the nomads had moved closer to the border. ACT met with the political leader of the nomads, who was still in the original camp. The camp was indeed quite empty in comparison to the previous visit. The political leader told ACT that he had urged his people to cross the border to a small piece of land that had been liberated by his resistance soldiers.[9]

ACT asked how many people lived in that area on the other side of the border and how many people were still on this side of the border. The representative also asked what had happened to the food. The political leader told ACT that part of the food had been given to the people in the liberated area and that another part of it was used to grow crops in that area.

The political leader proposed to visit this liberated area with ACT, so that they could see for themselves. Two of the staff went there with an armed patrol, while another staff member stayed in the camp to talk to the women. She was directed by the brother of the political leader to the 'woman in charge'. She tried to find out how the ACT supplementary food distribution had been used in the camp. The woman in charge told the ACT staff member that every family had received six or seven bags of supplementary feeding. Her children and grandchildren looked healthy. The government supplied water every other day. Then this woman took the ACT staff member to other women. They all looked healthy and well fed.

The two other staff members had a look in the liberated area, where they met various families that had just arrived from the neighboring country. These families were provided (bad quality) water, and the nomad resistance army gave them food, blankets, and a tent. They seemed sufficiently taken care of. The staff members also visited the farm, which was constructed by 'young men' as the doctor said. Later, the political leader admitted that these young men were soldiers who had received ACT food for constructing the farm. The staff members concluded from their own observations that indeed ACT food had been given to these soldiers.

The needed are found

Later that day, ACT met with the 'NGO doctor' in a hotel in a village close to the nomad camp. They talked extensively about possible future projects. Water, health, and (women's) education were mentioned as the most urgent needs. Since it was still unclear to the representative and his staff members what the exact needs were and where the need was highest, they returned to the camp with the doctor. The representative asked him where he could find nomads in need, since he had not found them while the doctor claimed there were many nomads who suffered from malnutrition and disease. The doctor brought them to three tents where they indeed saw some malnourished children. These families did not look very wealthy and lacked a male head of the household due to the fighting.

More discouraging stories

The doctor provided the ACT workers with information about the food distribution that contradicted the stories collected at the nomad camp. The doctor said that the supplementary feeding was only given to the elderly, to breast feeding mothers, pregnant women, and small children. Earlier that day, the staff members heard stories about families with small children that did not receive supplementary feeding at all, while the 'woman in charge' had told ACT that all families had received supplementary feeding.

For the ACT representative the situation became less clear with every bit of new information he heard. Part of the food seemed to be given to the resistance army or was spent on growing crops. It was not sure how the food and supplementary feeding had been distributed and to whom. It was not sure whether the water supply would continue and what other aid was exactly needed, where, for whom, and for how many. In addition, the ACT representative knew from the doctor that a medicines distribution to this nomad group by another NGO had partly failed, because there had been a conflict between the nomads and other members of the umbrella resistance group that the nomads were part of. This conflict had to do with customs fees and the ownership of the medicines. The medicines therefore had to stay in the port and expired. In the camp, the staff members found thrown away medicines and medical material in front of the hospital tent and dispersed throughout the camp, indicating a careless attitude towards the aid distribution. This did not look well for future aid distributions.

A commitment to continue

Still, the doctor made an enthusiastic impression on the representative. This man was clearly working very hard for these people. Why would he do that, if these people did not need it? The ACT representative saw no reason to doubt this person's evaluation of the situation. The ACT representative felt he did not have enough information to stop working with the nomads, but he also did not have enough reliable information about existing needs that should be addressed in the future. The only decision he felt he could make was to send an ACT staff member once again and let him observe the situation for a longer period of time, before the office would decide whether to continue working with the doctor and his nomad group.

Innocent until proven guilty

From the above, we conclude that coincidence was an important factor for this project to begin: a simple note left in a mailbox. In the beginning, the ACT representative did not even think of working with this man, since he was not a 'member of the family'. When it appeared problematic to find 'members of the family', the ACT representative became more open to new initiatives. The ACT representative tried to work according to a logic of consequence in order to decide if and how to work with this man and his project. He could only find out whether this man was reliable by giving him a small amount of money to start a project, since nobody knew this man and his project. Later, the ACT representative visited the project site and tried to collect information about the effectiveness and efficiency of the project and the man who initiated it. However, the information he could collect was incomplete, contradictory, or not very reliable. The ACT representative found himself caught in a dilemma: he either could stop funding this NGO, taking the risk that he might make a mistake. It might later appear that this group of people really needed aid. He could also continue to fund the nomads and give the doctor the benefit of the doubt, with the knowledge that some of the aid would be diverted to soldiers and without knowing for sure whether all these people really needed it. The only option left in order to get more information was to have one of his staff members go there again to observe the situation for a longer period of time and to do a survey. The consequential decision-making mode was no longer of use, since relevant information was missing or contradictory. Even the garbage can decision-making mode did not have any use, because the ACT representative could not (yet) establish whether this project matched ACT's work method and outlook. In the end, the ACT representative applied a typical ACT appropriate decision rule: he gave the project the benefit of the doubt and declared the man 'innocent until proven guilty'.

The law of diminishing alternatives

From the above, we conclude that the starting point for decision-making in the ACT field office in this country was the logic of appropriateness, which was the standard way of working in the ACT head office. This country was a logical country to work in for ACT, because of the long-lasting relationship between ACT and the population.

However, the possibilities for aid provision in the ACT tradition were limited, a factor that apparently was not weighed in the head office before deciding to work in this country. Due to a lack of local NGOs, the ACT field office was limited in its possibilities to initiate projects based on past experiences. Only the first ethnic group discussed was a clear member of the family, which could therefore make mistakes before ACT would do something about it. The commitment of ACT in this case might be remarkable, but is comparable to cases discussed in the previous chapter. After some time, after many reports of mismanagement of aid, the ACT representative proposed to organize a mission in order to collect more information that should help to decide on the future of the relationship with this organization. However, the area was still inaccessible.

One way to solve the lack of alternative local partners was to start working through governmental institutions, a very unusual thing to do for ACT. However, since ACT had a long-lasting relationship with this government, this is understandable because the government used to be the former resistance army that had been extensively supported by ACT in the 1980s and 1990s. This decision is therefore an appropriate way of acting. Another way to deal with the lack of local NGOs was to support small, individual initiatives. The representative chose a strategy of trial and error financing, applying a consequential decision mode to decide on the continuation or termination of relationships. Nevertheless, this approach did not always provide the required results in terms of clear facts about the performance of an NGO.[10]

This all illustrates how contextual constraints influenced the possibility of applying certain preferred modes of decision-making. Here we see once again that a lack of alternatives for action made a humanitarian aid worker to use another decision-making mode than usual to find options for action. Again, this search process was in the end characterized by solutions looking for problems. The ACT representative started looking for problems that fitted ACT's solutions. The role of the individual became more important since the ACT representative had room to maneuver. Coincidence and timing became other important factors as well, of which the note in the mailbox is a typical example. Hence, garbage can decision-making became prevalent.

Interestingly, the case described here also shows that garbage can decision-making can only be a last resort as long as there are problems that match the solution offered by the humanitarian aid NGO. When this no longer can be established, as was the case in the nomads' project, ACT reverted to a 'toned down' version of the logic of appropriateness.

From preferred to less preferred decision-making modes

The decision-making process concerning new(er) partner organizations was characterized by consequential decision-making dynamics as long as capable partner organizations were available as well as the means to establish whether potential partners were trustworthy. When it is difficult to establish the trustworthiness of an organization and the need for intervention, ACT Netherlands' decision-making processes are more garbage can in character. Here we see how contextual constraints once again limited a humanitarian aid NGO to work according to its preferred decision-making mode, just as was the case within MSF Holland.

We hypothesized that ACT Netherlands would either have an appropriate or a garbage can decision-making mode. In any case, the analysis of the organizational features would predict that the logic of consequence would be absent in this organization. Based on the observations presented in this chapter, we have to refute that hypothesis, since consequential decision-making dynamics were indeed important within ACT Netherlands when it concerned the selection of new partner organizations. This implies that consequential decision-making is not necessarily related to the organizational features. This conclusion is strengthened by the observation that ACT Netherlands' 'organization in action' shows more resemblence to Selznick's institution than to Simon's admninistrative organization or March and Olsen's ambiguous organization.

However, it could be argued that the logic of appropriateness is in principle the preferred decision-making mode within ACT Netherlands. Only if the preferred decision-making mode was impossible to apply, due to limited alternatives for action and a lack of reliable information, other decision-making modes came into play. The logic of consequence seemed to be a second best option to decide on partner organizations, while garbage can decision-making came into play when both the logic of appropriateness and the logic of consequence could not be applied. Garbage can decision-making was induced due to a lack of alternatives for action, which made the consequential work method useless to the ACT representative. Interestingly enough, ACT reverted to the logic of appropriateness when no information was available at all to decide on the quality of the match between problems identified and solutions available.

Notes

1 In total, there were 18 interview cases concerning the approval and rejection of project proposals submitted by unknown organizations.
2 In 8 out of 12 initiation cases, the project officers approved the proposal because they were convinced the organization had the capacity to implement the project effectively, indicating an attempt to maximize the organizational goals.
3 In 4 cases it was mentioned that there was a clear need for intervention.
4 In 6 out of 12 initiation cases, missions were organized to establish this. In another 5 cases, other information gathering instruments were used to determine the trustworthiness of the applicant organization.
5 This was the case in 4 out of the 12 interview cases.
6 In 4 out of 6 rejection cases, this was the reason for rejecting project proposals: the project officer thought the organization lacked the capacity or the project proposal was problematic.
7 For reasons of anonimity, the name of this NGO was changed into EEC (Earthquake Emergency Committee).
8 LoC dimensions in decision-making concerning 'strangers'

Table 11.3   LoC dimensions in decision-making concerning 'strangers'

The number of cases in which	start (12)	reject (6)	total (18)
There were attempts to maximize the organizational goals	8	4	12
Assessments were mentioned as an information gathering instrument	6	2	8
The importance of information collection other than assessments was stressed	5	1	6
The involvement of experts was mentioned	4	1	5
A clear need for intervention was mentioned/ there was no reason to intervene (anymore)	4	0	4
The decision-making process was described in terms of sequentiality	4	0	4
Alternatives for action were formulated	3	1	3
The proposed activities were related to the organizational policies	1	1	2
Prospective reasoning was established	0	1	1
Total number of cases = 18			

Table 11.4   No. of LoC dimensions for the unknown partners interview cases

No. of LoC dimensions mentioned in interviews→	0	1	2	3	4	5	6	7	8
	1	3	7	4	1	1	1	0	0

9   The nomads fight their own battle against the neighboring government and are sponsored by the government where the ACT field office is located. Having the nomads in the liberated territory had a political meaning, the political leader explained.

10 A final option is to implement projects under the management from the ACT field office itself, meaning that the field office becomes operational. However, this option only exists in the mind of the representative, and has not been realized yet. Nevertheless, the head office did not show any objections to this plan.

PART IV
Comparison and Conclusion

Chapter 12

Decison-Making Dynamics in MSF and ACT: Comparison and Discussion of Research Results

This study has shown how MSF Holland and ACT Netherlands decide on the locations and activities of their humanitarian aid projects. We argued that the complex context of humanitarian aid provision with all its situational and organizational constraints makes the work of these organizations almost an impossible job. If one wants to take into account all potential threats to effective intervention – such as safety risks, corruption, donor wishes, access problems, etc. – it would become very difficult, if not impossible, to come to any decisions about aid provision at all. Hence, the selection of humanitarian aid activities is always, in one way or another, a matter of choosing the lesser evil.

Humanitarian organizations are confronted with such dilemmas and hard choices every day. They cannot afford to take all the time they need to evaluate and prevent all potential risks. Most of the time, these risks are simply givens that cannot be prevented. In this study, the question was asked how humanitarian non governmental aid organizations decide about their aid activities, given these constraints and dilemmas.

Filling a void in NGO research

In order to answer the central research question of this study, we needed to open up the 'black box' of internal NGO dynamics. We reviewed the NGO literature and searched for insights about internal NGO work processes that could guide our research, but had to conclude that relatively little attention is being paid to this topic. There is more attention to explaining NGO behavior as if NGOs were a coherent group of actors, while the research question of our study directs our attention to the study of *differences* in NGO behavior and decisions.

Nevertheless, the NGO literature assisted in formulating some expectations for our research. First, it is argued in the literature that NGOs are characterized by loosely coupled structures, ambiguous goals, and internal conflict due to the pressure of muliple stakeholders demanding that NGOs strive for both instrumental and political objectives, which are contradictory in nature. Hence, we formulated the question whether this characterization of NGOs would also be found in our study of two cases. Second, the NGO literature that focuses on diversity in the NGO community states that differences in NGO operations can be explained by differences in the national contexts of the NGOs, their field of expertise, and their level of operation. Since we were interested in understanding the differences in selection outcomes of NGOs that shared the same orientation (i.e. humanitarian aid) and worked in the same national headquarters context (The Netherlands) and on the same level of operation (the international level), we hypothesized that these differences in outcomes might be related to differences in the *organizational set up* of these NGOs. We distinguished between two NGO categories often found in humanitarian aid, i.e. those NGOs that are operational, specialist, and oriented on welfare, next to NGOs that are non operational, generalist, and more developmental in character. We wondered whether such differences would help understand differences in selection outcomes of humanitarian NGOs.

An organizational decision-making perspective

In order to explore the differences in outcomes between the two categories of humanitarian aid NGOs described above, we needed a 'tool' to open up the black box of internal NGO dynamics. With help of three decision-making modes, we formulated a theoretical framework that served as a heuristic tool in this exploratory study of organizational decision-making processes. These three modes – i.e. the logic of consequence, the logic of appropriateness, and the mode of garbage can decision-making – not only contained characteristics of decision-making processes but also of the organizational structure connected to each decision-making mode.

We characterized the logic of consequence as a process of sequential and prospective reasoning; maximizing behavior; and information and expert driven decision-making. The logic of appropriateness was described in terms of instant and retrospective reasoning; obligatory and rule-based behavior; and decision-making by analogy. Finally, we typified garbage can decision-making as simultaneous reasoning without guidance by organizational goals or internalized values; entrepreneurial behavior; and decision-making by coupling.

We hypothesized that the logic of consequence is to be found in an organizational structure that resembles Simon's ideal type of the administrative organization, meaning a highly formalized, specialized and centralized organizational structure in which procedures, guidelines and expertise dominate the decision-making process. The logic of appropriateness would be connected to Selznick's ideal type of the 'institution', we argued, meaning an informally and decentrally structured organizational setting in which internalized values are guiding the decision-making process. Finally, we connected the logic of the garbage can to the ambiguous, institutionalizing organization, meaning that the goals and values of the organization are contested and formal structures do not guide organizational action because groups and coalitions are important actors in the organization. It is this latter organization type that resembles the dominant view on NGOs in the NGO literature most: NGOs as ambiguous and loosely coupled structures, characterized by internal conflict. Hence, based on the NGO literature, we would expect humanitarian NGOs resemble the ambiguous or institutionalizing organization most, deciding about humanitarian aid projects in the garbage can mode.

The two humanitarian aid providers compared

The theoretical framework was used to study decision-making processes in humanitarian aid NGOs. We selected two Dutch humanitarian aid NGOs for this study: ACT Netherlands and MSF Holland. They represent two organizational categories often found in the humanitarian aid NGO community: MSF Holland represents the *operational, specialist* NGO focused on *welfare*, while ACT Netherlands represents the *non operational, generalist* NGO that is more *developmental* in character. Hence, studying the decision-making processes in these two NGOs in relation to their organizational structures provided the opportunity of generalization to the theory (Yin, 1994): the research results with concern these two specific humanitarian NGOs might have a broader relevance to the study of (humanitarian aid) NGOs in general.

We studied MSF Holland's and ACT Netherland's selection pattern. Between MSF Holland and ACT Netherlands, two differences in selection patterns stood out:

1. MSF Holland had a fairly stable division of its budget over the continents, while ACT's expenditures over the continents varied more;
2. ACT spent its budget on a relative stable group of countries, while MSF's percentage of concentrated spending was decreasing.

By studying these two extremes with help of the theoretical framework, we aimed to account for the variation in the group of organizations that we studied, while at the same time it allowed us to look for common patterns. In the chapters following the theoretical part of this study, we described the selection outcomes, the organizational structure, and the dominant and secondary decision-making patterns for both MSF and ACT. Per organization, the following conclusions were formulated:

MSF Holland: consequentiality in humanitarian aid provision

The organizational structure of MSF Holland – a medical humanitarian aid organization found in the 1980s – resembled Simon's ideal type of the administrative organization to a large extent. The organization had a substantial number of guidelines, procedures, manuals, and policies. MSF headquarters consisted of various expert departments that focused on specific sub-themes in humanitarian aid. In addition, there was a clear formal line in authority and a hierarchical decision-making structure that was exercised when important decisions concerning the start, end, extension, or rejection of projects needed to be taken. Hence, MSF Holland did not resemble the picture of the ambiguous, institutionalizing organization, as often sketched in the NGO literature.

From this, we formulated the hypothesis that MSF's dominant decision-making pattern would resemble the logic of consequence. In Chapter 6, we presented the analysis of empirical data which indicated that the logic of consequence was indeed MSF's dominant decision-making mode. Based on this analysis one could therefore conclude that in this case the logic of consequence was connected to the features of the administrative organization. Hence, the hypothesis such as formulated in the theoretical chapter was confirmed. Once again, this picture did not resemble the claim in the NGO literature that NGOs are characterized by loosely coupled structures, ambiguous goals, and internal conflict.

However, not all the research material pointed to this conclusion. In Chapter 7, we presented the deviant cases in the research material. Although these deviant cases were relatively small in number, they implied the existence of secondary decision-making patterns within MSF Holland. First, we saw how MSF employees sometimes bypassed the formal structure or used the logic of consequence more as a persuasion and legitimizing strategy than as a 'sincere' method to come to a decision. Second, the logic of appropriateness was applied in cases in which MSF Holland felt an inside or outside pressure to commit to activities and projects that would have been rejected if a pure consequential decision-making had been applied. Third, the logic of the garbage can made its appearance in situations in which the alternatives for action became limited due to the absence of needs that could be defined as 'typical' MSF activities according to the organization's policies and mandate.

The above leads us to the conclude that the preferred decision-making mode in MSF Holland is indeed the logic of consequence. Nevertheless, consequential decision-making was not always possible. Several circumstances led to this. First, when there was lack of agreement on the organizational objectives, a different decision-making dynamic unfolded, such as the NGO literature suggests. Second, it was sometimes not possible to make decisions prospectively and in relation to the organizational goals because commitments of the past or pressures of the present stood in the way. Third, alternatives for action were sometimes lacking. This induced garbage decision-making. Hence, it was only in a minority of the decision occasions that we found decision-making dynamics as predicted in the NGO literature.

ACT Netherlands: Working with 'the family'

ACT Netherlands – an ecumenical humanitarian aid organization found in the 1950s – appeared to have anything but a relation to Simon's administrative organization. There were little procedures, policies, and guidelines, and the organization was not hierarchically structured very much. The organization had some degree of specialization because the project officers were responsible for specific regions in the world.

From this, we predicted that we would not find the logic of consequence to be the dominant decision-making mode. However, we could not hypothesize in advance what other decision-making mode would then be dominant. In Chapter 10, we presented the analysis of the empirical data and concluded that ACT's dominant decision-making mode was the logic of appropriateness (and not garbage can decision-making, as predicted by the NGO literature). The decision-making process was characterized by retrospective reasoning and rule-based and obligatory behavior. The longer ACT worked with a partner organization, the more difficult it was to terminate the relationship, even though there were serious problems concerning project implementation.

The research material also gave evidence of deviations from this dominant decision-making pattern. The logic of consequence emerged as a secondary pattern when ACT decided to work in areas in which it had no (reliable) partner organizations. Whenever potential partners were found, their trustworthiness was tested by means of a consequential process of trial and error. In cases in which alternatives for action – i.e. local partner organizations – were scarce or absent, we observed garbage can decision-making. So, once again, garbage can decision-making was only found in a minority of the ACT decision occasions.

From the above, we concluded that the preferred and dominant decision-making mode within ACT Netherlands was the logic of appropriateness. The longer the relationship with a partner, the more appropriate behavior we observed. Only if partner organizations were absent or not to be found, different decision-making dynamics emerged.

The organization 'in action' showed most resemblance to Selznick's idea of an institution. The project officers within ACT had internalized the organization's values and made their decisions almost instantly. They did not need guidelines, policies, or decision-making criteria to decide, since they shared the same kind of organizational values. Existing policies lagged behind the reality of decision-making and reflected the organizational values more than it prescribed them. Hence, it could be argued that the logic of appropriateness was indeed connected to Selznick's ideal type of the institution, as was hypothesized in the theoretical framework. The analysis of the organization 'in action'also showed that ACT Netherlands did not resemble the ambiguous, institutionalizing organization, such as suggested in the NGO literature.

Selection through decision-making

Now we have established that MSF and ACT hade different dominant decision-making modes and that they were related to different organizational settings, the question arises if and how this influences the selection outcomes.

MSF's main focus was on the African continent, while ACT focused more on Europe and the Middle East. MSF had a group of 15 countries in Africa, Asia, and Latin America that continuously received aid, while ACT had a group of 21 countries receiving continuous aid on these three continents. Within this group of countries, ACT's expenditures fluctuated more irregularly than MSF's spendings. Within MSF, the expenditures on countries receiving continuous aid had been decreasing consistently after 1998, the year in which a new a Mid Term Policy was being formulated. Within ACT, expenditures on the African and Latin American countries of continuous aid also had decreased, whereas for Asia it had increased. Still, a substantial percentage of the aid budget was reserved for these permanent receivers. Another interesting observation is that the two NGOs selected different countries for their permanent funding relationships: only Sierra Leone, Sudan, Afghanistan and Peru received aid continuously in both NGOs. Relevant to this research is the question to what extent these selection outcomes resulted from a specific decision-making mode.

The logic of consequence made MSF search for those places in the world where MSF thought medical humanitarian crises required their intervention most. Within MSF Holland, the amount of money spent on a country reflected the perceived need for and costs of intervention. The decrease in spending on the countries of continuous aid reflected the aim of the new Mid Term Policy of 1999 which stated that MSF should return to its core business of providing aid in humanitarian *and* medical emergencies. Before 1998/1999, MSF had a number of projects that did not match this criterion of the humanitarian *and* medical emergency. In addition, there was a group of countries where MSF seemed to have a permanent presence: this group of countries of continuous aid occupied between 70 and 80 percent of the total budget per continent in 1998 (see Chapter 6). A few years later this percentage had declined because MSF was more inclined to stop working in countries once the situation changed for the better. Hence, there were less countries receiving continuous aid, occupying a smaller percentage of expenditures of the total budget. If they did receive aid for a longer period of time, this reflected the fact that the need for intervention is continuous. Hence, it could be argued that the consequential work method within MSF redirected MSF's expenditures and led to a limitation of countries that received continuous aid.

Within ACT Netherlands, it was not the amount of money spent that was important, but the fact that a family member received permanent support. This explains why the yearly expenditures per continent and per group of countries of continuous aid fluctuated more within ACT than within MSF Holland. In some cases, expenditures to these permanent partners were more symbolic than substantial. They confirmed the permanent relationship between ACT and some of their partners. The appropriate work method also explained why ACT has a bigger group of countries of continuous aid than MSF had. The commitment towards these partner organizations was substantial, resulting in obligatory behavior and therefore more stability in the aid locations. ACT's actions were much more determined by its past; once a partner had become a family member it had more chance to receive aid continuously. This observation seems to be confirmed by the fact that ACT funded partner organizations in countries that were not suffering from severe humanitarian crises anymore (such as Kenya and Mexico). Thus, the appropriate decision-making mode seems to explain why ACT had a bigger group of countries receiving continuous aid, why certain countries were on that list, and why the organization had a less stable expenditure pattern.

One exception should be noted, however. This is the decision ACT made to work more intensively in Turkey and Kosovo. The fact that ACT's expenditures on Europe have increased so substantially is the result of the crises in these two countries. In both countries, ACT did not have family ties to rely on. Hence, ACT's main focus on Europe cannot be explained by means of the appropriate decision-making style.

Different as night and day?

From the above, it can be concluded that MSF Holland and ACT Netherlands actually represent two extremes in the community of humanitarian aid NGOs. In addition to their differences in selection outcomes, and their different outlook and work method, they have different preferred and dominant modes of decision-making. In addition, the organizations differ in the way they are structured organizationally. Nevertheless, we also observed some similarities in their decision-making processes.

'Partir, c'est mourir un peu'

A first similarity found in both organizations was related to the termination of project activities. When MSF or ACT had to decide about ending project activities somewhere in the world, we saw more evidence of obligatory behavior and feelings of commitment when compared to the decisions to initiate project actvities. This especially became evident when the organization had a long-lasting relationship with a partner or a country. Although ACT's decision-making processes were more appropriate in character than MSF decision-making processes, both organizations apparently found it hard to stop working in countries where they had established long-lasting relationships.

The law of diminishing alternatives for action

Both organizations' preferred decision-making modes were abandoned due to constraints that are inherent to these decision-making modes. For example, applying the logic of consequence is only possible if one agrees on the organizational goals, has enough reliable information to decide on, and has enough alternatives for action to choose from. If one of these factors is missing, consequential decision-making is very difficult. The logic of appropriateness requires that there are past experiences and commitments that can guide the decision-making process. If these are absent, it is hard to determine what is the appropriate action to take.

Both ACT Netherlands and MSF Holland could not always apply their preferred decision-making mode. ACT Netherlands shifted to consequential decision-making if it had no family ties in a country where the organization wanted to work. In other words, there was lack of previous experiences and rules of appropriate behavior that could guide the decision-making process. MSF Holland already made her decisions consequentially. However, there were cases when commitments from the past or expectations in the present changed the decision-making process towards the logic of appropriateness.

Then there were cases in which MSF humanitarian aid workers in the field concluded that MSF intervention was not needed, based on the consequential work method. For one reason or another, this did not lead to the decision to stop working in the country by the headquarters. Instead, MSF employees in the field were urged to continue looking for potential activities. The same goes for ACT Netherlands. There were also occasions when ACT Netherlands decided to start working in a country although reliable partner organizations were lacking. An attempt was made to select new partner organizations through a consequential work method. However, in some cases, this did not work out. For both organizations, the alternatives for action sometimes became so limited that neither appropriate nor consequential decision-making was possible anymore. Then the 'law of diminishing alternatives' was induced, meaning that both organizations started to look for problems that matched their solutions. The decision-making processes became garbage can in character.

Garbage can decision-making as a last resort

Garbage can decision-making was always the last decision-making mode in both organizations, more as a last resort than as a consciously chosen decision-making method. Garbage can decision-making was only found in circumstances in which headquarters had decided to continue the field presence, while the field had problems finding potential projects that matched the organization's goals and standards. Within ACT, the decision to intervene in the case that was discussed in Chapter 11 was related to previous commitments and experiences: ACT used to work in the country for years and it had close ties with the new government, the previous resistance army. How to explain headquarters' persistence within MSF is more difficult. It seems to be related to the fact that the 'window of opportunity' finally opened, after years of waiting.

The garbage can decision-making mode was certainly not the preferred way of working. It was more a last resort – however not consciously chosen - since other work methods were not possible to apply. Garbage can decision-making resulted from the fact that alternatives for action were lacking due to contextual and organizational constraints. In the one case in which both MSF's and ACT's decision-making processes were studied, these constraints consisted of the presence of many other aid organizations; a national government pulling the strings of humanitarian aid provision, thereby restricting the freedom of aid organizations to do what they seemed was needed; and safety concerns, especially access problems due to landmines. The operational space became so small that potential activities were either absent or already taken care of by others. There were no alternatives for action to chose from or no family to work with. Then, both organizations picked the first problem they found that matched their solutions to a certain extent, before others would do so.

Evaluating the theoretical framework of this study

In the theoretical chapter of this book we touched upon a number of issues concerning the three logics of decision-making used in this study that might have influenced the results and conclusions of this study. To what extent have these issues influenced indeed the conclusions of the study presented above?

Different decision-making units

The different methods of data collection helped to deal with the fact that the logic of the garbage can focuses on the organizational level as decision-making unit, where the other two logics focus on the individual. We did not hear many 'garbage can' stories in the interviews. This could imply that respondents have tried to rationalize their actions in interviews. From this, one could conclude that by focussing on the individual as the central decision-making unit in the interviews, we have not collected valid data. However, the access to files and email communication, and the fact that we were able to visit project teams on the ground, helped to partly overcome this problem. Using other data collection methods helped to focus on both the individual and the organization as a decision-making unit.

One could argue that decision-making in these two NGOs might be more garbage can in character than is argued here, due to the methodological pitfall mentioned above. Nevertheless, we hope to have shown, from the interviews, the documents, and the observed decision moments, that both consequential and appropriate decision-making were more dominant decision-making modes than garbage can decision-making.

How consequential decisions can be appropriate and not

In this study,we tried to distinguish between three modes of decision-making: the logic of consequence, the logic of appropriateness, and the garbage can decision-making mode. In the theoretical framework of this study we acknowledged the fact that these three decision-making modes each have a different level of abstraction. On the one hand, there is the logic of consequence, which is an ideal type that prescribes behavior according to clear rules for action. The logic of appropriateness, on the other hand, is an ideal type that presumes certain rules for behavior, but does not give a concrete interpretation of what the contents of these rules can be.

It was therefore argued that a consequential work method could also be the appropriate decision-making mode in an organization, since a person could identify a situation as a situation in which he or she was expected to behave consequentially.

This complicated the study of decision-making processes in this book. However, we made the distinction between consequential and appropriate decision-making more clear by defining characteristics such as prospective versus retrospective reasoning and maximizing versus obligatory behavior. Therefore, it was possible to label MSF Holland's work method to be consequential and ACT Netherlands' work method to be appropriate.

On a higher level of abstraction, we can conclude that MSF Holland's consequential work method could be seen as appropriate behavior. MSF employees were expected to work according to consequential decision-making elements based on MSF's organizational values: to be 'present, relevant, and effective in the major humanitarian crises of the day' and to 'show compassion to populations in need' (MTP 1999:6). To ignore the consequential work method would be inappropriate and undesirable within MSF. One could therefore argue that MSF's consequential work method represents only one category of appropriate behavior.

This being said, MSF's decisions taken on the concrete level of initiating, terminating, rejecting, and extending project activities were clearly consequential in character. A clear distinction could be observed between prospective and retrospective reasoning, maximizing and obligatory behavior, and sequential and instant decision-making. Hence, it was consequentiality in action that resulted in MSF's selection outcomes as discussed, and hardly previous commitments towards countries or populations or outside pressures.

From this study, it can be concluded that 'appropriateness' can have many manifestations. The most dominant manifestation of appropriate behavior was observed towards the countries and populations receiving aid. In addition, appropriate behavior was also observed towards the Dutch society (citizens, politics and the media). Finally, appropriate behavior was observed among colleagues inside the organization.

Three mutually exclusive logics?

This study indicates that the three logics are not mutually exclusive. The three decision-making logics coincided in two different organizational settings. The decision-making shifted from dominant to secondary patterns due to constraints inherent to the assumptions of the preferred decision-making mode.

The decision-making mode applied was clearly related to the number of alternatives of action available. The less alternatives for action available, the more garbage can – like the decision-making process became. This observation draws our attention to the fact that both the ideal type of consequential and appropriate decision-making carry with them assumptions about the information needed in order to make decisions. This is done in terms of goals, alternatives, costs, rules, or past experiences. The logic of consequence assumes that there is always a possibility to collect (reliable) information and that this information is helpful in the decision-making process. The logic of appropriateness assumes the existence of former experiences that can guide decision-making. Hence, both models assume the existence of alternatives for action. These two models do not really give an answer to the question how decisions are made when alternatives of action are lacking, a situation which was real in its consequences for both the ACT and MSF field office in the cases described earlier. Hence, although the three logics are not mutually exclusive within organizations, it could be argued that the three logics are mutually exclusive in certain decision occasions, depending on the number of alternatives for action available.

Connecting decision-making processes to organizational structures

In the theoretical framework of this study, we assumed that certain decision-making modes would be more likely to be present in certain organizational settings than in others. It was assumed, for example, that consequential decision-making would be present in an organization that showed resemblance to Simon's administrative organization.

MSF Holland's organizational features showed a striking resemblance to the ideal type of the administrative organization, while ACT Netherlands' organizational structure had features of the institution. These differences in organizational setting seemed to be connected to the preferred mode of decision-making in both organizations. From this, it could be concluded that for these two organizations the assumptions formulated in the theoretical framework have not been proven to be wrong. Since neither of the two NGOs showed resemblance to the institutionalizing organization, it could not be studied to what extent garbage can decision-making would be dominant. What may be concluded is that the features of the organizational setting influence the contents of the *preferred* decision-making mode. Whether the preferred decision-making mode will actually become the dominant decision-making mode is constrained by the circumstances in which these decisions need to be taken.

Still, the three logics coincided within one organizational setting. Moreover, the presence of characteristics of Simon's administrative organization and Selznick's institution seemed to actually have induced garbage can decision-making. This happened when the consequential and appropriate decision-making mode was applied in contexts in which alternatives for action were absent. The consequential or appropriate decision-making mode kept guiding the decision makers in the field. Based on these dominant decision-making methods, they decided that there were no suitable options for action. However, headquarters was persistent: the teams should be present in these countries. This is what led the teams to look for problems that matched their solution.

This conclusion might be in dissonance with Cohen, March and Olsen's argument that the less structured the organization, the more chance garbage can decision-making occurs. MSF Holland, for example, could be labeled as a fairly tight hierarchical access structure through the position of country managers, heads of mission, operational directors, and the MT. ACT Netherlands also has a segmented access structure (the project officer is the first to know about problems and solutions). If decision-making modes stem from the organizational structure, this study results in the conclusion that garbage can decision-making occurred *as a result of* a persistence to apply consequential or appropriate decision-making modes in situations that did not allow for it. It was not a lack of decision-making structures that induced garbage can decision-making. This would leave us with a new insight into what circumstances lead to garbage can decision-making.

Now that the black box is open ...

From above, we conclude that the theoretical framework of this study has proven to be of value for the purpose of this study: we gained more understanding of the internal operations of two NGOs that had the same field of expertise (humanitarian aid), the same level of operation (international), and the same national headquarter context. This study showed how the differences between the organizational set up of the two NGOs – in terms of orientation, channel of implementation, and type of aid – were related to the ideal types developed in the theoretical framework (see Figure 12.1 for a summary). This helped us understand the differences in selection outcomes.

Organizational setup	MSF	ACT
National headquarter's context	The Netherlands	The Netherlands
Level of operation	International	International
Field of expertise	Humanitarian aid	Humanitarian aid
• **Orientation**	• welfare	• development
• **Channel of implementation**	• operational	• non operational/ partners
• **Type of aid**	• specialist, technical (medical)	• generalist
⇩	⇩	⇩
Dominant decision-making mode and organizational structure	Logic of Consequence in the Administrative Organization	Logic of Appropriateness In the Institution
Pattern in selection outcomes	Selection and budget reflect humanitarian needs: • few continuous countries of aid • flexible project portfolio: often 'new' countries and projects, whenever budget allows so	Selection and budget reflect commitments and solidarity: • many continuous countries of aid • stable project porfolio: new partners that fit the organizational mandate do not get access easily

Figure 12.1 Comparing MSF and ACT on their similarities and differences

External dimensions in the country of aid provision
- access
- security
- misuse of aid
- type of needs
- number of aid agencies present

⇩

law of diminishing alternatives

⇩

garbage can decision-making dynamics

⇧

pressure to work according to preferred decision-making mode

⇧

Organizational setup	MSF	ACT
National headquarter's context	The Netherlands	The Netherlands
Level of operation	International	International
Field of expertise • **Orientation** • **Channel of implementation** • **Type of aid**	Humanitarian aid • welfare • operational • specialist, technical (medical)	Humanitarian aid • development • non operational • generalist
Organization size	Large	Small
Degree of institutionalization	Relatively low	Relatively high
⇩	⇩	⇩
Dominant decision-making mode & organizational structure	Logic of Consequence in the Administrative Organization	Logic of Appropriateness in the Institution
Pattern in selection outcomes	Selection and budget reflect humanitarian needs: • few continuous countries of aid • flexible project portfolio: often 'new' countries and projects, whenever budget allows so	Selection and budget reflect commitments and solidarity: • many continuous countries of aid • stable project porfolio: new partners that fit the organizational mandate do not get access easily

Figure 12.2 The interplay between consequential, appropriate, and garbage can decision-making

This study implies that an often found assumption in the organizational NGO literature – stating that NGOs have common characteristics which result in common behavior – does not hold for the two cases studied. Even though we identified some common experiences shared between these two NGOs – such as a tendency towards appropriate decision-making regarding project termination, the law of diminishing alternatives for action, and garbage can decision-making as a last resort – these were opposite to the expectations formulated after the NGO review: garbage can decision-making was not the dominant decision-making mode. However, when garbage can decision-making dynamics occurred these were indeed related to internal disagreement, such as suggested in the NGO literature. Nevertheless, these dynamics were also the result of diminishing alternatives for action, which was related to the situation on the ground. So, it was the combination of external and internal factors that induced garbage can decision-making (see Figure 12.2). External factors were not part of the theoretical framework but proved to have impact in specific circumstances.

By and all, this study resulted in answers to the question how these two non governmental humanitarian aid organizations decided on the initiation, rejection, extension, and termination of project activities. The theoretical framework proved its value: it facilitated the opening of the 'black box of decision-making' and allowed us to explore the relationship between organizational features and decision-making outcomes and processes more precisely. The comparative case study method and the method of maximum variation led to a research design that allowed to compare extreme organizations in order to explore their differences in relation to the theoretical framework, while at the same we could study common patterns in different settings. Together, this enabled us to find an answer to the central question of this study.

Nevertheless, one question remains and that is how to interpret the results of this study of two cases in relation to the existing knowledge about the wider community of humanitarian NGOs and even of the NGO community in general. This question will be addressed in the final chapter of this book.

Chapter 13

A Look Beyond the Horizon: Identifying Steps towards Theoretical Generalization

This study focused on decision-making processes in MSF Holland and ACT Netherlands and tried to answer the question how these processes are related to their organizational features and the outcomes of decision-making. Now we have gained more insight in these three factors, there is some ground to take a look beyond the horizon of this study. A relevant question to ask, after the presentation of the empirical and theoretical conclusions in the previous chapter, is to what extent these conclusions are valid for the larger community of humanitarian NGOs or beyond.

Before an attempt of theoretical generalization can be made, it is important to relate this study to the larger NGO literature. A relevant remark in this respect is that this study is predominantly focused on NGOs as *organizational* entities which is quite a specific focus in NGO research. As stated in Chapter 2, the NGO literature is just as diverse and multidisciplinary as the NGO community itself; for example, NGOs are not only studied as organizational entities but also as social movements, voluntary organizations, non state actors, etc. Because this study had a specific focus on the organizational aspects of humanitarian NGOs, the research results should be treated with caution when attempting to make theoretical generalization to the wider NGO community because other potential valuable perspectives are not taken into account.

Having mentioned this, however, a relevant question remains to what extent such an organizational perspective on humanitarian NGOs could be of help in understanding their behavior and internal dynamics, especially when focusing on NGO diversity. In this chapter we will reflect on the value of this organizational perspective for the study of humanitarian NGOs. Questions for future research will be formulated which could be of assistance in exploring the potential applicability of the research findings for the wider NGO community.

An attempt of theoretical generalization from an organizational perspective

What can we learn from this study about decision-making processes and outcomes in NGOs in general and humanitarian aid NGOs in particular? Previously, we argued that MSF Holland and ACT Netherlands represent two NGO categories often found in humanitarian aid: the operational, specialist, welfare-oriented NGO (MSF) and the non operational, generalist, development-oriented NGO (ACT). We studied the relationship between the NGOs' organizational setup, decision-making processes, and selection outcomes without the interference of variation in the national headquarter context and the level of operation – mentioned as other potential intervening variables in the literature – because these two variables were equal for both NGOs. In summary, the two cases studies led to the following results:

Organizational setup	MSF	ACT
National headquarter's context	The Netherlands	The Netherlands
Level of operation	International	International
Field of expertise • **Orientation** • **Channel of implementation** • **Type of aid**	Humanitarian aid • welfare • operational • specialist, technical (medical)	Humanitarian aid • development • non operational/partners • generalist
	⇩	⇩
Dominant decision-making mode and organizational structure	Logic of Consequence in the Administrative Organization	Logic of Appropriateness In the Institution
Pattern in selection outcomes	Selection and budget reflect humanitarian needs: • few continuous countries of aid • flexible project portfolio: often 'new' countries and projects, whenever budget allows so	Selection and budget reflect commitments and solidarity: • many continuous countries of aid • stable project porfolio: new partners that fit the organizational mandate do not get access easily

Figure 13.1 Comparing MSF's and ACT's similarities and differences (1)

What do the above results imply for the humanitarian aid NGO community as a whole? Since MSF and ACT represent two common categories humanitarian aid NGOs, we can attempt to project the specific research results of ACT and MSF to these two categories of humanitarian aid NGOs (Yin, 1994). This requires us first to formulate questions for future research, before one can organize new research into a more representative group of humanitarian NGOs and draw any definite conclusions.

The research results of this study may be a source of inspiration to formulate questions for future research in the following way: to what extent will humanitarian NGOs that are operational and have a specialist and welfare-oriented approach resemble the administrative organization and show logic of consequence decision-making processes? Will such organizations be characterized by budgets that represent the needs around the world as well as by few continuous aid relations, just as within MSF? Will there be hardly any problems to terminate project activities when the project aims have been met or the need for intervention has decreased?

In addition, we could formulate questions for future research for humanitarian NGOs that work with partners, provide a diverse range of aid (generalist aid), and are development-oriented. Will such organizations resemble Selznick's institution and show appropriate decision-making processes, just as in the case of ACT? Will we find that a large percentage of the budget is spent on countries and partners that receive continuous aid and that new partners do not find access easily? Will relationships hardly be stopped and if so, only after long deliberation processes? Is the budget used as a way to express solidarity?

If it is correct that MSF and ACT in all aspects represent two common categories of NGO in the humanitarian community – something which should be studied further in the future – the relationship between the organizational setup of NGOs and their dominant decision-making pattern could be hypothesized as follows:

Orientation: Welfare vs development

Organizations that have a welfare orientation focus on the shorter term dimension of humanitarian crises and therefore have less chance to become involved in appropriate decision-making dynamics since there is little time to develop commitment and obligations. Organizations that focus on longer term aid in humanitarian crises have more chance to become involved with the people they help. This might induce obligatory behavior and feelings of commitment.

Channel of implementation: Operational vs non operational

Organizations that are operational will have to deal with the distance between headquarters and field. Therefore, more coordination, reporting, and accounting is needed than in organizations that work through partners. Formal coordination mechanisms and policy criteria are needed to facilitate concerted action and control. Hence, in this kind of organizations there might be more chance of features of the administrative organization and a tendency towards consequential decision-making. In organizations that work with partners for a longer period of time, there is more chance of appropriate behavior. Through time, contacts might deepen, friendships evolve, mutual trust develops, and feelings of commitments emerge. This might induce instant decision-making and retrospective reasoning.

Type of aid: Specialist vs generalist

If an organization provides a specialized form of aid, such as medical aid, its employees will predominantly be experts who are trained and raised in a certain tradition. One could argue that expert training often involves aspects of reporting, research, and data collection. Hence, it could be argued that especially in expert aid organizations, the tendency toward consequential decision-making will be more likely.

This study indicates that the presence of a specific decision-making mode is related to internal determinants such as the NGO's organizational structure, which in turn, is connected to the organization's orientation, channel of implementation, and the type of aid the organization provides. So, the dimensions 'specialist aid', a 'welfare orientation', and 'operationality' all three seem to induce an administrative organization and the logic of consequence. The other way around, the dimensions 'generalist aid', a 'development orientation', and 'working through partners' seem to induce the institution and hence the logic of appropriateness. Future research into the larger humanitarian NGO community, and based on the questions formulated above, needs to establish to what extent these hypothesized relationships hold.

Other organizational explanations for NGO diversity

The abovementioned variables are not the only potential organization variables that might explain differences in the behavior of NGO. If we take a closer look at the two NGO selected for this study, we see that they differ on two other internal determinants as well: organization size and degree of institutionalization (see Figure 13.2).

Organizational setup	MSF	ACT
National headquarter's context	The Netherlands	The Netherlands
Level of operation	International	International
Field of expertise	Humanitarian aid	Humanitarian aid
• **Orientation**	• welfare	• development
• **Channel of implementation**	• operational	• non operational
• **Type of aid**	• specialist, technical (medical)	• generalist
Organization size	Large	Small
Degree of institutionalization	Relatively low	Relatively high
⇩	⇩	⇩
Dominant decision-making mode & organizational structure	Logic of Consequence in the Administrative Organization	Logic of Appropriateness in the Institution
Pattern in selection outcomes	Selection and budget reflect humanitarian needs: few continuous countries of aid flexible project portfolio: often 'new' countries and projects, whenever budget allows so	Selection and budget reflect commitments and solidarity: many continuous countries of aid stable project porfolio: new partners that fit the organizational mandate do not get access easily

Figure 13.2 Comparing MSF's and ACT's similarities and differences (2)

To what extent can the differences in selection outcomes between the two NGOs be explained by these two variables? And what does that mean for the findings of this study? In the two cases studied, the dimension 'organization size' and 'degree of institutionalization' coincide with the other dimensions. In other words, in the case of the larger, less instutionalized organization (MSF) all dimensions point to the logic of consequence, while in the case of the smaller, more institutionalized organization (ACT) all dimensions result in the logic of appropriateness. The question is to what extent the two dimensions 'organization size' and 'degree of instutionalization' have influenced our research findings. How could these two dimensions be related to an organization's structure and decision-making modes? This relationship could be hypothesized as follows:

Organization size

A small organization does not require an administrative organization for it to function. Personal contacts and informal coordination will do. Bigger organizations will have more coordination problems, for which the structure of the administrative organization is a solution. Bigger organizations also might feel the pressure towards professionalization and specialization.

Degree of institutionalization

One could argue that the higher the degree of institutionalization in the organization, the more chance decision-making will follow a logic of appropriateness. In less institutionalized organizations, either garbage can or consequential decision-making might be found. If there is lack of consensus on organizational goals, procedures, and work methods, garbage can decision-making will most likely emerge. If agreement over goals and methods exist, but has not yet been engrained in the individual, formal procedures, coordination mechanisms and decision-making criteria are needed to come to concerted action. As the institutionalization process evolves, these goals and norms might become internalized and decision-making can become more instant and rule-based.

The pattern described above urges us to be careful about the generalizations previously suggested. Ideally, the above hypotheses should be explored in humanitarian NGOs that approximately have the same scores on the dimensions 'organization size' and 'degree of institutionalization' in order to determine to what extent these two dimensions have influenced the organizations' structures, decision-making modes, and selection outcomes.

One should also study the impact of these two dimensions in combinations with the previously mentioned variables 'type of aid', 'implementation channel', and 'orientation'. For example, one should also study organizations that are fairly small and hardly institutionalized but that are operational, specialist, and welfare oriented. What kind of decision-making processes and selection outcomes would we expect then? How would such NGOs decide about their projects? We could hypothesize that humanitarian NGOs that are confronted with internal contradictory demands – in terms of size, degree of institutionalization, type of aid, etc. – will resemble the ambiguous, institutionalizing organization, because internal disagreement about the organization's priorities and wished-for structure may exist. Hence, we exptect to find garbage can decision-making dynamics. This hypothesis could be verified by conducting a critical case study of an NGO that is characterized by a mix in scores on the dimensions 'type of aid', 'channel of implementation', 'orientation', 'organization size', and 'degree of institutionalization' (Patton, 1990; Yin, 1994).

Before we conclude that the *internal organizational determinants* 'operationality', 'type of aid', and 'orientation', or 'degree of institutionalization', and 'organization size' explain the presence of certain decision-making modes and structures in an NGO, we need to analyze the impact of *external determinants* as well. This is discussed in the next section.

The impact of external factors: The crisis context and the stakeholders

This study indicates that especially the presence of garbage can decision-making is dependent upon external, contextual constraints. The law of diminishing alternatives *in combination* with a persistent organization to continue working according to the preferred decision-making mode led to garbage can decision-making as a last resort in some of the cases studied. This had to do to with external dimensions in the country of aid provision, as discussed in Chapter 1. We have seen how these circumstances led to a lack of alternatives of actions to chose from. This obstructed both consequential and appropriate decision-making, even though preferred in the organizations studied.

Since we have observed these dynamics in both organizations and they were linked to contextual constraints often experienced by humanitarian aid NGOs, we hypothesize that the law of diminishing alternatives and garbage can decision-making as a last resort might be a more common phenomenon experienced by humanitarian aid providers. A future relevant research question would be if other humanitarian NGOs that face limited alternatives as well as internal pressure to follow the preferred decision-making mode will also experience garbage can decision-making. The question then is to what extent humanitarian aid NGOs have an inclination to continue to work according to their preferred decision-making mode and to what extent these NGOs are influenced by external constraints, both in the headquarters'country and in the project country. In other words, to what extent is the law of diminishing alternatives for action a coincidental or a general phenomenon in humanitarian aid NGOs?

The crisis context

Before we can conclude that the law of diminishing alternatives for action can be expected to be a general phenomenon in humanitarian aid NGOs, we need to analyze the situation in the field. The more politicized the humanitarian crisis is in which the NGO intervenes, the more it is expected that the contextual constraints related to access, security, and misuse of aid will be present. In addition, we expect that the more media attention a humanitarian crisis receives, the more humanitarian organizations will be present, thereby resulting in diminishing alternatives for action.

The stakeholders

In addition to the crisis context, we need to analyze the situation in the headquarters' national context. What are the wishes and demands of the donors of the NGO? What do the media ask for and how does the public think about the NGO? How strong is the competition with other NGOs? What the internal decision-making processes and selection outcomes look like might be dependent upon the power constellation in the external environment. In such circumstances, the stakeholder demands might be of more influence than the internal organizational dynamics. A stakeholder analysis is therefore an appropriate analytical approach to study what has caused the presence of a specific decision-making mode.

We hypothesize that the presence of garbage can decision-making in an organization might also be the result of multiple stakeholders that have contradicting demands. We expect that NGOs that experience contradicting demands from their environment will try to suit all these demands simultaneously (at least, if there is not one dominant stakeholder) and hence, a mix of decision-making dynamics will occur. There may be a lack of agreement on the preferred decision-making mode, and hence, garbage can decision-making will occur. Hence, the occurence of garbage can decision-making does not necessarily mean that the organization is confronted with diminishing alternatives for action.

In this study we have not gained much insight into the role and influence of stakeholders. This might mean two things: 1) these external dimensions did not matter as much as is often thought; or 2) the research methodology and methods of data collection have not been able to bring this dimension out into the open. It is difficult to judge which of the two explanations holds for this study. Most probably, it is a mix of both.[1] Overall, we have not found strong evidence for the power of the media, competition, or donor driven action in this study. This leads to the conclusion that this kind of external constraints did not play a large role in the decision-making process about starting, ending, rejecting and extending project activities in the cases studied for this research.

One explanation of this lack of stakeholder influence might be that the stakeholders of MSF and ACT all want the same. In the case of MSF and ACT these demands might not have been contradictory, they might have been either instrumental or political in character. For other NGOs the situation might be different. Nevertheless, we wonder whether ACT and MSF are surrounded by a group of unified, coherent stakeholders, since ACT and MSF are both not simply instrumental actors (service providers) or solely political actors. They both engage in political activities, such as advocacy and lobbying, as well as in service provision. Another explanation might be that ACT and MSF have been effective in creating a buffer to their environment, which allows them to follow their own preferred decision-making mode (Pfeffer &

Salancik, 1978; Oliver, 1991). For example, organizations are capable of decoupling potential contradicting activities as a way to obtain the wishes of their stakeholders simultaneously (Meyer & Rowan, 1977; Oliver, 1991). By means of decoupling the core of the organization – i.e. the decision-making processes about and implementation of project activities – can be protected from stakeholder's wishes. Hence, the organization can pursue their preferred decision-making mode. A final explanation might be that ACT and MSF are not very much dependent upon their external stakeholders or that their stakeholders are quite dispersed which prevents them from having any influence (Hasenfeld, 1983).

Future research into these matters should pay attention to the use and strengths of buffering strategies of humanitarian aid NGOs in order to establish if and how stakeholders influence the internal decision-making dynamics in NGOs.

Combining internal and external determinants of organizational decision-making

The focus on the internal organization in this study has resulted in more concrete hypotheses about the interplay between various organizational dimensions of humanitarian aid NGOs as well as between the internal organization and the organization's environment. These dimensions are summarized in Table 13.1.

Table 13.1   Combining internal and external determinants of organizational decision-making

---

Internal determinants

1. the internal organizational set up in terms of
    a.   the type of aid: specialist vs generalist
    b.   the orientation: development vs welfare (kunnen ook andere dimensies zijn)
    c.   the channel of implementation: operationality or partners as well as
    d.   the organization's size
    e.   the degree of institutionalization as well as
    f.   the relationship between these dimensions: do they coincide or do they conflict?
2. the buffer strategies and capabilities of the organization

External determinants

3. the demands and power of the organization's stakeholders (contradictory or not, instrumental and/or political, dispersed or not)
4. the characteristics of the humanitarian crises the NGO
   is involved in (highly politicized or not)

We hypothesize that the presence of a specific decision-making mode in a humanitarian aid NGO is related to a combination of internal as well as to external determinants. Hence, an organization can only have a coherent decision-making mode – such as the logic of consequence or appropriateness – if the organization's internal determinants coincide with the external determinants, or the organization has been able to buffer contradicting external determinants from its internal determinants.

Garbage can decision-making occurs when the internal and external demands do not coincide. We have identified three sources of garbage can decision-making. First, we expect garbage can decision-making to happen in organizations that have a mixed score on organizational dimensions such as the channel of aid, orientation, the type of aid, etc. In these organizations we expect to find evidence of the ambiguous, institutionalizing organization. Second, we hypothesized that garbage can decision-making will also occur in organizations that are confronted with multiple stakeholders that have contradictory demands while at the same time the organization is unable to create a buffer to these external demands. Third, organizations that resembled Simon's administrative organization or Selznick's institution could also be characterized by garbage can decision-making because of the law of diminishing alternatives for action in combination with a persistence to continue following the preferred decision-making mode (i.e. consequential or appropriate decision-making).

Exploring directions for future research in the broader NGO community

Now we have discussed the potentional relevance of the research findings of this study of two specific humanitarian aid NGOs for the wider humanitarian aid NGO community, the question arises whether this study may also have wider implications for NGOs that operate in other countries and fields of expertise as well as on other levels of operation and with a different orientation. This urges us to be even more cautious because of the wide range of NGO activities and tasks.

However, the two NGO categories constructed for this study and the research results connected to these two categories might serve as a source of inspiration for other organizational studies into the wider NGO community. The dimensions used to construct these categories may be helpful to guide our thinking about differences in decision-making characteristics of various NGO categries. For example, one could explore the differences between specialist and generalist or operational and non-operational NGOs in other fields of expertise, such as the environment or human rights, while taking into account their organization size and degree of institutionalization.

The relevance of the results of this study for NGOs that have different orientations, such as research, networking, or development education (Vakil, 1997) cannot be determined beforehand. This study implies that the dimension 'orientation' (welfare vs development) within a shared field of expertise (humanitarian aid) may be quite defining when understanding diversity in NGO behavior. Hence, further study should establish if the distinctions used in this study may have wider relevance.

Another direction to explore is to what extent the sources of garbage can decision-making identified in this study can be found in NGOs that have different fields of expertise and orientations. We could hypothesize that NGOs that experience mixed scores on the organizational dimensions or that are confronted with contradicting external demands – and that are unable to buffer these – will be characterized by features of the ambiguous, institutionalizing organization and garbage can decision-making. We also may formulate an expectation to find garbage can decision-making in organizations that are confronted with the law of diminishing alternatives of action, especially if NGOs persist in following their preferred decision-making mode while the context does not allow such a mode to work properly. Hence, the question is if the law of diminishing alternatives could be found in NGOs that work in other fields of expertise or orientations, even though the contextual constraints might differ. It must be said, however, that the field of humanitarian aid provision might be so specific that this phenomenon of diminishing alternatives for action might be unique to this specific field of expertise. Further research has to point out whether this third source of garbage can decision-making is specific to humanitarian aid only or not.

A final direction for future research is to study to what extent the above conclusions have value for NGOs that operate in other countries than The Netherlands. The NGOs of this study were Dutch, although both NGOs were also part of a large international network and operated on the international level. The question is to what extent these two NGOs show similarites with other 'Western' or even 'non-Western' NGO, or whether specific national or cultural differences are of importance in understanding differences in NGO behavior. In other words, to what extent are the dimensions orientation, type of aid, organization size, etc, 'neutral'or culturally defined organizational features?

In short, one needs to remain cautious when connecting the internal and external determinants of organizational decision-making (and the degree to which they coincide) as identified in this study to the wider NGO community.

Concluding remarks

We started this study with the question how to explain diversity in NGO behavior, even though they operate in the same national headquarter context and in the same field of expertise. Current NGO research suggests that NGOs are a coherent group of actors, characterized by loosely coupled structures and internal conflict. This study has shown that this assumption is incorrect for the two humanitarian aid NGOs of this study, which represent two important categories of humanitarian aid NGOs. This study brought evidence to the fore in favor of the 'academic hunch' found in NGO research that the organizational setup of NGOs is related to their decision-making processes and decision-making outcomes. In this final chapter, we made an attempt to specify this 'hunch' by formulating more precise hypotheses, distinguishing between internal and external determinants of humanitarian aid NGO decision-making practices. We have explored if and how the insights gained from this study may be of relevance to the wider NGO community. We hope that this study will generate more systematic organizational research into the internal dynamics of this very relevant and interesting category of organizations of which we do so little.

Notes

1   On the one hand, it could be that the data sources did not reveal much about the impact of external factors, such as the role of the media, since it is not a formal reason to go somewhere. Hence, people might not use 'media arguments' in files or interviews. In addition, the field work period might have been too short to uncover the influence of the media and other contraints from the home country through the observation of decision-making moments. Since we did not sit in very often, we continued to be a strange face in the group, which might have prevented that people brought these kind of arguments up.

On the other hand, there were some (though little) indications that media pressure led to the decision to enter a country, in which later appeared that the needs were not as high as thought or where others were already covering the area. This then induced garbage can decision-making.

Epilogue

Complexity Reduction through Decision Making: Intended and Unintended Consequences in Humanitarian Aid

This study has given us a glimpse behind the scenes of humanitarian aid provision by two Dutch NGOs. The results of this study are of interest to various groups of readers. This book is informative for those who know little about the internal dynamics of humanitarian aid NGOs. For academics, the book is interesting to read because it connects well-known literature on organizational decision-making to the rather unfamiliar field of humanitarian aid operations. Besides, the study explores the relationship between decision-making processes, and organizational structures, theoretically and empirically. Donors, be they private or public, have the opportunity to learn more about the organizations they sponsor and support.

A fourth and very relevant group of readers involves the humanitarian aid NGOs themselves. For this group, probably little news is to be found in this book. They know their own work methods, decision-making processes and the context they work in. They know their fellow NGOs and what makes them different. To these organizations, this book might be one of those academic exercises that state the obvious. There is hardly any new insight to be gained from, since the most important question of interest to practitioners – and donors as well - is not answered in this book: how should we judge decision-making processes in humanitarian aid NGOs? Are they good or bad? Should they be improved and if so, can they be improved? This question has not been the heart of this study.

In the introduction chapter of this book, we explicitly stated that this was not an evaluation of the performance of humanitarian aid NGOs. Before we can evaluate, we need to know more about the internal work processes of these organizations, we argued. Since this study was not organized to be evaluative, evaluative remarks are hard to make in a responsible, academic way. That is why we did not do it.

However, the question remains: what results of this study could be relevant to practitioners in the field? What have we gained from studying decision-making processes in humanitarian aid organizations from the perspectives of the logic of consequence, appropriateness, and the garbage can? What is the use of knowing what the dominant and secondary mode of decision-making is in an NGO? We would argue the following: knowing the dominant and secondary decision-making patterns in your organization gives you clues about the strengths and weaknesses of your organization's decision-making capacities. In the remainder of this epilogue we explore how one could look at the results of this study and what their value to practitioners might be, with the reservations made in the previous chapter in mind.

Reducing complexity through decision-making processes

In the introductary chapter of this book, it was argued that the field of humanitarian aid provision is often approached in a normative way. In the theoretical chapter of this book, we concluded that the logic of consequence is often evaluated to be the 'best' decision-making method to apply. Respondents often talked about organizational decision-making processes in terms of 'good' or 'bad'. The logic of consequence was often perceived to be the 'right' way of deciding. Any deviation from an ideal-typical consequential decision-making process was considered to be 'wrong'.

We do not have a normative stand on what decision-making logic is good or bad to apply while deciding on humanitarian aid activities or other issues. What we want to do is to present an alternative view on the functioning of these three decision-making logics in the setting of humanitarian aid provision.

What is so striking in this study is that the decision-making processes in both NGOs were fairly structured, while the context in which the decisions need to be taken are so complex, uncertain, and sometimes chaotic. In our view, this is no coincidence. Both the logic of consequence and the logic of appropriateness could be seen as complexity reducing mechanisms that helped these two NGOs grapple with the multifaceted reality of humanitarian aid provision. This study implies that the logic of consequence and the logic of appropriateness proved to be helpful complexity reducing mechanisms to accomplish this. In other words, the logic of consequence is not better than the logic of appropriateness, it is just a different way of dealing with complexities.

Complexity reduction through consequentionalization

MSF Holland's decision-making processes were characterized by mostly consequential decision-making elements. This can be understood as an attempt to rationalize and structure the complex context of their work. MSF Holland tried to grasp these complexities by collecting and analyzing information with help of experts. Goal maximization, by establishing those areas most in need and the most effective interventions possible, is another indicator for their attempt to deal with a sometimes chaotic work situation.

MSF Holland dealt with the complexities of their work by means of numbers, figures, and methods of analysis. By doing this, the organization simplified its operations to a certain extent in order to cope with the world they work in. Thinking in morbidity and mortality rates, nutritional data, and prevalence rates, is a way to think in a more distant way about who needs what aid most. It means that some of the stressing aspects of humanitarian crisis are reduced to facts and figures. And even if that is done, decision-making is still difficult, since there remains more than enough to disagree, discuss and negotiate about, as we saw in Chapters 7 and 8.

Hence, the use of the logic of consequence within MSF Holland can be looked at as a way to create distance to deal with the complexities of the humanitarian aid context. Consequentionalizing the complexity and severity of humanitarian crises is a way of doing this. If the organization did not do this, it would may have experienced difficulties to make a selection out of all potential interventions. This could, in the end, jeopardize the effectiveness of the organization and hence ultimately its legitimacy and the future survival of the organization.

Complexity reduction through blood ties

ACT Netherlands tried to deal with the same complex context by relying on their family ties. These family ties were at one time developed by means of consequential decision-making processes, but once in the family, appropriateness took over the dynamics of decision-making. The slogan of the organization seemed to be 'once a family member, always a family member'. A family member was trusted and treated with respect. Family commitments resulted in obligatory behavior and long periods of investing in the partners, even if projects were really problematic. A partner would only be excluded from the family after huge misbehavior was proven and could not be ignored anymore.

By doing this, ACT reduced the complexities of their work by limiting their work to trustworthy partner organizations. ACT did not itself deal with all the facts and figures of the context their partners worked in, but required their partners to describe the reality in the form of project proposals. These proposals did not need to be very detailed, since the trustworthiness of the family member had already been proven and therefore automatic approval could follow. In addition, proposals of strangers were easily put aside because they were not part of the family. In a situation of heavy work load, little time, and too much to do, appropriate decision-making was a helpful mechanism for the ACT project officer to make swift decisions about very complex matters.

Complexity reduction through coincidence?

The logic of the garbage can is often – by its name alone – disregarded as a useful or 'good' decision-making method. However, one could wonder whether garbage can decision-making might be just as useful as a complexity reducing mechanism as the logic of consequence and the logic of appropriateness.

Garbage can decision-making reduces complexity because it is the solution that defines the search for problems, and not the other way around as is the case in consequential decision-making. This inverse rationality in decision-making might help an organization to reduce the complexities of the context they work in. For example, it might be very difficult to establish the needs for humanitarian intervention or the trustworthiness of partner organizations. Information might not be available and when it is, it might be unreliable, incomplete, or contradicting. One option could be not to go. Hence, external pressure might be so strong, that the organization cannot choose this option. Another option could then be to diminish the costs of information collection and to simply decide to go somewhere and see for yourself whether the solutions the organization has to offer can be matched with the problems in the country. If this is the case, a project can be initiated. If it is not the case, the organization can decide to pull out. One difficult question will remain, however, and that is how long the search for problems is continued before one decides to pull out of a country.

Intended and unintended consequences of complexity reduction

If one considers the logics of consequence, appropriateness, and the garbage can as complexity reducing mechanisms, the question becomes evident what the consequences of this complexity reduction will be. Reducing complexity implies that some parts of reality will be simplified or ignored.

Each logic simplifies and ignores (parts of) reality in its own way. This can create various intended and unintended consequences (Merton, 1957; Sieber, 1981). In the following paragraphs we will discuss some of these consequences per logic for the case of humanitarian aid provision. However, before we can discuss the unintended consequences of these logics, we need to formulate what the intended consequences of humanitarian aid provision are. In general, the world expects humanitarian aid provision to be fast, flexible, effective (relieves the suffering), efficient (is affordable), accountable, appropriate, and transparent. Let us see what that means for the three logics of decision-making. To be clear, the intended and unintended consequences we describe below are not the result of the empirical research done in the two NGOs. They are the result of a 'thought experiment'.

The pitfall of delay, goal displacement, and rational myths

If an NGO has a dominant decision-making mode that resembles the logic of consequence to a large extent, decision-making will be effective and efficient if you have the time and expertise to collect information and alternatives to decide on. Decision making will be swift and productive if the NGO members agree on the organizational goals and mandate. This trust in information and cost-benefit analysis of alternatives of action is both a strength and a weakness of this decision-making mode.

On the one hand, it ensures a transparent and well-considered deliberation process, which guarantees accountability. On the other hand: sometimes it is very hard to collect sufficient and reliable information in humanitarian crises, especially when there is a serious time constraint. Contradictory evidence may complicate the analysis of data tremendously. Sometimes it is difficult to collect any information at all. If information is needed before a decision is taken, data collection can thus become very expensive and time-consuming and hence very inefficient. If there are information problems, the fact finding process might slow down the decision-making process. This might also happen because NGO members can disagree about the interpretation of the information collected; they then need time to find consensus. Hence, the organization runs the risk of being too late all the time. This might mean that either the emergency is getting worse (or already over ...), while the NGO is still trying to decide. Or other humanitarian aid agencies have already stepped in and the momentum has been missed.

In addition, if consequential decision-making takes place in an 'administrative organization', there is the risk of goal displacement (Merton, 1957). A reporting and monitoring culture adds to the accountability and transparency of the organization's actions, but also runs the danger of becoming a goal in itself. Hence, the field might be more focused on filling in the forms and doing the statistics than on doing the real job.

Another category of goal displacement can be the creation of so-called 'rational myths' (Meyer & Rowan, 1977). NGO employees might not sincerely use the logic of consequence to come to decisions, but use it to rationalize their actions with the benefit of hindsight, after projects have been launched. In other words, the transparency and accountability can be fake, a result of manipulated reality. Too much emphasis on facts and numbers has the danger of creating an illusion of certainty (Stone, 1997). This make-believe world of certainty might fit the wishes of the donors and the donating public and therefore guarantee the survival of the organization (don't we all trust organizations with a consequential work method more than one without?). Nevertheless, it makes one wonder whether this increases the flexibility and effectiveness of aid provision activities. Holding up the rational myth demands a lot of energy, which could instead be directed to the people in need.

In summary, a striving for maximizing behavior might lead to exactly the opposite, i.e. delay and extra costs, while the purpose of accountable and transparent action induces goal displacement and rational myths. This all can obstruct fast, flexible, effective, and efficient action.

The pitfall of mismatch, paralysis, and entrapment

If decision-making processes in an NGO resemble the logic of appropriateness, decision-making processes will work effectively if the organization has former experiences and guiding rules, so that employees can match the situation to a rule. Relying on former experiences and developing guiding rules are very effective and efficient mechanisms. They promote swift action, especially when NGOs work with partners. When there is a crisis in an area of a well-trusted partner you only have to transfer some money and that's it.

However, there are risks involved in doing this. Employees can make a mismatch between the situation at hand and the rule to apply (Reason, 1990), initiating the wrong course of action. Another potential unintended consequence is that crises might occur in areas where the NGO is inexperienced, for example, because they do not have a partner working there. Or, the situation at hand is new, and no applicable rule is available. Then the organization runs the risks of becoming paralyzed since they have no options for action: there are no partners to rely on or no rules to apply. Hence, the organization cannot respond to the needs and no effective, swift, and efficient aid operation can be launched. So, the logic of appropriateness inhibits the danger of being an inflexible decision-making mode. People do not know what to do if the new situation cannot be matched to old situations and existing rules for action.

A third problem might arise because of obligatory action and feelings of commitment. If an NGO has a long-lasting partner, there is a risk of entrapment (Otten, 2000), meaning that there might be legitimate reasons to stop working with a partner, but feelings of commitment prevent this from happening. It might occur that partners take advantage of the trust they receive from the NGO and once this is discovered, it might be difficult to end the relationship. Or, the need for intervention has disappeared, but the ties of friendship are so strong that the NGO keeps on transferring funds to its partner. The longer the NGO is involved with such a partner, the more difficult it is to terminate the relationship. Hence, the NGO is supporting an ineffective and inefficient NGO when compared to the organization's mandate. These long-lasting relationships might also prevent potential new and effective partners from entering 'the family'. Since NGOs as a rule have limited budgets, there is little room for new partners in new areas if most of the budget is spent on 'old friends'.

In summary, the logic of appropriateness might induce mismatches between situations and rules, paralysis when unfamiliar situations occur, and entrapment because of obligatory behavior. This might lead to ineffective, inefficient, inflexible, and questionable aid provision.

The pitfall of backing the wrong horse

If garbage can decision-making is the dominant decision-making mode in an organization, this works well if the organization is able to couple its solutions (its own work methods and mandates) to the right problems (humanitarian crises). This inverse rationality can be very effective and efficient because it requires less time for information collection than in the consequential aid NGO and is more flexible than the appropriate aid NGO.

But deciding in this manner also involves an element of gambling. In order to discover whether your solution matches the problem you need to go to the country and see for yourself. There is a chance that the first gamble to go was wrong and there is no need to intervene. Then the NGO already has spent some money in going there and therefore might be inclined to stay a little bit longer to search for relevant problems. This might become a 'tour' around the country, which is another form of entrapment, since the longer the NGO is in the country without finding matching problems, the more it might put its energy in finding one. The NGO might start looking for a needle in a haystack. If this needle cannot be found, the NGO has nothing else to do than return to the home country after spending lots of money on its search process and the risk of losing face. Hence, garbage can decision-making can result in expensive and inefficient search processes that never result in action, which can seriously compromise the organization's credibility.

Weighing pitfalls

The 'thought experiment' described above shows that each logic of decision-making has its own potential intended and unintended consequences. In a way, this short discussion of unintended consequences might help NGOs to think over their own pitfalls in aid provision. Pitfalls can never be prevented. Unintended consequences are part of the deal. As long as the dominant decision-making mode does not create the above-mentioned pitfalls too often, the strengths can outweigh the weaknesses.

Nevertheless, being aware of one's pitfalls and discussing them in the organization, gives insight in the organization's strengths and weaknesses. Just knowing them might facilitate decision-making in instances that these pitfalls occur (for example, an NGO spends a lot of time collecting information about a crisis; an NGO keeps on funding a partner in a situation in which the need to intervene has disappeared; or an NGO keeps on looking for a problem that matches its solution). These thoughts might help to stimulate discussion and facilitate learning. If there is a contribution that we can make on a more practical level of aid provision, it is this one.

'Dismoralizing' the good Samaritans

For this book, we deliberately chose to study humanitarian aid provision outside its moral context. We argued that it was time to study the actions of humanitarian aid agencies with the idea in mind that the context they work in is very complex. Humanitarian aid provision is almost an impossible job to fulfill effectively and efficiently. This does not mean that we judge humanitarian aid provision to be ineffective and inefficient. We simply argue that the conditions for successful aid provision are limited. We therefore should not expect that aid agencies are always successful in their work. There are many constraints.

This study describes how difficult it is to make decisions about humanitarian aid interventions. Consequently, we should keep the following things in mind when evaluating the performance of the humanitarian aid community. First, we have to take into account the conditions these organizations have to work in, before we come to harsh conclusions. We plead for evaluating the humanitarian aid sector on its own merits, just like any other policy program, such as upholding a medical system in our own country. We find it striking that humanitarian aid projects are sometimes judged quite harshly, while these organizations work in extreme difficult circumstances. If we are not able to solve our national problems – such as medical care, crime and unemployment – how can people expect humanitarian aid providers to do better? Especially, since our national context is so much simpler, more structured, and well-organized, compared to the context of humanitarian aid provision?

Second, we should not forget that we are all part of the humanitarian aid community, responding to dramatic news flashes, donating money, formulating criteria for donor funding, and evaluating the performance of aid providers. We partially make up the organizational constraints mentioned earlier. In addition, many of us uphold the idea that consequential decision-making is the only 'right' way to decide. One might wonder whether this will always result in effective and efficient decisions. So, part of the behavior of and decisions by these organizations are the result of our own expectations and actions.

This is not a plea for a placid attitude towards the performance of humanitarian aid agencies. On the contrary, a critical attitude remains needed, just as it is for our national policies. However, it should be done realistically and fairly ('what's sauce for the goose is sauce for the gander'). In this book we tried to provide an in-depth view into the internal dynamics of humanitarian aid NGOs in their decision-making regarding where to go and what to do, as an attempt to present a realistic and fair picture of the world of humanitarian aid provision. We sincerely hope that more will follow.

Research Methodology, Data Collection, and Operationalization

In this appendix, I describe the research methods used for this study, as well as issues concerning data collection and operationalization. This appendix serves as a means to open up the 'black box' of decision-making with regard to my own research process and is aimed to make the research process of this study transparent. First, I discuss the comparative case study method used for this study, followed by a discussion of the data collection process. Then I discuss the attempt to triangulate research methods and its consequences for the reliability and validity of this study. I end this appendix by presenting an operationalization of the three decision-making modes.

The comparative case study method

This study is an example of the comparative case study method. The choice for the case study method stems from the exploratory character of this study.

Exploring decision-making with help of theory

Since little is known about the internal operations of humanitarian aid NGOs, I could not construct a thorough theoretical framework that, in advance, could lead to the formulation of hypotheses and expectations about research results. This, however does not mean that this study is not guided by theory. I have developed a theoretical framework that has an heuristic function and has guided the data collection process. This theoretical framework focuses on the character of decision-making processes and their relation to the organizational structure. Where the three logics of decision-making help to understand *how* decision-making processes work and how they relate to decision outcomes, the relation with the organizational structure might help to understand *why* the processes worked the way they worked. In that sense, this study combines ambitions of exploration with some attempts of explanation. In other words, this study falls within the category of the 'interpretative' (Lijphart 1971) or 'disciplined-configurative' case study (Eckstein (1975) in Kaarbo & Beasly, 1999) since 'theory is used to direct the examination', but 'although there maybe some feedback from the case to theory ... the focus is still mainly on the case' (Kaarbo & Beasly, 1999).

The theoretical framework chosen for this study combines three logics of decision-making in order to see whether they provide a useful heuristic instrument to study decision-making empirically, which has not often been done. The feedback on the theory in this study therefore focuses on the usefulness of the logics for empirical research. Besides, I reflected on the presumed relationship between organizational decision-making processes and organizational structures in these three logics.

Structured, focused comparison of decision occasions

The study meets the requirements of a 'structured, focused comparison' to a large extent (George & McKeown, 1985). It is focused because I have defined a specific class of events that will be studied: decisions regarding the initiation, rejection, extensions, and termination of project activities. I have collected data on all these four decision categories.

It is structured because I have studied this class of events with help of a limited set of independent variables, i.e. the characteristics of the organizational decision-making process and the organizational structure. This theoretical framework has guided all observations in the study. Although I chose to focus on the relation between decisions, decision-making processes, and organizational structure, this does not mean that I have not been sensitive to other potential explanatory variables, such as contextual factors, but they have not been the point of departure for this research.

It is comparative because I compare two organizations and their decision-making processes and 'cases within cases'. I have studied decision-making processes by collecting data on so-called 'decision occasions' (Paige, 1968; Stern & Sundelius, 2002). Decision occasions are 'those points in the decision process when there is a felt need by those involved to take action, even if the action is the choice to do nothing or to search for more information' (Hermann, 2002:5). Concerning the research question of this study, relevant decisions occasions are those decisions about the initiation, rejection, termination, and extension of project activities. The collection of information on a number of decision occasions led to numerous (decision) cases within the cases (the organizations), which could be analyzed and compared.

Pattern matching and process tracing

I analyzed these decision occasions by comparing the predicted patterns of decision-making and organizational characteristics in the theoretical framework with the patterns found in the cases (Kaarbo & Beasly, 1999). I also studied those instances that did not match the predicted patterns, for example, those decision-making processes that were not related to the organizational setting as predicted in the theoretical framework. I have attempted to establish a dominant decision-making pattern in each organization and described to what extent this pattern resembled any of the three logics (if at all). I separately studied and described those instances that did not match the predicted pattern and described them as secondary decision-making patterns.

One particular form of pattern matching is *process tracing*. George and McKeown (1985) argue that *process tracing* is a useful way to study organizational decision-making, because it helps to reconstruct decision-making processes throughout time by focussing on the stimuli of decision-making, the process that leads to a decision, the behavior that then occurs, and the impact of various institutional arrangements and other factors on attention and behavior. In other words, it is a way to open the black box of decision-making. Process tracing

> involves both an attempt to reconstruct actors' definitions of the situation and an attempt to develop a theory of action. The framework within which actors' perceptions and actions are described is given by the researcher (George & McKeown, 1985:35).

In this study, the three logics of decision-making and the characteristics of the organizational structure provide this framework in which the actors' perceptions and actions are described.

The data collection process

The data of this study were collected by means of qualitative interviews, document analysis, and observation during a two month field work period in each of the organization's headquarters and a three week visit to an African country in which both organizations were providing humanitarian aid. During this visit I conducted interviews, studied documents, observed decision-making in action, and visited project sites.

Fieldwork at the headquarters

At the headquarters of both organizations, I conducted two categories of interviews. First, I conducted background interviews that provided general background information about the organization's history, structures, and work methods. I conducted two of these background interviews with ACT Netherlands employees and nine with MSF Holland employees. Second, I conducted interviews that focused on decision occasions. I collected 90 MSF decision occasions and 39 ACT decision occasions.

I used a qualitative method for the interviews about decision occasions and the processes that led to them (Weiss, 1994). The questions asked in the interviews were fairly open. I asked the respondents to talk about examples of the various decision categories mentioned above and the processes that led to them as detailed as possible. In addition, I asked for 'business as usual decisions' and decisions that, in their view, clearly deviated from the organization's usual way of working. By asking them for typical and a-typical cases, I gained more insight in what was perceived to be 'normal' and 'abnormal' decision-making in the organization.

Whenever possible, I taped the interviews. Within ACT, I could tape all the interviews. However, within MSF, six interviews were not taped because some respondents did not feel comfortable having their interview taped or the context in which the interview was held did not allow for the taping of the interview (for example, during lunch in a busy cafeteria or in a shared office). Part of the interviews were in Dutch and others in English. In the previous chapters, some quotes were therefore translated from Dutch to English.

Even though the interviews were taped, I always took additional notes. These notes were the point of departure for the analysis of the data, but I did a check on the reliability of my notes by comparing fragments of the interviews to my notes. Even though I did not write down the literal wording of the respondents, the tenor of the notes matched the literal wording on tape. For example, all the quotes mentioned in the following chapters were checked on tape (whenever available). I only had to remove one quote because the tenor of my notes differed from the literal wording on the tape.

We selected employees for the interviews on decision occiasions who were directly involved in decision-making processes concerning the initiation, termination, rejection, and extension of project activities (see Figure 4.2). I tried to interview employees from various hierarchical layers in the organization: from the frontline officer in direct contact with the target population to the directors at the headquarters. Within MSF Holland, I interviewed 18 employees at the headquarters about decision occasions. Ten of them actually worked in the field but happened to be in the country because of the yearly 'Co-days' (MSF coordination meetings). Within ACT Netherlands, I interviewed the head of the department and all ACT Netherlands project officers responsible for project decision-making.

	ACT Netherlands	MSF Holland
Headquarters	Project officers (6, of whom 4 were interviewed twice)	Operational Directors (4) Health advisors (2) Humanitarian affairs/former country manager Emergency Desk member
Field	–	Country managers (7) Medical coordinators (3)

Figure A.1 Respondents interviewed in the fieldwork period at the headquarters

The document analysis consisted of a study of general documents, such as annual plans, annual reports, policy papers, guidelines, manuals, and minutes of meetings. When available, I studied the project files pertaining to the examples mentioned by informants in the interviews. At most, the files consisted of exploratory mission reports, project proposals, progress and monitoring reports, trip reports, situation reports, evaluations, and email correspondence. At least, they consisted of project proposals and formal progress reports (see also the section on the quality and quantity of the data). Nine very informative MSF country files – containing a wide variety of documents, offering a chronological picture of decisions regarding various projects – were used for the case descriptions in the proceeding chapters. These nine files contained information about 38 decision occasions. The files of six partners – which comprised information on different decision categories in a period of one or more years – were used for the case descriptions in the ACT chapters.

I observed decision-making moments in headquarters whenever possible. Within ACT Netherlands, I was present at six weekly meetings in which project proposals were discussed. Within MSF Holland, I was able to sit in at Operational Support meetings five times, as well as at two MT meetings.

Data collection in the field

During my visit to the field I also conducted interviews, analyzed documents, and observed decision-making moments. I held qualitative interviews with the MSF country manager of the country visited and the medical coordinator, both members of the country management team. During a stopover on my way home I was able to collect some extra data from another MSF team by interviewing the country manager, the logistical coordinator, and two project managers from a MSF team.[1] Within the ACT office, I interviewed the ACT representative (twice) and his project manager. In these interviews, I predominantly focused on decision occasions, although more general background topics were also discussed.

In the field, I was not able to sit in at MSF Holland meetings, due to time constraints and the fact that MSF Holland was preparing to leave the country. However, the project files were so full of information that I was able to reconstruct the decision-making process concerning this project country, based on the documentation and the results of the interviews held with the MSF team members. Within ACT, I sat in at a staff meeting within the ACT Netherlands liaison office and three meetings between ACT and other members of the humanitarian aid community. I studied the project files of all current projects (10) and visited three ACT project sites in the country.

The data collected in the field served as input for the MSF case presented in Chapter 7 (postwar intervention in Africa) and the ACT case in Chapter 10, in the section 'Working without alternatives for action: a case'.

Quality and quantity of the data collected

When comparing the results of the data collection phase, there are some differences in the quantity and quality of the data collected within MSF and ACT. Overall, I was able to collect more data within MSF by means of interviews and document analysis, while I could collect more observation data within ACT.

I conducted more interviews within MSF than within ACT. However, I was not able to interview all relevant MSF staff members. Since ACT is a smaller organization, there were fewer employees to interview. Nevertheless, I interviewed all employees in ACT, except one project officer who had just started his job at ACT very recently. In order to enlarge my data set, I used interviews that I had conducted in the pilot phase of the study in 1999, resulting in a total of 11 interviews. Four employees were interviewed twice.

The MSF files also comprised more information than the ACT files. MSF files often contained formal documents (project proposal, quarterly reports, reports of field visits, evaluation reports, etc) as well as parts of email communication between headquarters and field. ACT files predominantly consisted of a (brief) project proposal, some monitoring reports, and a bit of communication between headquarters and field. Some files did not contain more than a project document. This observation in itself indicates that MSF values filing and reporting more than ACT (which fits the idea of the administrative organization).

On the other hand, I was able to observe more decision-making moments within ACT than within MSF. Within ACT Netherlands I had unrestricted access to weekly and bilateral meetings. Moreover, I had a desk in the office in which five of the seven project officers had their workplace. This gave me the unique opportunity to follow decision-making on the spot for two months in a row. Within MSF, it was not possible to follow decision-making processes so closely. My desk was in the library, for example, which made it more difficult to observe spontaneous decision-making moments. Although I had unrestricted access to expert meetings, I did not have the same arrangement for the highest decision-making level in the organization. In two months time, I sat in at two management team meetings. This created some difficulties in my attempts to understand decisions taken at the management team level, even though I interviewed all MT members about decision-making processes in the organization.

During the field research, it became evident that email is an important communication channel with the field in both organizations. Unfortunately, it was exactly this communication channel that I had hardly any access to. The main reason for this is that email is not collected and stored centrally in these organization. If I had wanted to get access, I would have had to ask all relevant actors to allow me to access their email. This was an impossible job and for privacy reasons not very proper to ask.

A final comment should be made about the field visit. The field visit was an eye-opener to me in various ways. Experiencing part of the reality of the humanitarian aid worker, if only for such a short time as I did, was most valuable and necessary for the interpretation process of the data collected. In addition to this, I found an MSF file of practically all email communication between headquarters and the field in this particular country, which had been missing during my fieldwork at the headquarters. This file not only helped me understand the decision-making dynamics of this specific country, but also contextualized email communication I found in the files of other project countries. In other words, once I had seen the complete communication picture for one file, I felt I could better interpret incomplete files. Within ACT, the project files were not extensive and often lacked information relevant for this research. The field trips and visits to meetings within the humanitarian aid community compensated for the lack of documents to a large extent.

Attempts at triangulation: Reliability and validity issues

The original research strategy of this study was to triangulate interview material with document analysis and observation moments as much as possible. The aim was to study the files of decision occasions mentioned in the interviews, and to see whether these could be matched to observation notes of decision-making in action.

The method of triangulation is often advised to reduce bias and to increase the validity of the research (Patton, 1990; Blaikie, 1991; Yin 1994). However, I could only match all three data sources in three MSF project countries and although there were more possibilities of triangulation within ACT, the files often contained hardly any information to triangulate with. Beside, different data sources sometimes provided different insights into the decision-making processes studied. For example, formal standardized documents resembled the formal decision-making procedures, while email communication was more informal, and therefore revealed more of the informal dynamics of decision-making in the organizations. The interviews produced stories about decision-making processes which resulted in a collection of perceptions on decision-making processes. These stories might have contained elements of rationalizations of certain decisions and actions.

Hence, the use of three methods of data collection might not have decreased the danger of bias or increased the validity of this research to the extent that I had hoped for in advance. Nevertheless, the different data collection methods gave me the chance to confront the different results these methods produced. For example, I could ask respondents about decision-making moments that I had observed earlier, thereby checking to what extent the stories told by respondents resembled my own perception of the decision-making moment observed. Or, I could ask for projects that I had read about in a file. Moreover, the presentation of the dominant and secondary decision-making patterns of MSF and ACT in the empirical chapters of this study are derived from all these sources.

In conclusion, I have not met the aim of triangulation. Nevertheless, the use of three different data collection methods helped me to confront conflicting research results. In addition, our interpretation of the dominant and secondary decision-making patterns were confirmed by data resulting from all three methods (interviews, observation, document analysis). Hence, the use of different data collection methods added to a more in-depth and complete picture of decision-making on humanitarian aid in these organizations (Swanborn, 1996).

Reliability and validity issues

Various impediments in the data collection process may have influenced the reliability and validity of this research. The fact that I did not have access to email communication may have steered my interpretations. The one complete file of email communication I found during my field visit pointed to garbage can decision-making dynamics, but it is difficult to judge to what extent this case is representative for MSF's complete project portfolio. An extensive study of more email communication might have led to a somewhat different or more diverse picture of decision-making in both organizations.

The lack of access to particular decision-making moments prevented me from acquiring a complete picture of decision-making within MSF, especially at the management team level. At this level, it was therefore difficult to come to conclusions based on the research I had done. I therefore decided to avoid such conclusions as much as possible, even though I recognize that this is an omission in my research.

The fact that the three data collection methods could not be applied evenly in both organizations might have influenced the analysis of the data as well, especially in cases in which different data sources sometimes pointed to different research results. However, when possible, I tried to confront the data from different sources.

I have attempted to improve the validity and reliability of this research in various ways (see also Yin, 1994). I asked all respondents about all categories of decisions (initiation, rejection, termination and extension). The framework of analysis presented in Chapter 3 was always the point of departure for the data collection and the analysis. I already mentioned the use of three data collection methods in order to deepen my understanding of both organizations. The fact that all three methods pointed to the same dominant and secondary patterns in most instances studied adds to the validity of this study. In addition, I have not only looked for patterns in decision-making, but I also studied and reported on the exceptions to these patterns. These exceptions – here called the secondary patterns in decision-making – helped to specify conclusions about the dominant decision-making patterns in both organizations.

Identifying the decision-making modes

I collected data regarding various types of decisions: initiating activities, rejecting proposed activities, extending activities, and ending activities.

Identifying consequential decision-making

In Figure A.3, a characterization of consequential decision-making is given. If problems were first formulated in the data before alternatives for action and their potential consequences were articulated, followed by a decision, I established that this was sequential reasoning. If interview and document fragments or decision-making in practice showed proof of a consideration of future consequences of alternatives for action and if was described how actors in decision-making anticipated on future developments, I called this prospective reasoning. If certain costs were weighed against perceived benefits of (proposed) project activities or the effectiveness and efficiency of projects was related to decisions to start, stop, reject, or extend project activities, I labeled the data as an attempt to maximize behavior. The same goes for data which clearly linked the decision taken to organizational goals, procedures, and policies. The decision-making process was considered to be information driven if the use of information gathering instruments was mentioned such as assessments, reports, an analysis of numbers and facts about the situation at hand, etc. Finally, if the role of experts was emphasized, I labeled this as expert decision-making.

Decision-making dimensions	Indicators
Sequential reasoning	• first problems are formulated, then alternatives for action, then the consequences of these alternatives, before a solution is chosen
Prospective reasoning	• anticipatory action: consideration of future consequences of actions
Maximizing behavior	• importance of effectiveness and efficiency criteria • actions are related to organizational objectives by using formal policies, procedures and guidelines in order to decide
Information-driven Decision making	• use of information gathering instruments • emphasis on data collection and fact finding • use of data for decision-making • use of monitoring mechanisms

Figure A.2   Identifying consequential decision-making

Identifying appropriate decision-making

If decisions were taken that were a 'natural' way to decide ('we always do it this way', 'of course I decided to approve this project'), without considering other alternatives for action, I established that this was instant reasoning. The decision-making process was labeled retrospective if the data included evidence of related past experiences to situations in which a decision made much later was described ('we have been doing this for years now'). I established obligatory behavior if the decision to initiate, end, extend, or reject project activities was connected to feelings of commitment towards the people in need, the public, or other internal or external groups ('it was unacceptable not to go', 'we could not leave these people behind!', 'we simply had to be there'). The decision-making process was considered rule-based if the decision was linked to certain internalized rules within the organization in which people and events were categorized in such a way that decisions could instantly be taken. If decision occasions were linked to comparable decision occasions in the organization, I called this decision-making by analogy (see Figure A.4).

Decision-making dimensions	Indicators
Instant reasoning	• a direct and almost unconscious application of an internalized rule system
Retrospective reasoning	• use of past experiences to make decisions in the present
Obligatory, rule-based behavior	• expressions of commitment • expressions to live up to other people's expectations, internally or externally
Rule-based decision-making	• actions are based on organizational values and an internalized rule system • categorization of people and events
Decision making by analogy	• decision-making by comparing current situations with other situations with the same features

Figure A.3   Identifying appropriate decision-making

Identifying garbage can decision-making

I considered the decision-making process to be simultaneous if a clear order in the process could not be established and solutions or choice opportunities, for example, existed before problems had been formulated (see Figure A.5). If the decision taken was not related to the organizational goals or an internalized value system, I labeled this as an absence of collective goal rationality. As soon as the data pointed to the role of particular actors in the decision-making process, in that they were the ones persuading or negotiating project proposals or other decision categories, or the decision-making process contained elements of negotiation and persuasion, this was called entrepreneurial behavior. Finally, I labeled the process as decision-making by coupling, if I could establish that solutions, choice opportunities, and actors were actively coupled to each other by decision-making actors and if timing and coincidence played a role in the coupling process.

Identifying organizational features

I also tried to establish the features of the organizational setting of both NGOs studied on the basis of interviews, observation data, and documents. The difficulty of labeling the two NGOs according to these dimensions was that some of these features could only be derived from the organization's formal structure (or blueprint) while other dimensions could only be established by studying the organization in action. In addition, the formal features of an organization do not necessarily need to be characteristic for how an organization functions in practice.

Decision-making dimensions	Indicators
Simultaneous reasoning	• problems, solutions, choice opportunities and actors are presented simultaneously or semi-randomly
Individually or departmentally prospective reasoning	• there is an absence of collective goal rationality; this gives organizational members room to drive for their personal or departmental goals
Entrepreneurial, persuasive behavior	• actors are crucial in the decision-making process in order to connect actors to solutions, problems and choice opportunities • group dynamics determine the decision-making outcome • decision-making is characterized by persuasion, negotiation and compromise
Decision making by coupling	• a decision is taken if a solution can be matched to a problem, an actor, and a choice opportunity • timing and coincidence are important factors that facilitate the possibilities for coupling

Figure A.4   Identifying garbage can decision-making

As a solution to this, I chose to describe the organization's formal structure first (see Figure 3.5) and then hypothesized what kind of decision-making could (not) be expected from this description.

Then, I proceeded to analyze and characterize the decision-making process. Finally, I tried to establish whether the description of the formal structure was indeed representative for the 'organization in action' and to what extent the organizational features (being a combination of the formal structure and the 'organization in action') were related to the hypothesized decision-making mode. With this strategy I established:

- what the role of the formal structure in decision-making was
- what compliance mechanisms were present and in use in the organization
- how coordination was achieved (or not)
- what the role was of decision-making fora in the organization
- what the nature was of the dominant decision makers involved in the process
- to what extent decision-making was characterized by conflict or consensus
- how the organization related to its environment.

	Simon's administrative organization	Selznick's institution	March & Olsen's ambiguous organization
Degree of centralization	High: centralized, hierarchical decision-making through policies and procedures	Low: decentralized decision-making through internalized ways of working	Low: unstructured work processes and decentralized decision-making
Degree of specialization	High: presence of specialized units involved in decision-making	Low: hardly any specialization	Low: unclear technology, hence little specialization
Degree of formalization	High: substantive and procedural coordination mechanisms	Low: little formal coordination mechanisms	Low: problematic preferences, hence little formalization

Figure A.5   The formal organizational structure in the 3 decision-making models

Notes

1   I was also able to interview a country manager from another European MSF branch. This gave us interesting insight into the different work methods and perspectives within the various MSF branches. However, this interview could not serve as input for the study of MSFH decision-making processes.

Bibliography

Aall, P., Miltenberger, D. and Weiss, T.G., 2000. *Guide to IGOs, NGOs and the Military in Peace and Relief Operations*. Washington: United States Institute of Peace Press.

Albala-Bertrand, J.M. 2000. 'Complex Emergencies versus Natural Disasters: An Analytical Comparison of Causes and Effects', *Oxford Development Studies*, 28(2):187–204.

Allison, G. and P. Zelikow. 1999. *Essence of Decision, Explaining the Cuban Missile Crisis*. New York: Longman.

ALNAP. 2002. *Humanitarian Action: Improving Performance through Improved Learning*. London: Overseas Development Institute.

Anderson, M. 1999. *Do No Harm, How Aid Can Support Peace– or War*. Boulder/London: Lynne Riener Publishers.

Anheier, H.K. 1990. 'Institutional Choice and Organizational Behavior in the Third Sector', in Seibel & Anheier, *The Third Sector: Comparative Studies of Nonprofit Organizations*, Berlin/New York: De Gruyter, pp 47–52.

Ashforth, B.E. and F. Mael. 1989. 'Social Identity Theory and the Organization', *Academy of Management Review* 14(1):20–39.

Badelt, C. 1990. 'Institutional Choice and the Nonprofit Sector', in Seibel & Anheier, *The Third Sector: Comparative Studies of Nonprofit Organizations*, Berlin/New York: De Gruyter, pp 53–64.

Barrow, O. and Jennings. M. (eds). 2001. *The Charitable Impulse: NGOs and Development in East & North-East Africa*. Oxford:James Currey/Bloomford: Kumarian Press.

Beigbeder, Y. 1991. *The Role and Status of International Humanitarian Volunteers and Organizations, The Right and Duty to Humanitarian Assistance*. Dordrecht: Martinus Nijhoff Publishers.

Bendor, J., Moe, T.M., and Shotts, K.W. 2001. 'Recycling the Garbage Can: An Assessment of the Research Program', *American Political Science Review* 95 (1):169–198.

Benthall, J. 1993. *Disasters, Relief and the Media*. London/New York: I.B. Tauris & Co.

Berendsen, L. 1996. *Kroniek van Artsen zonder Grenzen*. Alkmaar: Van Duuren & Van der Linden.

Biddle, B.J. 1986. 'Recent Developments in Role Theory', *Annual Review of Sociology* 12:67-92.

Biggs, S. and Neame, A. 1996. 'Negotiating Room for Manoeuvre: Reflections Concerning NGO Autonomy and Accountability Within the New Policy Agenda', in Edwards, M. and Hulme, D. (eds), *Non Governmental Organisations:*

Performance and Accountability, Beyond the Magic Bullet, London: Earthscan Publications/Save the Children, pp. 31–40.

Blaikie, N.W.H. 1991. 'A Critique of Triangulation in Social Research', *Quality and Quantity* 25:115–136.

Boin, A. 1998. 'Integration: Institutions and Leadership', in *Contrasts in Leadership, an Institutional Study of Two Prison Systems*. Delft: Eburon.

Boin, A. 2001. *Crafting Public Institutions, Leadership in Two Prison Systems*. Boulder/London: Lynne Rienner Publishers.

Borton, J. 1993. 'Recent Trends in the International Humanitarian System', *Disasters* 17(3):187–201.

Brett, E.A. 1993. 'Voluntary Organizations as Development Organizations: Theorizing the Problem of Efficiency and Accountability', *Development and Change* 24:269–303.

Brown, L.D. and Moore, M.H. 2001. *Accountability, Strategy, and International Non-Governmental Organizations*, Working Paper No. 7 (April), The Hauser Center for Non Profit Organizations, The Kennedy School of Government, Harvard University.

Browne, M. 1993. *Organizational Decision Making and Information*. Norwood: Ablex Publishing Company.

Brunsson, N. 1985. *The Irrational Organization. Irrationality as a Basis for Organizational Action and Change*. Chichester/New York: John Wiley & Sons.

Brunsson, N. 1989. *The Organization of Hypocrisy. Talk, Decisions and Actions in Organizations*. Chichester/New York: John Wiley & Sons.

Burnell, P.J. 1991. *Charity, Politics and the Third World*. New York: St. Martin's Press.

Burns, T.R. and H. Flam. 1987. *The Shaping of Organization, Social Rule System Theory with Applications*. London: Sage Publications.

Burns, T. and Stalker, G.M. 1961. *The Management of Innovation*. London: Tavistock.

Calabresi, G. and Bobbitt, P. 1978. *Tragic Choices, The Conflicts Society Confronts in The Allocation of Tragically Scarce Resources*. New York: Norton.

Capelleveen, J.J. van. 1999. *Als Het Te Laat is om te Bidden. Geschiedenis van de Stichting Oecumenische Hulp*.Utrecht: Stichting Oecumenische Hulp.

Carley, J. 1980. *Rational Techniques in Policy Analysis*. London: Heinemann.

Charlton, M.W. 1997. 'Back to Humanitarianism: The Global Food Aid Regime in the Post-Cold War Era', *The Canadian Journal of Development Studies* 18:3.

Choo, C.W. 1998. *The Knowing Organization. How Organizations Use Information to Construct Meaning, Create Knowledge, and Make Decisions*. Oxford: Oxford University Press.

Choudhury, E. and Ahmed, Shamima. 2002. 'The Shifting Meaning of Governance: Public Accountability of Third Sector Organizations in an Emergent Global Regime', *International Journal of Public Administration* 25(4):561–588.

Christensen, S. and Molin, J. 1996. 'The Humanitarian Foundation, Revitalizing an Old Organization', in Chevalier, F., and Segalla, M., *Organizational Behavior and Change in Europe*, London: Sage Publications.

Clarke, G. 1998. 'Non-Governmental Organizations (NGOs) and Politics in the Developing World', *Political Studies,* XLVI:36–52.

Clusky, Mc, J.E. 2002. 'Rethinking Nonprofit Organization Governance: Implications for Management and Leadership', in *International Journal of Public Administration* 25(4):539–559.

Cohen, M.D., March, J.G., and J.P. Olsen. 1972. 'A Garbage Can Model of Organizational Choice', *Administrative Science Quarterly* 17(1).

Cohen, M.D., March, J.G., and J.P. Olsen. 1976. 'People, Problems, Solutions, and the Ambiguity of Relevance', in March, J.G. and J.P. Olsen (eds), *Ambiguity and Choice in Organizations,* Bergen/Oslo: Universitetsforlaget: 294–334.

Cohen, M.D., J.G. March and J.P. Olsen. 1988. 'A Garbage Can Model of Organizational Choice', in J.G. March, *Decisions and Organizations*, London/New York: Basil Blackwell, Inc.

Corder, K. 2001. 'Acquiring New Technology, Comparing Nonprofit and Public Sector Agencies', in *Administration & Society* 33(2):194–219.

Cuny, F. 1983. *Disasters and Development*. New York/Oxford: Oxford University Press.

Denhardt, R.B. 1993. *Theories of Public Organizations*. Belmont: Wadsworth Publishing Company, pp. 80–105 and 178–219.

DiMaggio, P.J. and Anheier, H.K. 1990. 'The Sociology of Nonprofit Organizations and Sectors', *Annual Review of Sociology* 16:137–159.

DiMaggio, P.J. and Powell, W.W. 1983. 'The Iron Cage Revisited: Institutional Isomorphism and Collective Rationality', *American Sociological Review* 48:147–160.

DiMaggio, P.J. and Powell, W.W. 1991. *The New Institutionalism in Organizational Analysis*. Chicago: University of Chicago Press.

Douglas, J. 1987. 'Political Theories of Nonprofit Organization', in Powell, W.W. (ed.) 1987. *The Nonprofit Sector, A Research Handbook*. New Haven: Yale University Press, pp. 43–54.

Downs, A. 1967. *Inside Bureaucracy*. Boston: Little Brown.

Duffield, M. and Prendergast, J. 1994. *Without Troops and Tanks: The Emergency Humanitarian Desk and the Cross Border Operation into Eritrea and Tigray*. Lawrenceville NJ: The Red Sea Press.

Dijkzeul. D. and Beigbeder, Y. (eds) 2001.*Rethinking International Organizations, Pathology and Promise*. New York: Berghahn Books.

Ebrahim, A. 2003. *NGOs and Organizational Change, Discourse, Reporting and Learning*. Cambridge: Cambridge University Press.

Eckstein, H. 1975. 'Case Study and Theory in Political Science', in Greenstein, F.I. and Polsby, N.W. (eds), *Handbook of Political Science*, Reading, MA: Addison-Wesley, pp. 79–138.

Edwards, W. 1954. 'The Theory of Decision Making', *Psychology Review* 51(4):380–417.

Edwards, M. 1997. 'Organizational Learning in Non-Governmental Organizations: What Have We Learned?', in *Public Administration and Development* 17:235–250.

Edwards, M. and Hulme, D. (eds) 1996. *Non-Governmental Organisations: Performance and Accountability, Beyond the Magic Bullet*. London: Earthscan Publications/Save the Children.

Etzioni, A. 1967. 'Mixed Scanning', *Public Administration Review* 27:385

Field, J.O. (ed.). 1993. *The Challenge of Famine: Recent Experiences, Lessons Learned*. West Hartford: Kumarian Press.

Fisher, J. 1998. *Non Governments, NGOs and the Political Development of the Third World*. West Hartford: Kumarian Press.

Fisher, W.F. 1997. 'Doing Good? The Politics and Antipolitics of NGO practices', *Annual Review of Anthropology* 26:439–464.

Fitz-Gerald, A.M. and Walthall, F.A. 1999. 'An Integrated Approach to Complex Emergencies: The Kosovo Experience', *The Journal of Humanitarian Assistance*, www.jha.ac.

Fowler, A. 1996. 'Assessing NGO Performance: Difficulties, Dilemmas and a Way Ahead', in Edwards, M. and Hulme, D. (eds), *Non Governmental Organisations: Performance and Accountability, Beyond the Magic Bullet*, London: Earthscan Publications/Save the Children, pp. 143–116.

Frederickson, J.W. 1986. 'The Strategic Decision-Making Process and Organizational Structure', *Academy of Management Review* (11):280–297.

George, A.L. and McKeown, T.J. 1985. 'Case Studies and Theories of Organizational Decision Making', *Advances in Information Processing in Organizations* 2:21–58.

Goldmann, K. 2005. 'Appropriateness and Consequences: The Logic of Neo-Institutionalism', *Governance: An International Journal of Policy, Administration, and Institutions* 18(1):35–52.

Gordenker, L. and Weiss, T.G. 1997. 'Devolving Responsibilities: A Framework for Analysing NGOs and Services', *Third World Quarterly*, 18(3):443–455.

Grandori, A. 1984. 'A Prescriptive Contingency View of Organizational Decision Making', *Administrative Science Quarterly* 29:192–209.

Grath, G.M., Mc and and More, E. 2001. 'The Greta System: Organizational Politics Introduced to the Garbage Can', *Decision Support Systems* 31:181–195.

Haan, A, de. 1995. *Artsen zonder Grenzen, Tien Jaar Noodhulp Wereldwijd*. Utrecht: Bosch & Keuning.

Haghebaert, B. 1996. 'Noodhulp: Failliet van de Ontwikkelingssamenwerking?', in K. Lieten and F. Van der Velden, *Grenzen aan de Hulp*, Amsterdam: Het Spinhuis.

Halperin, J.J. and R.N. Stern (eds). 1998. *Debating Rationality, Nonrational Aspects of Organizational Decision Making*. Ithaca/London: Cornell University Press.

Hansmann, H. 1987.' 'Economic Theories of Nonprofit Organization', in Powell, W.W. (ed.) 1987. *The Nonprofit Sector, A Research Handbook*. New Haven: Yale University Press, pp. 27–41.

Hansmann, H. 1990. 'The Economic Role of Commercial Nonprofits: The Evaluation of the Savings Bank Industry', in Seibel & Anheier, *The Third Sector: Comparative Studies of Nonprofit Organizations*, Berlin/New York: De Gruyter, pp 65–76.

Harriss, J (ed.). 1995. *The Politics of Humanitarian Intervention*. London/New York: Pinter/Save the Children.

Hasenfeld, Y. 1983. *Human Service Organisations*. Englewood Cliffs: Prentice Hall.

Heller, F., Drenth, P., Koopman, P. and Rus, V. 1988. *Decisions in Organizations, A Three-Country Comparative Study*. London: SAGE Publications.

Hermann, M. P. 2002. 'A Guide to Doing Comparative Case Studies, Maxwell Style', draft paper.

Hickson, D.J., Butler, R.J., Cray, D., Mallory, G.R., and Wilson, D.C. 1986. *Top Decisions: Strategic Decision-Making in Organizations*. London: Basil Blackwell.

Hilhorst, D. (ed.). 2002. 'Being Good at Doing Good? Quality and Accountability of Humanitarian NGOs', *Disasters* 26(3): 193–212.

Hilhorst, D. 2004. *The Real World of NGOs*, London: Zed Books .

Holmstrom, B.R. and Tirole, J. 1989. 'The Theory of the Firm', in Schmalensee, R. and Willig, R.D. (eds). *Handbook of Industrial Organization, Volume 1*, New York: Elsevier, pp: 61–133.

Houghton, D.P. 1998. 'Analogical Reasoning and Policymaking: Where and When is it Used?', *Policy Sciences* 31:151–176.

IOV. 1994. *Humanitarian Aid to Somalia, Evaluation report 1994*. Ridderkerk: Ridderprint BV.

Iriye, A. 1999. 'A Century of NGOs', *Diplomatic History* 23(3): 421435.

James, E. (ed.). 1989. *The Non Profit Sector in International Perspective, Studies in Comparative Culture and Policy*. Oxford: Oxford University Press.

James, E. 1990. 'Economic Theories of the Non Profit Sector: a Comparative Perspective', in Seibel & Anheier, *The Third Sector: Comparative Studies of Nonprofit Organizations*, Berlin/New York: De Gruyter, pp 21–30.

Kaarbo, J. and Beasly, R.K. 1999. 'A Practical Guide to the Comparative Case Study Method in Political Psychology', *Political Psychology* 20(2):369–391.

Kahneman, D, Slovic, P,. and Tversky, A. 1982. *Judgment under Uncertainty. Heuristics and Biases*. Cambridge: Cambridge University Press.

Kaufman, H. 1960. *The Forest Ranger: A Study in Administrative Behavior*. Washington: Resources for the Future.

Kingdon, J.W. 1984/1995. *Agendas, Alternatives, and Public Policies*. New York: Longman.

Koopman and Pool. 1992. *Management van Besluitvorming in Organisaties. Een Strategisch Perspectief*. Assen/Maastricht: Van Gorcum.

Korten, D.C. (ed.). 1986. *Community Management, Asian Experience and Perspectives*. Bloomford: Kumarian Press.

Korten, D.C. 1990. *Getting to the 21rst Century: Voluntary Action and the Global Agenda*. West Hartford: Kumarian Press.

Kreps, D.M. 1990. *A Course in Micro-Economic Theory*. Princeton, NJ: Princeton University Press.

Kriger, M.P. and Barnes, L. B. 1992. 'Organizational Decision Making as Hierarchical Levels of Drama',*Journal of Management Studies* 29:439–457.

Kunreuther, H. and Meszaros, J. 1997. 'Organizational Choice Under Ambiguity: Decision Making in the Chemical Industry following Bhopal', in Shapira, Z., *Organizational Decision Making*, Cambridge: Cambridge University Press.

Lai, S-K. 2003. 'Effects of Planning on the Garbage Can Decision Processes: A Reformulation and Extension', *Environment and Planning* 30:379–389.

Levitt, B. and Nass, C. 1989. 'The Lid on the Garbage Can: Institutional Constraints on Decision Making in the Technical Core of College-Text Publishers', *Administrative Science Quarterly* 34:190–207.

Lewis, D. 2001. *The Management of Non-Governmental Development Organizations*. London/New York: Routledge.

Lewis, D. 2003. 'Theorizing the Organization and Management of Non-Governmental Development Organizations', in *Public Management Review* 5(3):325–344.

Lijphart, A.. 1971. 'Comparative Politics and the Comparative Method', *The American Political Science Review* 65:682–693.

Lindblom, C.E. 1959. 'The Science of Muddling Through', *Public Administration Review* 19(1):79.

Lipshitz, R. 1994. 'Decision Making in Three Modes', *Journal for the Theory of Social Behavior* 24(1):47–65.

Macrae, J. and A. Zwi (eds). 1994. *War and Hunger: Rethinking International Responses to Complex Emergencies*. London: Zed Books.

March, J.G. 1981. 'Decision Making in Perspective, Decisions in Organizations and Theories of Choices', in Van de Ven, A.H. and Joyce, W.F., *Perspectives on Organization Design and Behavior*, New York: John Wiley & Sons.

March. J.G. (ed.). 1988. *Decisions and Organizations*. Oxford/New York: Basic Blackwell Ltd.

March J.G. 1994. *A Primer on Decision Making, How Decisions Happen*. New York: The Free Press.

March, J.G. 1997. 'Understanding How Decisions Happen', in Shapira, Z. (ed.). *Organizational Decision Making*. Cambridge: Cambridge University Press.

March, J.G. and J.P. Olsen. 1989. *Rediscovering Institutions*. New York: The Free Press.

March, J.G. and Shapira, Z. 1982. 'Behavioral Decision Theory and Organizational Decision Theory', in Ungson, G.R. and Braunstein, D.N., *Decision Making: An Interdisciplinary Inquiry*. Boston: Kent Publishers:92–115.

Merton, R.K. 1957. *Social Theory and Social Structure*. New York: The Free Press.

Messick, D.M. 1999. 'Alternative Logics for Decision Making in Social Settings', *Journal of Economic Behavior and Organization* 39:11–28.

Meyer, J.W. and Rowan, B. 1977. 'Institutionalized Organizations: Formal Structure as Myth and Ceremony', *American Journal of Sociology* 83:340–363.

Miller, J. 1994. *The Social Control of Religious Zeal*. New Brunswick: Rutgers University Press.

Mintzberg, H., Raisinghani, D, and Théorêt, A. 1976. 'The Structure of 'Unstructured' Decision Making Processes', *Administrative Science Quarterly,* 21 (June): 246–275.

Mintzberg, H. 1983. *Structures in Fives. Designing Effective Organizations.* Englewood Cliffs:Prentice Hall.

Milliano, J., de. 1991. *Tussen Korenvelden en Puinhopen: Onderweg met Artsen zonder Grenzen.* Amsterdam: Balans/Lannoo.

Morgan, G. 1986. *Images of Organization.* Beverly Hills: SAGE Publications.

Mucciaroni, G. 1992. 'The Garbage Can Model and the Study of Policy Making: a Critique', *Polity* 14(3):459–482.

Natsios, A.S. 1997. *US Foreign Policy and the Four Horsemen of the Apocalypse: Humanitarian Relief in Complex Emergencies.* The Washington Papers No. 170.

Neustadt, R.E. and May, E.R.. 1986. *Thinking in Time. The Uses of History for Decision-Makers.* New York/London: McMillann Press/Collier McMillan Press.

Noordegraaf, M. 2000. *Attention! Work and Behavior of Public Managers Amidst Ambiguity.* Delft: Eburon Publishers.

Nutt., P. 1984. 'Types of Organizational Processes', *Administrative Science Quarterly*, 29:414–450.

Nutt, P. 2000. 'Decision Making Success in Public, Private and Third Sector Organizations: Finding Sector Dependent Best Practice', *Journal of Management Studies* 37(1):77–108.

Nutt, P. 2005. 'Search During Decision Making', *European Journal of Operational Research* 160:851–876.

ODI Briefing Paper. 2002. *International Humanitarian Action: A Review of Policy Trends.* London: Overseas Development Institute.

Oliver, C. 1991.'Stragetic Responses to Institutional Processes', *Academy of Management Review*, Vol.16:145–179.

Otten, M. 2000. *Verstrikt in Grote Projecten: Hoe de Stadhuizen in Amsterdam en Apeldoorn tot Stand Kwamen.* Den Haag: VNG.

Padgett, J.F. 1980. 'Managing Garbage Can Hierarchies', *Administrative Science Quarterly* 25:583–602

Paige, G.D. 1968. *The Korean Decision.* New York: Free Press.

Patton, M.Q. 1990 (2nd edition). *Qualitative Evaluation and Research Methods.* Newbury Park: SAGE publications.

Perrow, C. 1986. *Complex Organizations, a Critical Essay.* New York: McGray-Hill.

Peters, G.B. 1999. *Institutional Theory in Political Science, The 'New Institutionalism'.* London: Pinter.

Pfeffer, J. and Salancik, G.R. 1978. *The External Control of Organizations, A Resource Dependence Perspective.* New York: Harper & Row Publishers.

Pinfield, L.T. 1986. 'A Field Evaluation of Perspectives on Organizational Decision Making', *Administrative Science Quarterly* 31:365–388.

Pool, P.L. 1992. *Management en Besluitvorming in Organisaties: Een Strategisch Perspectief.* Assen: Van Gorcum.

Powell, W.W. (ed.) 1987. *The Nonprofit Sector, A Research Handbook.* New Haven: Yale University Press.

Powell, W.W. and Friedkin, R. 1987. 'Organizational Change in Nonprofit

Organizations', in Powell, W.W. (ed.) 1987. *The Nonprofit Sector, A Research Handbook*. New Haven: Yale University Press, pp180–192.

Prendergast, J. 1996. *Frontline Diplomacy, Humanitarian Aid and Conflict in Africa*. Boulder/London: Lynne Rienner Publishers.

Quade, E.S. 1975. *Analysis for Public Decisions*. New York: American Elsevier Publishing Company.

Randel, J. and German, T. 2002. 'Trends in the Financing of Humanitarian Assistance', in Macra, J. (ed.), *The New Humanitarianisms: A Review of Trends in Global Humanitarian Action*, HPG paper 11, Oxford: Overseas Development Institute.

Reason, J. 1990. *Human Error*. Cambridge: Cambridge University Press.

Salamon, L.M. 1994. 'The Rise of the Nonprofit Sector', *Foreign Affairs*, July/August, no.4.

Salamon, L.M. and Anheier, H.K. 1997a. *Defining the Non Profit Sector: a Cross-National Analysis*. Manchester/New York: Manchester University Press.

Salamon, L.M. and Anheier, H.K. 1997b. *The Emerging Nonprofit Sector, An Overview*. Manchester/New York: Manchester University Press.

Salamon, L.M., Sokolowski, S.W., and List, R. 2003. *Global Civil Society, an Overview*. The Johns Hopkins University Institute for Policy Studies, Center for Civil Society Studies.

Schick, F. 1997. *Making Choices, a Recasting of Decision Theory*. Cambridge: Cambridge University Press.

Schreurs, P. 2000. *Enchanting Rationality, an Analysis of Rationality in the Anglo-American Discourse on Public Organizations*. Delft: Eburon.

Scott. W.R. 1987. 'The Adolescence of Institutional Theory', *Administrative Science Quarterly* 32:439–511.

Scott, W.R. 1992. *Organizations. Rational, Natural and Open Systems*. Engelwood Cliffs: Prentice-Hall Publishers.

Scott, W.R. 1995. *Institutions and Organizations*. Thousand Oaks: Sage Publications.

Seaman, J. 1996. 'The International System of Humanitarian Relief in the "New World Order"', in Harriss, J. *The Politics of Humanitarian Intervention*. London/New York: Pinter/Save the Children.

Searing, D.D. 1991. 'Roles, Rules, and Rationality in the New Institutionalism', *American Political Science Review* 85(4):1239–1260.

Seibel, W. and Anheier, H.K. 1990. *The Third Sector, Comparative Studies of Non Profit Organizations*. Berlin/New York: De Gruyter.

Selznick, P. 1957. *Leadership in Administration: A Sociological Interpretation*. New York/London: Harper & Row Publishers.

Shapira, Z. (ed.). 1997. *Organizational Decision Making*. Cambridge: Cambridge University Press.

Shawcross. 1983. *The Qualities of Mercy: Cambodia, Holocaust and Modern Conscience*. New York: Simon & Schuster.

Shrivastasa, P. and Grant, J.H. 1985. 'Empirically Derived Models of Strategic-Decision Process', *Strategic Management Journal* 6:97–113.

Sieber, S.D. 1981. *Fatal Remedies, The Irony of Social Intervention*. New York/ London: Plenum Press.

Simon, H. 1945/1997. *Administrative Behavior, a Study of Decision-Making Behavior in Administrative Organizations*. New York: The Free Press.

Skjelsbaek, K. 1971. 'The Growth of International Nongovernmental Organization in the Twentieth Century', *International Organization* 25(3):420–442.

Smillie, I. 1995. *The Alms Bazaar: Altruism under Fire, Non-Profit Organizations and International Development*. London: Intermediate Technology Publications.

Smith, B.H. 1996. 'More than Altruism: the Politics of European International Charities', in Edwards, M. and Hulme, D. (eds), *Non Governmental Organisations: Performance and Accountability, Beyond the Magic Bullet*, London: Earthscan Publications/Save the Children, pp. 319–338.

Sommer, J.G. 1994. *Hope Restored? Humanitarian Aid to Somalia, 1990–1994*. Washington, D.C.:RPG.

Sproull, L.S., Weiner, S. and Wolf, D. 1987. *Organizing an Anarchy*. Chicago: University of Chicago Press.

Stern, E. and Sundelius, B. 2002. 'Crisis Management in Europe: An Integrated Regional Research and Training Program', *International Studies Perspective* 3:71–88.

Stone, D. 1997. *Policy Paradox, The Art of Political Decision Making*. New York: W.W. Norton & Company.

Swanborn, P.G. 1996. 'A Common Base for Quality Control Criteria in Quantitative and Qualitative Research', *Quality and Quantity* 30:19–35.

Tandon, R. 1996 'Board Games: Governance and Accountability in NGOs', in Edwards, M. and Hulme, D. (eds), *Non Governmental Organisations: Performance and Accountability, Beyond the Magic Bullet*, London: Earthscan Publications/ Save the Children, pp. 41–49.

Thompson, J.D. and A. Tuden. 1959. 'Strategies, Structures, and Processes of Organizational Decision', in J.D. Thompson and P.B. Hammond. (eds), *Comparative Studies in Administration* pp195–216. Pittsburgh: University of Pittsburgh Press.

UNHCR. 2005. *Global Report 2005*.www.unhcr.org.

Uphoff, N. 1996. 'Why NGOs are not a Third Sector: A Sectoral Analysis with Some Thoughts on Accountability, Sustainability and Evaluation', in Edwards, M. and Hulme, D., (eds) *Non-Governmental Organisations: Performance and Accountability, Beyond the Magic Bullet,* London: Earthscan Publications/Save the Children, pp. 17–30.

Vakil, A. 1997. 'Confronting the Classification Problem: Toward a Taxonomy of NGOs', *World Development* 25(12): 2057–2070.

Waal, A., de. 1997. *Famine Crimes: Politics and the Disaster Humanitarian Industry in Africa*. London/Bloomington/Indianapolis: African Rights, The International African Institute and Indiana University Press.

Weick, K. 1976.'Educational Organizations as Loosely Coupled Systems', *Administrative Science Quarterly* 21:1–19.

Weiss, R.S. 1994. *Learning from Strangers, The Art and Method of Qualitative Interview Methods.* New York: The Free Press.

Weiss, T. G. and Gordenker, L. (ed.). 1996. *NGOs, the UN, and Global Governance.* Boulder/London: Lynne Rienner.

West, K. 2001. *Agents of Altruism, The Expansion of Humanitarian NGOs in Rwanda and Afghanistan.* Aldershot: Ashgate.

Whitman, J. and D. Pocock. 1996. *After Rwanda, the Coordination of United Nations Humanitarian Assistance.* London/New York: MacMillan Press/St. Martin's Press.

Wills, F. 1996. 'Scaling-up, Mainstreaming and Accountability: the Challenge for NGOs', Edwards, M. and Hulme, D., (eds) *Non-Governmental Organisations: Performance and Accountability, Beyond the Magic Bullet,* London: Earthscan Publications/Save the Children, pp. 53–62.

Willemsen, J. 1996. *Van Tentoonstelling tot Wereldorganisatie, De Geschiedenis van de Stichtingen Memisa en Medicus Mundi Nederland 1925–1995.* Nijmegen: Vlakhof Pers.

Wood, A., Apthorpe, R. and Borton, J. 2001. *Evaluating International Humanitarian Action.* London: Zed Books.

Yin, R.K. 1994. *Case Study Research: Design and Methods.* Thousand Oaks, CA: Sage.

Zey, M. 1998. *Rational Choice Theory and Organizational Theory: A Critique.* Thousand Oaks: Sage Publications.

Zhou, X. 1997. 'Organizational Decision Making as Rule Following', in Shapira, Z. (ed.)., *Organizational Decision Making,* Cambridge: Cambridge University Press.

Name Index

Subject Index